"The fun of this nuts-and-bolts guide lies in Zobel's ability to comfort as well as educate."
—*San Francisco Chronicle*

"*Minding Her Own Business* gives you the necessary tools to take control of your finances and run a successful small business. Highly recommended."
—Salli Rasberry, coauthor of *Running a One-Person Business*

"Jan provides helpful information clearly, without jargon. Women business owners should not be without this book. It's like having a tax professional by your side at all times."
—Anna L. Marks, Publisher, *Bay Area BusinessWoman*

"*Minding Her Own Business* is a great addition to anyone's business library. Zobel has the ability to explain financial issues in a clear and understandable manner."
—Jane Applegate, nationally syndicated small business columnist and author of *201 Great Ideas for Your Small Business*

"Whether handling the paperwork herself or contracting out for tax preparation services, every woman entrepreneur should read *Minding Her Own Business*—and keep it handy for future reference as well."
—*Midwest Book Review*

"An excellent starting point for learning how to keep records effectively and becoming informed about the latest tax regulations."
—*Library Journal*

"*Minding Her Own Business* is right on target. It addresses all those frequently asked questions that people who are starting and running their own business have. It is written in a clear, concise, understandable manner that makes the information easy to use. I will highly recommend it to all my clients."
—Beth Wickham, Counselor, Business Development Center, Central Oregon Community College

"Making the tools we least like to use and the information we shy away from palatable and accessible is the great achievement of this book. Zobel has done women who aspire to mind their own business a great service—it's a mandatory resource for the serious entrepreneur!"
—Joline Godfrey, author of *Our Wildest Dreams* and *No More Frogs to Kiss* and founder of An Income of Her Own

MINDING
Her OWN
BUSINESS

The Self-Employed
Woman's Guide to Taxes
and Recordkeeping

Jan Zobel

Adams Media Corporation
Holbrook, Massachusetts

Copyright ©2000, Jan Zobel. All rights reserved. This book, or parts thereof, may not be reproduced in any form without permission from the publisher; exceptions are made for brief excerpts used in published reviews.

Published by
Adams Media Corporation
260 Center Street, Holbrook, MA 02343

ISBN: 1-58062-200-3

Printed in the United States of America.

J I H G F E D C B

Library of Congress Cataloging-in-Publication Data
Zobel, Jan.
Minding her own business: the self-employed woman's guide to taxes and recordkeeping / Jan Zobel.--Updated 3rd ed.
p.   cm.
Originally published: Oakland, Ca.: EastHill Press, c1998.
Includes index.
ISBN 1-58062-200-3
1. Income tax--Law and legislation--United States--Popular works.
2. Self-employed women--Taxation--United States. I. Title
KF6369.6 .Z63   2000
343.7305'2 21--dc21   99-046341
CIP

This publication is designed to provide accurate and authoritative information with regard to the subject matter covered. It is sold with the understanding that the publisher is not engaged in rendering legal, accounting, or other professional advice. If legal advice or other expert assistance is required, the services of a competent professional person should be sought.
— From a Declaration of Principles jointly adopted by a Committee of the American Bar Association and a Committee of Publishers and Associations

Note: Although this publication is designed to be accurate, as of the date it went to press, some of the information contained in it is subject to differences of opinion and interpretation. Furthermore, the scope of the subject matter, of necessity, has limited the amount of detail that can be presented. The information provided herein is not guaranteed or warranted to produce particular results, and the strategies outlined may not be suitable for every individual. Talk with a competent professional regarding the applicability of the information contained in this book to your particular situation. The author and Adams Media Press shall have neither liability nor responsibility to any person or entity with respect to any loss or damage caused, or alleged to be caused, directly or indirectly by the information contained in this book.

Cover photo courtesy of Adobe Image Library.

This book is available at quantity discounts for bulk purchases.
For information, call 1-800-872-5627.

Visit our exciting small business Web site at businesstown.com

Contents

DEDICATION

To my father, Jerome Zobel, who showed me what it means to be an entrepreneur; and to all the women who, with excitement and trepidation, are starting their own businesses.

Over and over again, courts have said that there is nothing sinister in so arranging one's affairs to keep taxes as low as possible.

—Judge Learned Hand

INTRODUCTION

Once upon a time someone decided that financial matters were men's domain. A woman's money and financial affairs were handled by her father and, after she married, they were handled by her husband. Many women overtly, or more subtly, received messages about money such as "You don't need to worry about that" or "It's not polite to talk about money" or "You don't really need a career, just something to fall back on until you get married."

Times have changed. Fortunately most women and girls are being more fully exposed to money principles. However, I still hear from many of the women I work with such statements as, "I've never understood anything about taxes" or "My father (or husband) has always handled my (our) finances" or "You'll probably think I'm dumb but . . ." Despite confusion and ambivalence about money and taxes, millions of women are starting their own businesses. According to the National Foundation for Women Business Owners, the number of women-owned businesses has more than doubled during the past twelve years. NFWBO reports that in 1999, there were 9.1 million women-owned businesses, representing 38 percent of all businesses, employing 27.5 million people and generating $3.6 trillion in sales annually.

If you've picked up this book, it probably means you're thinking about joining or already have joined the ranks of the self-employed. Congratulations! As head of your own business, you're in charge. You're the one who gets to make all the decisions—what type of clients and customers you want to attract, how much to charge, where to locate the business, what hours you want to work, and much more.

You're also the one who has the responsibilities of being self-employed. And high on that list is your responsibility for keeping good financial records and meeting your tax obligations. You may choose to get help with part or all of this. Ultimately, however, the buck stops with you, so it is important that you understand what's needed.

Elizabeth didn't realize that becoming self-employed meant her taxes would be different from what they were when she was an employee. It wasn't until she had her tax return prepared in March that she learned she could deduct all the business-related books and supplies she'd bought during the previous year. Unfortunately, by that time, she'd thrown away the receipts. As for all those miles she drove for her business last year, she had no idea she should have been keeping track of them. She tried to reconstruct what she could, but Elizabeth's taxes were higher than they would have been if she'd known how to keep track of her business expenses. Elizabeth owed so much on April 15 that the IRS penalized her for not having made tax deposits on a quarterly basis during the year.

You've probably picked up this book because you want to avoid Elizabeth's mistakes. Maybe you're frightened of the IRS and fear that a misstep could land you in jail. As you go through the pages of this book, I hope you will feel empowered by what you learn and able to use the information not only to avoid paying more than your fair share of taxes but also to create an ongoing financial picture of your business.

In Section 1 of this book, you'll learn why it was written specifically for women. You'll discover that although taxes have no gender bias, some women (and men) may be giving the IRS more than they need to. Section 1 will also help you get your business started correctly. You'll read about the different entities under which you can operate your business, and you'll get information about the licenses and permits you need to have. You'll find surprising answers to the questions "Do I need to have a separate bank account for my business?" and "Should I have a separate credit card for my business?" This section also answers the perennial question "How do I know when I've really started my business?"

Section 2 provides the information you need to know about keeping records. You'll learn easy methods to keep track of the money coming into and going out of your business. In Chapter 7 of this section, you'll find out what the IRS expects to see when they call a taxpayer in for an audit. Chapter 11 gives tips and warnings about using a computer to do the recordkeeping for your business.

The often confusing topic of employees versus independent contractors is the focus of Section 3. If you're currently working as an employee, as well as being self-employed, this section will explain the differences in your taxes. If you've recently become an entrepreneur after leaving your employee job, you'll be especially interested in learning what benefits were available to you as an employee that may no longer be available to you once you're self-employed. Taxes for independent contractors are also covered in this section. If hiring helpers is on your to-do list, you'll want to pay special attention to Chapter 15 (Is She an Employee or an Independent Contractor?) as well as the chapters on payroll withholding and issuing 1099 Forms.

Section 4 of this book is the one that many readers will turn to first—what can you deduct when you have your own business? Your car? Your travel? The costs you had in getting your business started? Read the requirements carefully and be sure to hold on to the necessary receipts. Even if you've been in business for awhile, take a close look at the chapter on deducting your home office. The rules have totally changed and you may now be eligible for this deduction even if you've never been able to take it before. If you've been thinking about starting a retirement plan, Chapter 32 will tell you about the different plans that are available and help you decide on the one that's best for you.

Section 5 is the central spoke of this book as it discusses and shows the tax forms used by self-employed people. Some of the concepts from earlier and later chapters will become even clearer as you see how they relate to your income tax forms. The focus here isn't to teach you to prepare your own tax return (although you may now have enough information to feel comfortable in doing that) but rather to help you see how all the pieces fit together on that page called the 1040 Form.

One of the most confusing areas for self-employed people is introduced in the chapters of Section 6—Making Quarterly Estimated Tax Payments and Calculating the Amount to Send Quarterly. The late comedian Red Skelton was once quoted as saying "I always send in my estimated tax payments anonymously. If the government expects me to guess how much I owe, they can guess who owes it." While you might not choose this tactic, you can avoid penalties by becoming familiar with our pay-as-you-go tax system. If, after reading this section, you need more information about quarterly payments, Appendix B provides a step-by-step calculation of estimated tax payments, along with an area for you to do your own figuring.

Section 7 wraps up this book by telling you where to get help. If you don't have enough money to pay your taxes, are looking for help with your business bookkeeping, are concerned about being audited, or wondering how long to keep records, this section will answer all your questions. You'll also learn about the different types of tax preparers and the pros and cons of using a computer tax program.

Appendix A walks you through the steps of reconciling a bank statement. If this is a skill you've never mastered, you can be assured that you're not alone. Running a business means that you need to be constantly in touch with your finances so it may be time to learn how to make your checkbook match the bank statement.

Appendix B provides detailed information about calculating estimated tax payments.

Appendices C and D contain lists of resources that will provide further help in running your business. You'll learn about small business organizations, helpful books and publications, and great places to travel on the Internet.

In many cases, round numbers are used as part of the examples in this book. This is not meant to imply that you should use round numbers in your recordkeeping or tax preparation. Rather, it's intended as a way to move the focus away from the numbers so that more emphasis can be placed on the concept being illustrated.

A great effort was made to include the most current tax information and forms available at the time this book went to press. In some cases, tax and deduction rates for the year 2000 were not yet available. Most of the tax rates and forms included in this edition are for 1999 and are applicable for returns being filed in 2000. The IRS's Web site and their annually updated publications are good sources of information about changes in tax law.

Running a business is an exciting adventure as well as a lot of hard work. Spending a little time learning the basics of recordkeeping and taxes will lessen your anxiety level and your work load, allowing you to spend more time doing the activities that led you to start your business in the first place.

—Jan Zobel

SECTION I
Getting Started

WHY A
TAX BOOK
FOR WOMEN?

Taxes don't differentiate between women and men: The complexity of the laws leaves everyone feeling confused! In my years as a tax preparer, however, I've found that many women (and some men, as well) have the added difficulty of number-phobia, usually as a result of not having been adequately exposed to math and finances while growing up. Number-phobia is the numbing or spacy sensation that occurs when encountering a tax form, a bank statement, or any other piece of paper that already contains figures or requires the filling in of numbers. This state of mind results in women telling me, as they frequently do, "Taxes are my greatest fear about starting a business," "I've never been good with numbers," or "Anything to do with money is a mystery to me."

Do number-phobic women pay more than their share of taxes? Maybe. Women as a group tend to be cautious about the business deductions they claim. Many of the women entrepreneurs whose tax returns I prepare have said to me, "I'd rather pay more taxes than be audited."

People who are unfamiliar or uncomfortable with finances make up a large portion of the more than 50% of Americans who have their tax return prepared by a professional. Those who don't understand where the numbers on their completed return came from have no way of knowing whether their desire to save taxes has been translated into a suitably prepared return.

Fortunately, this anxiety about numbers and taxes hasn't kept women from starting businesses at a rapid pace. In 1960, only 3% of this country's businesses were owned by women. Today, nearly 50% of all businesses are woman owned. This increase is due to women seeking out the information they've needed, financial and otherwise.

This book is designed to be another piece of that necessary information. It was written with the belief that anyone, no matter how unfamiliar with or afraid of numbers, can learn to take charge of her finances. Calculators and computers can deal with the numbers; our job is to learn how the numbers are used and what records we need to keep to make sure they're used to our advantage. This approach is designed to let those who are afflicted with number-phobia push it out of the way long enough to learn the underlying concepts that make up our tax system. Armed with that knowledge, fear of numbers is less likely to cause anyone to pay more than her share of taxes.

BUSINESS?

Anne is a technical writer for Cyberspace Company. Her job is to put together a manual to accompany Cyberspace's new software program. Anne was hired as an independent contractor (i.e., no taxes are withheld from her paycheck), not as an employee.

Maria opened a needlepoint shop last year. She has an employee who works part-time in the store.

Lenore sells skin care products at home parties. Also she recruits new people to sell the products. This type of business is called network, or multilevel, marketing, which means that when Lenore's recruits make their own sales, Lenore gets a percentage of the sales price.

Rochelle is a psychotherapist who is an employee at a counseling center. She also has a small private practice and sees clients in her home office.

All of these women are business owners, although they may not think of themselves that way. Often people who own a one-person service business (e.g., consultants, graphic artists, psychotherapists, house cleaners) may think of themselves as being self-employed without realizing that they've created a business of which they're the owner. While independent contractors may not think of themselves as business owners, the tax implications are the same as those for any other small business. That's because the IRS defines a business as being an activity you participate in regularly and continuously with the intent of making a profit. For tax purposes, the terms *self-employed, business owner* (if a sole proprietorship), and *independent contractor* all mean the same thing. (See the next chapter for information on sole proprietorships.)

WHEN IS SOMEONE CONSIDERED TO BE OFFICIALLY IN BUSINESS?

The IRS says once you are set up and ready (open) for business, you're considered to be in business. Ready for business means you have obtained all necessary licenses and permits; you have rented store or office space, if you're planning to do that; and you have told the public that your services or products are available. (In Chapter 4, we'll discuss the licenses and permits you might need.)

Although the IRS expects you to be aware of your tax obligations from the start, if you plan to operate as a sole proprietor without employees, there is no need to let the IRS know that you've opened a business. The IRS will be able to see that you are self-employed when you file your first income tax return after starting the business.

On the other hand, owners of partnerships or corporations *do* need to let the IRS know when they start a business because these entities are required to have a federal employer identification number (FEIN). This number is necessary because partnerships and corporations exist separately from the individuals who own them, whereas a sole proprietorship is intimately connected to its owner so can usually use the owner's social security number. (The differences between sole proprietors, partnerships, corporations, and limited liability companies (LLCs) are discussed further in the next chapter.)

SOLE PROPRIETOR, PARTNERSHIP, CORPORATION, OR LLC?

Choosing the entity for your business is an important decision. There are often both tax and nontax reasons for choosing one entity over another.

SOLE PROPRIETORSHIP

A sole proprietorship is a business owned by one person. The IRS usually allows a married couple to operate as a sole proprietorship, but this is the only exception to the one-person-only rules. Any other two (or more) people wanting to be in business together must choose an entity other than a sole proprietorship. Here's how you, as a sole proprietor, are connected to your business:

> You
> Your business

Your business and you are one. You can't borrow money from your business because you would be borrowing money from yourself. You can't have the business buy a car because it's really you buying the car. As the owner, you can't be treated as an employee of your business (more about this later). In Chapter 33, you'll see that the information about your business income and expenses is reported on Schedule C of your individual tax return, which is why the IRS refers to sole proprietors as Schedule C filers.

According to the IRS, nearly 80% of U.S. businesses are operated as sole proprietorships. That is because a sole proprietorship is the easiest, fastest, and cheapest way to set up and run a business. There are no government regulations that determine how the sole proprietorship is operated. Financial records are relatively easy to keep, and tax returns are simpler than they are for other entities. As a sole proprietor, you don't need to answer to anyone else; you can run the business in whatever way you choose.

One disadvantage to operating as a sole proprietorship is that it's hard to borrow money in the name of the business. Often sole proprietors are forced to use a personal asset (e.g., a home) as collateral when applying for a loan for the business. Another disadvantage is that the owner of the business is responsible for all financial risks. She has unlimited liability, which means that her personal assets are at risk if someone sues the business. Sole proprietors also aren't able to have fringe benefits (e.g., child care or health care costs) paid by the business, although they may offer these to any employees they have.

PARTNERSHIPS

A partnership is made up of two or more people in business together. As with a sole proprietorship, the partners can't be treated as employees of their business. There are different types of partnerships; sometimes all the partners are actively involved in the business, and sometimes one or more of the partners are investors or limited partners while the other partner or partners run the business. In either case, the partnership is a separate entity from the partners:

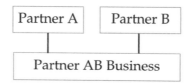

A partnership needs to have a federal identification number, which is issued by the IRS. The state may also require an identification number for the partnership. The partnership files a tax return, but no taxes are paid with the return; it's the partners who pay tax on the profits earned by the business. Each partner includes her share of the partnership income on her individual tax return. The profits (and losses) can be allocated unevenly, which may be helpful in reducing taxes for a high-income partner.

Like a sole proprietorship, a partnership is relatively free of government interference. However, the partnership tax return is more complex than the Schedule C, and the recordkeeping system needs to be more sophisticated (include more information) than the one needed for a sole proprietor.

A partnership allows you to work with one or more partners, which means that the responsibility of running the business is shared with others. Being able to work well with the partners you select is important.

There are disadvantages to operating as a partnership. Each partner is responsible for all the liabilities (e.g., loans) of the business. Also, it can be hard to sell or dispose of a partnership interest.

CORPORATIONS

Like a partnership, a corporation is an entity that is separate from those who own it:

```
┌─────────────────────────────────────────┐
│              ABC Corporation             │
└─────────────────────────────────────────┘

┌─────────────────────────────────────────┐
│                    You                   │
│        (Employee and Shareholder)        │
└─────────────────────────────────────────┘
```

A corporation must be registered with the IRS and the state in which it operates. As part of the registration process, the corporation will be given identification numbers by these agencies. The incorporation process is done at the state level. Many states charge corporations an annual fee for the privilege of doing business in their state. California's fee, for example, is $800 a year, whether the corporation makes any money during the year or not.

In addition to the expense and time involved in becoming incorporated, the shareholders (owners) must adopt bylaws, elect officers, and conduct and keep records of regularly scheduled meetings. Financial recordkeeping and tax returns for a corporation also can involve significant time and expense.

Some people choose this way of operating a business because they feel that incorporating gives the business a sense of legitimacy. Another major nontax reason for incorporating is that the shareholders are protected from personal liability if someone sues the corporation. If you own a home and operate your business as a sole proprietor or partnership, you could lose this asset if the business is sued. If you are incorporated, you are not likely to lose a personal asset unless the person suing you is able to prove that you didn't treat the corporation as a separate entity but, instead, commingled personal and business funds.

Other advantages of incorporating include the ease in which the business can be transferred to a new owner, the continuity of the business (it doesn't end if a shareholder dies or leaves), and the ability to sell shares of stock to raise money for the business.

Owners who work in the business are treated as employees of the corporation. This means that taxes are withheld from the owners' paychecks, just as if they were working for someone else. An incorporated business may or may not pay less tax than one operating as a sole proprietorship or partnership. This calculation is different for each business, since the tax benefits of incorporating will depend somewhat on the needs of the shareholders. This will be explained further in the descriptions of the different types of corporations—C-corporations, S-corporations, and personal service corporations.

C-corporations

When a tax return is filed for a C-corporation, the corporation pays taxes on the net profit of the business. One tax benefit of a C-corporation is that income splitting can be used. Shareholder salaries and dividends can be adjusted in such a way that taxes on the corporation's profits are split between the corporation and the shareholders. This strategy may reduce the total tax liability because the corporate tax rate is only 15% on the first $50,000 of profit. This is substantially less than the individual tax rate for a shareholder who has wages of $50,000. (There's more information about individual tax rates and brackets in Chapter 35.)

Since employee-owners of a C-corporation are treated like other employees, they are covered by whatever fringe benefits the business offers. These benefits could include health insurance; medical, child care, or tuition reimbursement plans; life, long-term care, and disability insurance; and retirement plans. The cost savings of being covered by these nontaxable fringe benefits may be enough of an incentive that incorporating will look inviting. Of course, these benefits reduce the profit of the corporation, and they must be available to all employees of the business.

A new business that expects to show a loss (have more expenses than income) for a year or more will probably not want to become a C-corporation. Any losses remain with the corporation and can only be deducted when the business begins to make a profit. This is unlike other entities in which losses from the business flow through to the owner's individual tax return, offsetting other types of income (e.g., wages or interest income) by the amount of the business loss.

S-corporations

An S-corporation is somewhat of a hybrid between a partnership and a C-corporation. While it files a corporate tax return, the profit (or loss) from the business is reported on the shareholders' (owners') individual tax returns. It is the shareholders, not the corporation, who pay tax on the profit. If the business has a loss, the shareholder can reduce other income (e.g., wages from another job) by deducting the loss. Some states impose a tax on the S-corporation even though the profits are being taxed to the shareholders.

An S-corporation differs from a partnership in that the profit is calculated after the salaries of the employee/owners have been deducted. Some S-corporations pay salaries based on actual profits so that by the time salaries have been deducted, there is no profit to be reported on the shareholder's individual return.

Some S-corporation employee/owners try to avoid paying the social security tax imposed on wages by taking money for themselves out of the business, not withholding taxes, and calling the distribution a dividend. The IRS is aware of this and expects owners to take a reasonable salary.

Children can be shareholders of an S-corporation, and income from the business can be split with them. This will be advantageous if you want to keep income from being taxed in your high tax bracket and, instead, want it taxed at their (usually) lower tax rate.

Unlike a C-corporation, fringe benefits are not available to employee/shareholders who own more than 2% of an S-corporation, although they can be available for any other employees of the business. As with a C-corporation, S-corporation shareholders are protected from personal liability for business errors and debts.

Personal Service Corporations (PSCs)

Professionals in the fields of health, law, engineering, accounting, performing arts, and consulting usually must be personal service corporations if they want to incorporate. Personal service corporations are taxed at a higher tax rate than other corporations. However, as with S- and C-corporations, a personal service corporation can adjust the shareholders' salaries so that there is no profit for the corporation and, thus, the higher corporate rate isn't paid. Instead, salary from the corporation, like all salaries, is taxed at the lower individual tax rate.

PSCs don't offer the same degree of protection from liability as other corporations. Individuals who are PSCs are usually personally liable for their own negligence.

Shareholders of PSCs are able to take advantage of some of the fringe benefits available to C-corporations. However, some of the benefits are only allowed if the corporation has more than one shareholder.

LIMITED LIABILITY COMPANIES (LLCs)

Limited liability companies are a fairly new kind of entity that combines the advantages of a partnership with the advantages of a corporation. Like partnerships, the profit from an LLC flows through to the owners who pay tax on it via their individual tax returns. The advantage of an LLC over a partnership is that, like corporation shareholders, all the owners of an LLC have limited personal liability for the business. In most states an LLC must have at least two members (owners). For IRS purposes, an LLC is treated like a partnership.

LLCs are especially appropriate for new businesses that expect to have a loss, since the loss will flow through to the individual member's tax return, reducing that taxpayer's total income.

Which Entity Is Best for Your Business?

It depends. There's no one right answer. Are you in a type of business in which lawsuits are common? Are you going into business with other people? Do you feel that you're not being taken seriously as a sole proprietor while your incorporated colleagues are getting all the business? Do you have large child care or medical expenses that could be covered by an employee benefit program if you were incorporated? Do you anticipate several years of losses before you start making a profit in your business?

A word of caution: Do not rush into creating an entity (a corporation, a partnership, or an LLC). They may be more difficult, expensive, and painful to get out of than they were to get into. Make sure you understand why you're making the choice you make. Too many people spend thousands of dollars to become incorporated in the hopes it will give them legitimacy, but they have no understanding of the tax implications of this decision. Often people move easily into a business partnership with lovers or friends. Sometimes working together causes strain on the personal relationship. Sometimes the relationship ends for other reasons. Whatever the reason, getting out of a business partnership is often messy. Don't go into business with anyone else, even your closest friend, without first discussing together the worst possible scenarios. What happens if one of you dies? Or wants out of the partnership? Or is working more/harder than the other one? These are things the two (or more) of you can talk about on your own, before meeting with an attorney. Make a list of your answers to such questions and then pay the attorney to look it over and write it up legally. You will never regret having taken the time and spent the money to prepare a written business agreement.

These are some of the questions that need to be answered before making this important decision. It's best to sit down with an accountant, a tax practitioner, or an attorney who is knowledgeable about the tax benefits, as well as the nontax implications (e.g., protection from liability and ease of selling the business), of the various entities.

NECESSARY
LICENSES AND
PERMITS

4

Now that you know you're a small business owner and you've chosen to operate as a sole proprietor, a partnership, an LLC, or a corporation, what's next? It's time to look into what licenses or permits you might need. If you are a professional (e.g., chiropractor, attorney, psychotherapist, contractor, real estate broker), most likely you already know what licenses are required before you can see clients or do work. Opening a restaurant or other food service requires meeting city health department guidelines. Any business that operates from a public facility, such as a store or office building, needs to be in compliance with the guidelines of the Americans with Disabilities Act (ADA). It is important to be aware of the regulations that apply specifically to your type of business, as well as those that are applicable to all businesses in your city or state.

If you set up your new business as a partnership, a corporation, an LLC, or a sole proprietorship with a business name that doesn't include your last name, you need to file a fictitious name statement. This is true also if such words as *associates*, *group*, or *company* are included in your business name, since those words imply that there are additional owners.

A fictitious name statement is generally filed with the county clerk's office. You pay a fee to register the name and then must run a public notice in the newspaper stating the business name and the name or names of those who own the business. The purpose of this is to protect consumers so that if they are cheated by a business, they can find out the names of the individuals who are responsible. Having a fictitious name means you are doing business as (DBA) a name other than your own.

Your city or county may require that you have a business license. Some cities require a license if you sell products or see clients in that city even if it's not your principal work or residence location. Some cities have zoning regulations and/or require a permit to operate a business out of your home. Find out what the rules are to be sure that you are operating within the regulations, before giving your home office address to anyone.

If you live in one of the forty-five states with a sales or excise tax and are responsible for collecting tax on your products or services, you need to register with the sales or excise tax agency. Generally, that agency also issues resale permits, which keep you from having to pay sales or excise tax on items you buy to resell to clients or customers. Some states require businesses to collect tax only on products sold within the state, whereas other states assess a sales or excise tax on all business transactions including professional services. Since each state has different regulations regarding sales tax and resale permits, you need to investigate this further on your own.

If you have employees (including yourself, if you're incorporated), you need to get a federal and a state employer identification number. The IRS and the state employment department will be able to tell you what taxes you must pay as an employer and what taxes must be withheld from employees' paychecks. This will include some combination of federal and state income taxes, social security tax, unemployment insurance, and perhaps mandatory disability and/or health insurance. A workers' compensation policy may be a requirement also. (Chapter 17 provides more information about payroll responsibilities.) Remember, if you're a sole proprietor or a partner in a partnership, you are *not* considered an employee of your business, so these requirements apply to you only if you hire employees to work in your business.

To find the local agencies that deal with the permits and taxes mentioned in this chapter, look in the government pages of your telephone book. The state section will list agencies that deal with employee and sales/excise taxes, and the city or county section will include those that handle zoning and business licenses.

What is a Federal Employer Identification Number?

A federal employer identification number (FEIN) is another name for an employer identification number (EIN). If you need an employer ID number, get it by applying to the IRS on Form SS-4. A sole proprietor is not required to have one unless she has employees or a Keogh retirement plan (see Chapter 32). When you open a business bank account, you may be told that you need a federal ID number, but you can tell the bank that you don't fall under the IRS requirements for having one. All business entities other than sole proprietorships must have an EIN whether they have employees or not.

BANK ACCOUNTS AND CREDIT CARDS

5

Most business books and classes will advise you that one of the first things to do when starting a business is to go to the bank and open a separate business checking account. At the risk of having to dodge a few tomatoes, I will say that I don't totally agree with that advice. Because many business owners find it helpful to have a separate business account, I'm not saying that you shouldn't do this; I'm simply saying that in many cases it is not a requirement.

At this point, the financial professionals reading this book may be grimacing, while many of the new business owners are probably breathing a sigh of relief. My client Barbara says, "I have a separate business checkbook, but whenever I'm at the office supply store, it seems like I always forget to take it with me, so I end up writing the check out of my personal account. When I'm at the grocery store, I always seem to have my business checkbook with me but not my personal one, so I end up writing checks to the grocery store out of my business checkbook." What she has at the end of the month is two checking accounts for which she has to pay fees and do reconciliations. Meanwhile, the expenses are all mixed up with business purchases in the personal account and personal purchases in the business account.

BANK ACCOUNTS

If you are going to have a separate business account, be sure to deposit all money from the business into that account, even if you later transfer it to your personal account. As much as possible, write business checks out of the business account and personal checks out of the personal account.

There are certain circumstances when you must have a separate business account, for example, when you operate as a corporation, a partnership, or an LLC. A separate entity requires a separate bank account. Also, if you're doing business under another name, other than your own, you may not be able to cash or deposit checks from your clients if you don't have a bank account in that name. Unless your bank is willing to give you an account called, for example, Jane Smith, DBA (doing business as) Smith's Carpeting, you need an account for Smith's Carpeting because clients will write checks to Smith's Carpeting, not to Jane Smith.

It's also a good idea to have a business bank account if you share a personal account with someone who is not your legally married spouse—for example, your mother, your roommate, or your domestic partner. If audited, you'll be asked to bring the bank statements from all accounts—checking and savings. If you bring in statements from an account you share with someone else, you will involve the other person in your audit. To minimize that involvement, keep your business income and expenses in a separate account even if the remainder of your finances are commingled. This is not an issue if you're married and have a joint account with your spouse; your spouse will already be part of your audit.

> **A money-saving hint:** If you decide to open a separate business account and your business name is the same as your personal name, consider opening another personal account. Fees for personal accounts are much lower than those for business accounts. Order checks for the second account in a different color so you can easily tell which checks go with which account.

CREDIT CARDS

Whether or not you have a business bank account, you may find it helpful to have a separate business credit card. The card does not need to be in the business name; just pick one of your credit cards as your business credit card. Many people find it easier to keep track of business expenses by using one credit card just for those expenses.

Also, while personal credit card interest is not deductible, business credit card interest is 100% deductible. By using one credit card exclusively for business, it will be much easier for you to determine how much interest you've paid on the business expenses you've charged. If you use a credit card for both personal and business expenses, you need to figure a way to prorate the interest, as it is deductible only to the extent that you can prove it's attributable to business expenses.

BALANCING YOUR CHECKBOOK

6

"I can't be overdrawn; I still have checks left."

—Slogan on a T-shirt

Do you call your bank on a regular basis to find out the balance in your account? Or do you close your current account and open a new one whenever your account balance is so muddled that you give up on ever reconciling it?

Balancing your checkbook (adding the deposits and subtracting the checks and withdrawals from the beginning balance) and reconciling your bank statement to your checkbook (making sure both have the same ending balance) are important steps in keeping track of your finances. By knowing your correct current bank balance, you avoid the embarrassment of not having enough in the account to cover checks you write, which can result in bounced checks. Also, you save yourself a substantial amount in bank charges, since each bounced check will incur an "insufficient funds" charge. In some states, the payee can sue you for three times the amount of a check that bounces. Most important, knowing the amount of money you have at any given time gets you out of a fog about money and is one more step in your money empowerment plan.

Each month you receive a bank statement from the institution where you have your account. Normally the bank statement lists all checks that have cleared (usually in numerical order), all withdrawals, and all deposits made during the prior 30-day period. Somewhere on the bank statement is the date of the last statement and the cutoff date for the current statement. The time between those two dates is the period covered by the statement. If you would find it easier to have a bank statement that ends on the last day of each month, ask the bank to change the statement ending date for your account.

Since the bank statement has an ending date, you need to look at the balance in your checkbook as of the same date. The checkbook balance should match your account balance as indicated by the bank statement. Chances are the two won't match. Reconciling your bank account is the process of finding out why the balances don't match.

The following are some of the reasons they may be different:

- Not all the checks you wrote have been cashed yet. Those that have not been cashed and returned to your bank are called outstanding checks. Outstanding checks will have been recorded in your check register but won't appear on the bank statement.
- You may have deposited some money in your account after the statement cutoff date. Although you recorded the deposit amounts in your check register, they are not included on your bank statement. These are called outstanding deposits.
- Your bank may charge a monthly service fee or pay monthly interest on your account. These amounts will be reflected on the bank statement but probably have not yet been entered in your check register.
- Automatic monthly payments may have been deducted from your account but may not have been recorded in your check register. This might also be the case with a regularly scheduled transfer made from one account to another. Also, you may have neglected to make note of ATM withdrawals (and any related fees).
- The amount of a check may have been entered differently in your check register than it was on the check itself. Typically, this is a transposition error (e.g., writing a check for $6.41 and entering it in your register as $6.14).
- The addition or subtraction in your check register may be incorrect.

You need to decide for yourself how much of a discrepancy you can live with. While it is always possible to get the balances to match to the penny, you may decide that it is not worth the time involved, and instead you'll accept the bank balance if it's within, for example, $3.00 of your own checkbook balance. If you want further help in getting the two balances to match, refer to the detailed instructions on bank statement reconciliations in Appendix A.

SECTION 2
Keeping Records

RECORDS DOES THE IRS EXPECT YOU TO HAVE?

7

If you're like most people, you have an innate dread of hearing from the IRS. Possibly one of your worst fears is receiving a letter that starts out, "Your return has been selected . . . " It's helpful to know what you would be expected to bring to an audit so that you can be sure to keep adequate records throughout the year.

If you should (and I hope you won't!) get called in for an IRS (or a state) audit, you will be asked to bring a number of items. In most cases the audit will focus on only 1 year. You will be asked to bring all bank statements for that year from all accounts, both business and personal. (If you have only one account, you'll obviously bring only the bank statements from that account.) The auditor will compare the deposits made to all your accounts with the amounts shown as income on your tax return. The IRS wants to make sure that no income from the business was deposited to personal accounts without having been included on your tax return.

Typically, an audit letter will ask you to bring all records of your business income and all canceled checks and receipts that verify the expenses you claimed for that year. If the bank doesn't return your canceled checks, this isn't a problem as long as the checks you use have carbon copies or your bank statement lists all the checks you wrote during the month, indicating payee name, amount of check, and date of payment. Most banks make available (generally, for a fee) a microfiche of your canceled checks should you need them. The auditor wants to see both your canceled checks and your receipts because the check shows that an item was paid for, while the receipt specifies what was bought.

> Lauren, a psychotherapist, was once "invited" for an audit. She had bought a lot of office furniture at a large department store, paying for it in installments. She had the canceled checks, on which she had written, in the memo section, "office furniture." Unfortunately, she had no receipts indicating what she'd bought. Who's to say she didn't buy an expensive stereo system or a new wardrobe rather than office furniture?

> Lynn Ann paid Betsy, a handyperson, to do some repairs around her office. In the memo section of the check to Betsy, Lynn Ann wrote, "office repairs," but she did not keep the receipt Betsy gave

her. How will she be able to prove that the check she wrote Betsy wasn't just a check to a friend? Will she be able to remember, if she is audited 2 years later, exactly what work Betsy did?

In addition to canceled checks and receipts, you also should have the original charge card receipts from any business expenses you charge. The monthly statement is acceptable if nothing else is available, but it gives no information about what was purchased. Also, the name shown as the payee on the monthly statement is sometimes different from the name of the business where you made the purchase.

Even the original charge card slip may not be sufficient when expenses for travel lodging are involved. The IRS wants to see the detailed receipt from the hotel so that they can be sure that the amount paid doesn't include personal items such as gifts.

You may have heard that you don't need to keep receipts if the amount of the expense is less than $75. This is true. However, you still need to record all information about the expense: how much it was, to whom payment was made, what type of expense it was, the date paid, and so on. Personally, I find it easier to just keep the receipt.

Receipts should be properly documented. For example, if you go to the drugstore and buy a roll of adding machine tape, the receipt may not indicate what was purchased. If it doesn't, you need to write "adding machine tape" on it. Otherwise, at the end of the year you'll have a pile of receipts showing the amounts of purchases but having no indication of what was bought. The IRS will accept the receipt with your notation as long as the amount and type of purchase are consistent with the kind of expense you need to have for your business.

What the IRS looks for in an audit is consistency. Does everything fit together? You can't always get receipts for money you spend, but if everything else seems to fit together, you shouldn't have any problems proving the expenses for which you don't have receipts. For example, you can't get a receipt for money you put in a parking meter, but if it's clear that you use your car in your work, the auditor will realize that you need to park somewhere, so this expense shouldn't be questioned. It's best, of course, if you enter parking meter costs in your car log (more about car logs in Chapter 25). The same is true with pay telephones; you won't be able to get a receipt for each call (unless you use a calling card). Although it's best to enter the amount spent in your calendar or appointment book, if the expense is consistent with the business you do, it shouldn't be a problem.

Your appointment book or calendar is an important part of your tax materials and should be kept with them from year to year. Notations on appropriate dates can provide backup information for such things as business mileage, meal expenses, parking meters, pay telephones, and business trips. In fact, if you're traveling at all for business, it's a good idea to record in your appointment book what activities you did each day you were away. This can be helpful should you ever need to prove that it was really a business trip.

Receipts, canceled checks, charge card slips, and appointment books can all be used to prove the expenses you had for your business. If you haven't been keeping all of these in the past, there's no sense worrying about it at this point, but you should make plans to do so in the future. That way, if necessary, you'll be able to show the IRS how you spent your money, and you won't miss out on the deductible expenses discussed in later chapters.

In addition to canceled checks, receipts, and appointment books, the IRS will ask in an audit to see all other records related to your business. These include payroll records if you have employees; copies of leases you have for store or office space, a car, or office equipment; your tax return for the year before and the year after the one being audited; copies of client or customer invoices; dimensions of your home if you claim office-in-home; and anything else related to the tax return being examined. This list is standardized, and some items may not apply to your business.

I recently received an e-mail from a woman who told me she'd just survived an IRS audit. "It was an incredible learning experience for me," she said. "What the taxpayer perceives as records and what the IRS interprets as records certainly are different." Her comment is very true. Although it's not necessary to live in constant fear of an audit (see Chapter 39 for information about your chances of being audited), being aware of what you'd be expected to bring if selected will enable you to keep ongoing records of those items the IRS would want to see.

As you'll read in the next chapter, the format in which you're keeping your business records may not exactly fit into the list of items the IRS wants to see in an audit. But if you're able to provide the backup documentation *in some form*, you (or your representative) can go to an audit with head held high.

KEEPING TRACK OF BUSINESS EXPENSES

8

You've now learned what documents the IRS expects you to bring to an audit. If you have just started your business, you may have little or no idea of how to begin keeping the required records. Or you may have been in business for a while and not be happy with the record-keeping system you've set up. Or perhaps you're one of those people who, just before last April 15, sat at the kitchen table, receipts and canceled checks spread out in front of you, saying, "There must be a better way."

The IRS does not require sole proprietors to have a formal book-keeping system. As long as you have the necessary backup materials, the method you use to record or store them is up to you. If you are comfortable keeping a sophisticated set of books, that's great. However, your situation may be more like Rachael's, a woman who recently came to my office.

> Rachael had met with an accountant several months before she came to see me. Hearing that she'd just started a new business, the accountant set up a comprehensive double-entry bookkeeping system for Rachael to use. Slightly embarrassed, Rachael confessed to me, "When I was in the accountant's office, I understood what I was supposed to do, but by the time I got home, I couldn't remember any of it, so I haven't been keeping any records for my business."

You probably didn't choose to go into business in order to learn book-keeping. If you have figured out some way of keeping records for your business and that system is working for you, I encourage you to continue it, no matter how "unsophisticated" it might seem. If you're currently using your checkbook as your record of expenses, that's fine. If you keep receipts filed by month or by type of expense or all collected together in a shoe box, that's fine too. What's not okay is to have some receipts in the kitchen drawer, some in the glove compartment of the car, and some on top of the TV.

This chapter provides an example of a simple but effective way of keeping track of your business expenses. If your business is a partnership, a corporation, or an LLC, you will need a somewhat more sophisticated recordkeeping system than the one described in this book. The principles are the same, but additional information is needed on an ongoing basis. Since you will probably consult a tax or accounting professional when establishing one of these entities, you will be able to get that person's suggestions for setting up an appropriate recordkeeping system.

The method shown in this chapter provides you with more information in a more accessible format than you have if a checkbook is the only record of your expenses. This system uses a disbursement sheet to record all money paid out. *Disbursements* is just another word for *expenses*. A disbursement sheet done on a computer is usually called a spreadsheet.

Whether you keep records by hand or on computer, I encourage you to read this chapter. The theory of recordkeeping is the same either way, so it's helpful to know how the process works, even if your computer program is doing the recording. (Chapter 11 discusses computerized recordkeeping.) Also, in the process of showing you how to use a disbursement sheet, I will be imparting some important tax information.

Look at the sample disbursement sheet (page 23). One advantage of using this method to keep track of expenses is that you can see at a glance all of your business expenses to date and whether they were paid by cash, check, or credit card. One of the potential problems in using only a checkbook as a record of expenses is that many times business purchases are made with a credit card or cash, and it's easy to forget to report those expenses. If they're for your business, those expenses are just as deductible as the ones paid for by check.

Additionally, a disbursement sheet provides information that will be helpful in making business decisions. At a glance you can see how much you've spent on advertising or postage. You can determine which months tend to bring in the most money and which months have the most expenses. Could you go on vacation next year during one of the months in which business seemed slow this year? Will you have enough income to cover the months that have extra expenses?

The disbursement sheet is made up of a series of columns. The first column is for the date the payment is made. The second column indicates the name of the person or company to whom payment was made. The next four columns are for the check number and amount for those things paid by check, the cash amount if paid in cash, and the charge amount if paid by credit card.

To the right of the double line are columns for some potential expenses. You already know or will determine the most common expenses in your business. Each of the most frequently occurring expenses should be given its own column. If you sell a product, you'll need a column called "Inventory" or "Merchandise Purchases" to record the amount of money spent in purchasing the product (or its components) before reselling it. Most

A DISBURSEMENT SHEET

Margie Leong, Computer Consultant

June 2000

Date	To:	Check Number	Amount of Check	Paid In Cash	Paid by Credit Card	Office Supplies	Client Expenses	Inventory Pruchases	Draw	Misc.	Description of Miscellaneous
6/3/9x	Minneapolis Paper Co.	101	40.09			40.09					
6/5/9x	Janet Jones	102	400.00							400.00	Office Rent
6/7/9x	Margie Leong	103	250.40			50.40				200.00	Travel
6/23/9x	North Airlines	104	116.18				116.18				
6/24/9x	Computer Shoppe	105	78.95					78.95			
6/25/9x	Third City Bank	106	560.72							500.00	Principal
										60.72	Interest
6/26/9x	Margie Leong	107	500.00						500.00		
6/26/9x	Petty Cash Reimbursement	108	45.03						8.93	20.00	Book
										13.20	Faxing
										2.90	Telephone
6/27/9x	VISA Credit Card	109	73.10							73.10	Entertainment
6/28/9x	Ace Furniture				300.00					300.00	Desk
6/30/9x	Third City Bank		7.50							7.50	Bank Charges
6/30/9x	The Office Store			30.19		30.19					
6/30/9x	Computer Shoppe			11.56				11.56			
			2,071.97	41.77	300.00	120.68	116.18	90.51	508.93	1,577.42	

businesses will have advertising or marketing expenses and office or computer supply costs. You may also pay for such things as professional dues, publications, and insurance. If you have employees, a column for payroll expenses will be used frequently, as will the columns for each type of tax withheld from the employees' paychecks.

If you use a manual bookkeeping system and you try to have a column for each possible business expense, you will end up with such a wide disbursement sheet that it will be totally unmanageable. This is not a problem with a computerized disbursement sheet, since you can have an almost unlimited number of columns. Computerized accounting programs also provide a generous (and sometimes unlimited) number of expense categories. With a manual system, however, you need to choose those expenses that occur most often, give them each a column, and then put the remainder of the expenses in the last two columns, which are called "Miscellaneous" and "Description of Miscellaneous."

On a tax return, you would never write that you had $1,577.42 worth of miscellaneous expenses (unless you're anxious to be audited). These columns are a temporary place to put infrequently occurring expenses. At the end of each month or at the end of the year, you will need to review the expenses listed in the "Miscellaneous" column and sort them into appropriate categories. The "Description of Miscellaneous" column will help you to do this.

Is it good to break down the expense categories into those shown on Schedule C?

Schedule C is the tax form used by sole proprietors to show business income and expenses. Many people think they need to use the same expense categories as are on Schedule C. You will see when we look at Schedule C that the IRS categories are not necessarily applicable to your business. Fortunately, the form has some blank lines to write in expense categories that are more appropriate for your business. I believe that the more you break down your expense categories, the less chance you have of being audited. Rather than listing, for example, $5,000 in supplies, divide the total amount into office supplies, computer supplies, small furnishings, and whatever other categories might apply. Of course, a lump sum of $5,000 in supplies for a business with gross income of $200,000 is looked at very differently than $5,000 in supplies for a business with $20,000 gross income.

HOW A DISBURSEMENT SHEET WORKS

The disbursement sheet on page 23 is for 1 month of Margie Leong's computer consulting business. Margie's business is primarily service oriented, but occasionally, when setting up a computer system for a client, Margie sells disks, software, or computer cables.

On the first line of Margie's disbursement sheet is a check for $40.09 to Minneapolis Paper Company for office supplies. The $40.09 is noted in the column labeled "Amount of Check," indicating how Margie paid for the expense. The same amount is also noted in the "Office Supplies" column, indicating what was purchased. Each expense is listed in two places: how it was paid and what was bought.

Next is a check to Janet Jones for $400.00. Margie pays office rent to Janet. This is not an in-home office, but an office outside the home. This expense has been entered in the "Miscellaneous" column. Since $400.00 is a large amount, you might wonder why rent doesn't have its own column. The reason is because, in most cases, office rent is due only once a month so isn't paid as frequently as many other types of expenses. Since her disbursement sheet has a limited number of expense columns, Margie allocates them to the expense categories for which she writes the most checks. It will be fairly easy at the end of the year to go through the "Miscellaneous" column and total the amounts for the twelve times office rent was paid. (Chapter 23 explains how office-in-home expenses are handled.)

Reimbursements

The next line on the disbursement sheet shows a check made out to Margie Leong. This check for $250.40 is reimbursement for $50.40 of office supplies and $200.00 of travel. Margie was at the office supply store and at the travel agency, and both times she had only her personal checkbook with her. She wrote the checks out of her personal checkbook and then went back to the office and reimbursed herself out of the business checkbook.

Even if Margie had not reimbursed herself, the expenses would still be deductible. It doesn't matter how you pay for something; if it's a deductible expense, it's deductible. Margie reimbursed herself to maintain a clear picture of her business and to be able to see at a glance what expenses she's had. Otherwise, she might forget about the expenses paid from her personal checkbook and think that her business has had fewer expenses than is really the case. Also, when it comes time to do her tax return, if Margie has reimbursed herself, she won't need to go back through her personal checkbook to see if there were business expenses paid out of her personal account.

If you're just starting your business, you may not have enough money in your business account to reimburse yourself for expenses paid from your personal account. Again, these business expenses are just as deductible, no matter which account was used to pay them. If you don't have a separate business account, you won't reimburse yourself, since, if you did, you'd be writing a check from your account and then depositing it right back into the same account!

The next line on the disbursement sheet shows another type of reimbursement. Margie paid for a plane ticket while doing work for one of her clients and will submit the bill to the client for reimbursement. Because she often has reimbursable client expenses, Margie has labeled one of her columns "Client Expenses." In Chapter 9, which covers money coming into the business, you'll see that Margie has a column called "Client Reimbursement." The two columns will cancel each other out (assuming that Margie gets reimbursed for all her client expenses), and there will be no tax ramifications. If Margie is not fully reimbursed for client expenses, she will deduct them on her tax return as if they were her own business expenses.

Inventory

Next on the disbursement sheet is the purchase of some computer cables from the Computer Shoppe. These are cables that Margie will resell to clients when she sets up their computer systems. When something is bought to be resold, it becomes part of inventory (more about inventory in Chapter 13). The $78.95 spent on cables is entered in the column called "Inventory Purchases."

Loans

The next line on the disbursement sheet shows a check made out to Third City Bank. Margie borrowed $7,000.00 from Third City Bank to buy a computer. The $7,000.00 loan is not considered income and is not reported on Margie's tax return. Every month Margie makes a loan payment of $560.72 to Third City Bank. Although she has a monthly expense of $560.72, $500.00 of this amount is a principal payment, repayment of a portion of the amount she borrowed. The amount that goes toward principal is not a deductible expense, whereas the $60.72 interest portion is.

The difference between how the principal is handled and how the interest is deducted is important to understand. When it's time to calculate her quarterly estimated tax payments (see Chapter 36), if Margie thinks her deductible loan expenses are $560.72 a month, her calculations will be incorrect. All she can deduct of the loan payment is the $60.72 monthly interest, not the entire $560.72 payment. Margie may or may not know during the year how much interest she's paying. Although her tax professional or a computerized financial program can create a loan payment schedule for her that shows the interest paid each month, Margie may not have the exact figure until the end of the year, when Third City Bank sends her a statement of interest paid.

Are you saying that the cost of the computer is not deductible?

No. The portion of the loan that is principal repayment is not deductible, but I haven't discussed the deductibility of the item on which the loan money was spent. In this case, the loan was used to buy a computer for Margie's business. The computer is fully deductible, but this is a separate issue from the deductibility of the loan that was used to purchase it.

Draw

Looking again at the disbursement sheet, you see that the next line lists a check to Margie Leong, the owner of the business. She has given herself $500.00 from her business. It is recorded in the column labeled "Draw." As a sole proprietor or a partner in a partnership, what you pay yourself is called draw.

Money you take out of your business that is for anything other than business expenses is called draw. If you're at the grocery store and you have your business checkbook with you, the check you write from that account for groceries is draw. If you give yourself $500.00 every week out of the business, that's draw.

If your business operates as a corporation, you are paid as an employee, just as you would be if you were working for someone else. But if you operate as a sole proprietorship or partnership, you cannot be an employee of your business, and you do not withhold taxes when you take money for yourself from the business.

If you use only one bank account, anything for which you write a check is either a business expense or draw. Draw is discussed further in Chapter 14, where you'll see that it is not a deductible expense. For that reason, you can choose whether or not to keep track of it. The main reason I encourage you to record the draw checks is so that you can see how much you take out of your business during the year. Often I say to a client, "Your profit was $40,000.00 from the business this year," and typically she responds, "I couldn't tell you where it went then, because I haven't seen it." By keeping track of your draw, you'll be able to see where the profit goes.

Petty Cash

Next on the disbursement sheet is a line for petty cash reimbursement. If you have a business that has frequent small purchases (e.g., a carpenter purchasing supplies or an editor making frequent trips to a nearby copy center), it may be helpful to have a petty cash account. It can be difficult to keep track of the money spent via a petty cash account, so you need to keep careful records.

Begin a petty cash account by putting a specified amount of money—for example, $50.00—into a petty cash box or envelope. Whenever money is taken out, replace it with a receipt or slip of paper, indicating how the money was spent. At any time, you should be able to add up the receipts and the remaining cash and have them equal the amount that was originally put in the box. When you run low on cash in the box, remove and total the receipts and replace the cash that has been spent.

In this example, a check for $45.03 is being written to restock the petty cash fund. By looking at the expense columns, you can see that $20.00 was spent on a book, $13.20 was spent on faxing at the local copy center, $8.93 was draw (Margie took money out of petty cash one day to buy lunch), and $2.90 was spent on pay telephone calls. What's entered on the disbursement sheet is the breakdown of how the $45.03 was spent. When Margie adds the amount of this check to what remains in the petty cash box, the total cash will again equal $50.00. Note: There is no such expense as petty cash; the money was spent on *something*.

Credit Card Purchases

The next line on the disbursement sheet is a payment to VISA® Credit Card. When Margie's credit card bill came, the total due was $73.10, which had been spent on business entertainment. Margie pays the credit card bill and enters the amount of the check under business entertainment. Unfortunately, most credit card bills aren't so simple. What if the credit card bill had been for $573.10, of which $73.10 was for business entertainment and $500.00 was for something personal? Margie would have several choices about how to pay that bill:

- Since she has separate business and personal accounts, she could write two checks: $73.10 from the business account and $500.00 from her personal account. She would then send both checks in payment of her bill.
- She could write one check from her personal account for $573.10, then reimburse herself from the business account for the $73.10.
- She could write one check from her business account for $573.10, of which $73.10 is for business entertainment and $500.00 is draw. Remember, paying for something personal from the business is draw.

What if Margie pays off her credit card bill by sending $50.00 or $100.00 a month? How does she know whether that amount is paying for the business entertainment or the personal item or for some other expense? The next line on the disbursement sheet demonstrates a way to handle this.

That line indicates a $300.00 purchase from Ace Furniture that was paid by credit card. Margie bought a desk for her office, and the date listed is the date she charged it. As far as the IRS is concerned, the date you charge something is the date it's considered paid for. If you charge something before December 31, you can deduct it on that year's tax return even though you won't be paying the credit card bill until the following year. If you pay off your credit cards in monthly payments, record the full amount of the purchase at the time you charge the item so that you can deduct the expense in the current year. Don't worry about the fact that you're not actually going to be paying it off until sometime next year. If you record your credit card purchases this way, the checks you write each month to make payments on your credit card bill should be listed under "Draw" to avoid recording the expense twice.

Assets

Look again at the Ace Furniture line on the disbursement sheet. Margie's purchase of a desk is listed in the "Miscellaneous" column. A desk, a computer, a fax machine, and similar items are called assets. A business asset is something of value that you use in your business. When you buy an asset for your business and the asset is expected to last for more than a year, the IRS says you must depreciate the item over a period of years.

Depreciate means that instead of deducting the full cost of the item in one year, you deduct the cost over a period of years. Chapter 22 explains depreciation more thoroughly, but what you should note here is that when you file your tax return, you need to list the assets purchased during the year. By recording the asset in the "Miscellaneous" column rather than including it under, for example, office supplies, it will be easy at the end of the year to compile a list of the assets purchased for your business in that year.

What about the credit card interest?

As mentioned earlier, interest on credit cards used for business expenses is 100% deductible. You can either record the interest monthly or wait until you get the statement from the credit card company at the end of the year telling you how much interest you paid during the previous year. Remember, interest paid on a credit card used for both personal and business expenses can be deducted only if you can prove how much interest was incurred on the business purchases.

If I pay off my credit cards on time, there is no interest to deduct. Is it better for a business not to pay them off in full each month?

It's never better to spend money in order to save money. If you spend $23.00 on interest, that doesn't equal a $23.00 tax savings. Don't get into the trap of thinking you should spend some money in order to have a deduction. Just remember, you don't save $1.00 in tax when you spend $1.00 on a deductible expense. If you don't spend it, you'll have more money in your pocket!

Bank Charges

In keeping track of your expenses, don't forget bank charges. If your checking account is for business only, deduct 100% of the service charge. If it's part business, part personal, you need to prorate the amount in some equitable manner. Margie has listed her bank charges on the next line of the disbursement sheet.

Cash Expenditures

The last two lines of the disbursement sheet are expenses that Margie paid for in cash. Each purchase has also been listed in one of the expense categories.

Totaling the Disbursement Sheet

When Margie adds together columns 4, 5, and 6 (which indicate the amount spent and the method used to pay for the expense), they should equal the total of the columns on the right side of the double line (which indicate what was purchased). This confirms that every transaction has been correctly entered in two places on the disbursement sheet.

KEEPING TRACK
OF THE MONEY
COMING INTO YOUR BUSINESS

The opposite of disbursements (money out) is receipts (money in). Although you may think of receipts as something you get when you pay for groceries, it is also a technical term used by bookkeepers and accountants to refer to money that comes into a business. If the word *receipts* confuses you, just think of it, when used in this context, as "money in."

As with your disbursements, if you already have a system of keeping track of the money coming into your business, that's great—keep it up. If you haven't yet set up a system, this chapter will help you get started.

The most important thing you should know about receipts is that you need a record of every single deposit made to all bank accounts. At the least, there should be a notation in your checkbook summarizing the source of each deposit. Some people keep a duplicate deposit slip and write the source on that. You can also use a receipts spreadsheet (discussed later in this chapter).

Whichever method you use, it is important to record all money coming in, whether it is taxable or not. This record is necessary for your personal as well as your business account. If you are self-employed but also work as an employee, make a note when you deposit your paycheck that it was the source of the deposit. Make note also of which deposits are from client fees, which are a birthday gift from Mom, which is reimbursement from a colleague for a dinner you paid for, and so on. *Wherever it came from and whichever bank account it's deposited into, every single dollar should be recorded.*

 Is the birthday gift I received from my mother taxable?

 No. Any person can give any other person up to $10,000 per year, and the money is neither taxable nor shown on either person's tax return. That doesn't mean, however, that you shouldn't keep track of any monetary gifts; you wouldn't want the IRS to think it was income from your business that you failed to report. If you receive a large amount of frequent gifts, I recommend that you ask the donor to enclose a letter with each check, making mention of the gift. You may also want to make a copy of the check to avoid any problems should you be audited.

Sole proprietorships file a Schedule C with their tax return, showing their business income and expenses. For this reason, the IRS calls sole proprietors Schedule C filers. Schedule C filers are audited more often than other people because the IRS thinks they may not be reporting all their income. There is less focus on businesses that don't have a lot of cash transactions than there is on businesses such as restaurants and hair salons, where much of the business is done in cash. Nevertheless, all businesses need to keep good records.

The IRS also expects you to keep track of and report any bartering you do. If you are an auto mechanic and you fix Paige's car in exchange for a dress from her dress shop, you have taxable income. The value of the dress is the amount that needs to be included with your income. If, instead of giving you a dress, Paige does some bookkeeping for your business, you must report the value of the bookkeeping as income. Since the work was done for your business, you can deduct as a business expense the value of the car repair you did. This is because you could have deducted the bookkeeping if you had paid money for it. Although most people don't think about recording their barter "income," you can be assured that one question asked at every audit is, "Did this taxpayer participate in barter transactions?"

In an audit the IRS looks at the monthly statements from all bank accounts. They add up the deposits made to all the accounts and compare the total to the income reported on your tax return. If more money went through your bank account than shows up as income on your tax return, you need to have a good explanation for the difference. Neither the gift from Mom nor the computer loan from Third City Bank are taxable, but unless you keep a record indicating the source of that money when you deposit it, the assumption will be that it was income you didn't report. *Keeping track of your money coming in is at least as important, if not more so, as keeping track of your expenses.*

Remember, if you have a separate business bank account, all business income should be deposited into that account and then transferred, if you wish, to other accounts. Similarly, the paycheck from your work as an employee and the birthday gift from Mom should be deposited into your personal account.

USING A RECEIPTS SHEET

A receipts sheet, like a disbursement sheet, allows you to see at a glance what business activity has occurred. Like the disbursement sheet, the receipts sheet is made up of columns. The total amount of each deposit is noted, and then, to the right of the double lines, the amount is noted again in the appropriate column to indicate the source of the money.

As with the disbursement sheet, choose column headings that most accurately reflect the sources from which you get money. In Margie's business, "Receipts from Clients" is one column heading and "Retail Sales" is another.

If clients reimburse you for expenses, as Margie's do, you may have a column labeled "Client Reimbursements." Theoretically these reimbursements should equal the "Client Expenses" column on your disbursement sheet, which is where you would record those expenses for which you expect to be reimbursed. Sometimes the end of the year comes before

A RECEIPTS SHEET (MONEY IN)

Margie Leong, Computer Consultant

July 2000

Date	From:	Total Amount of Deposit	Retail Sales	Sales Tax Collected	Client Fees	Client Reimbursement	Transfer from Savings	Misc.	Description of Miscellaneous
7/3/9x	North Airlines reimbursement	116.18				116.18			
7/5/9x	Computer supply sales	200.90	190.00	10.90					
7/7/9x	Transfer from City Bank	850.00					850.00		
7/10/9x	Client fees	600.00			600.00				
7/24/9x	Bounced check	(70.00)			(70.00)				
7/25/9x	Client fees	80.00			70.00			10.00	Bank Charges
		1,777.08	190.00	10.90	600.00	116.18	850.00	10.00	

you've received a reimbursement for something you paid for late in the year, so the two column totals may not always be identical. The first line in the receipts sheet on page 32 shows the reimbursement Margie received for the $116.18 North Airlines ticket.

If you sell a retail product (i.e., you sell something directly to the person who will use the product), you may, like Margie, have a column labeled "Store Sales" or "Retail Sales." The second line in the example shows a deposit of $200.90 from computer supply sales. Of that total, $190.00 is the amount received for the items that were sold, and $10.90 is the sales tax collected. (In your state, the sales tax may be called excise tax, or you may live in a state where no sales or excise tax is paid.) The sales tax collected is not your money. You collect the tax when you make a sale, but you are serving as the intermediary who will pass it on to the state or city agency that is actually assessing the tax. The reason for listing the sales amount separately from the tax collected is so that you don't make the mistake of thinking you made $200.90 today when in reality you made $190.00.

Next on the receipts sheet you'll see a line indicating a transfer from Margie's savings account. Transferring money from one account to another is not a taxable transaction. It's already your money; you're simply transferring it from one place to another. If you don't keep track of the transfer of money, however, an IRS auditor could assume it was income you didn't report, so it's best to record it in some way.

The next line on Margie's receipt sheet shows client fees received. Client, patient, or customer fees are the amounts received by service businesses such as plumbers, consultants, doctors, and artists. Margie received $600.00 in client fees and deposited them that day. A few days later she received a notice from her bank telling her that one of those checks, in the amount of $70.00, had bounced. On the next line Margie records the bounced check by entering the $70.00 amount in parentheses to indicate, in bookkeeping language, that the amount is to be subtracted out. Margie subtracts the $70.00 as if she'd never received the check. After the amount has been subtracted, the total of the deposits is $70.00 less, and the "Client Fees" column now totals $530.00, instead of $600.00. Then Margie contacts the client, saying, "Your check bounced, and my bank assessed a service fee of $10.00. Please come to my office with $80.00 in cash to cover your original check and to reimburse me for the bank charge." Once the client comes with the money, Margie starts all over again, depositing the $80.00, of which $70.00 is recorded in the "Client Fees" column and $10.00 in the "Miscellaneous" column as a bank service charge reimbursement.

When you total the deposits column (column 3), it should equal the total of all the columns to the right of the double line. This confirms that each deposit has been entered correctly in two columns.

A 6-Column Pad with Address Space

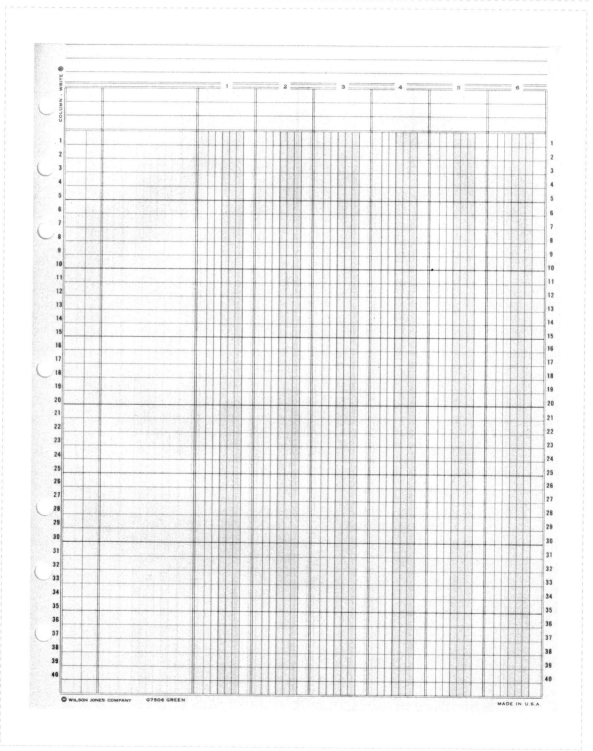

LEDGER BOOKS AND RECORDKEEPING SYSTEMS

10

A manual disbursement sheet might look like the example on page 23. In an office supply store, you will find many different types of ledger books available for use in recording disbursements in this format. Some of the books will have preprinted expense column headings. If you own a very small business, you may find that the categories of expenses listed are not pertinent to you. For example, unless you have employees, an expense column labeled "Employee Pension Plan" won't be useful. For that reason, you may find it easier to use a book with blank column headings so that you can enter your own expense categories.

One option is to use a columnar pad (see page 34). Columnar pads come in many different widths: two-column, six-column, thirteen-column widths, and so forth, are readily available. Typically, these pads are light green. The width most commonly used to record disbursements is a 13-column pad with address space, which is an especially wide column on each page. This wide column can be used to record to whom payment is made or from whom payment is received. The narrow columns next to the address space can be used to record the date and check number, if payment is made by check. The remaining columns can be labeled with your business's most frequently occurring expenses.

A columnar pad with fewer columns is often sufficient for keeping track of receipts (money in). *List money in and money out on separate sheets of paper; you'll confuse yourself if you try to include them both on one sheet*. The individual sheets on a columnar pad can be torn out easily. By putting them in a three-ring binder, you'll have a very adequate set of business books.

ONE-WRITE SYSTEMS

Another way of keeping manual records is to use a one-write system. Safeguard® and McBee® are two brand names of one-write systems, and other brands are available through dealers, mail order companies, and your bank. You can't go into an office supply store and buy a one-write system off the shelf because the checks need to be coded to your bank account. The checks in a one-write system have a strip of carbon on the back of them so that the date, the payee's name, the check number, and the amount of the check are entered automatically on the disbursement sheet as you write the check (see page 36). All you need to do to complete your expense records is to label the columns of expenses on your

A Safeguard® One-Write System Disbursement Sheet with Checks
One of the checks is folded over to show the carbon strip in the back.

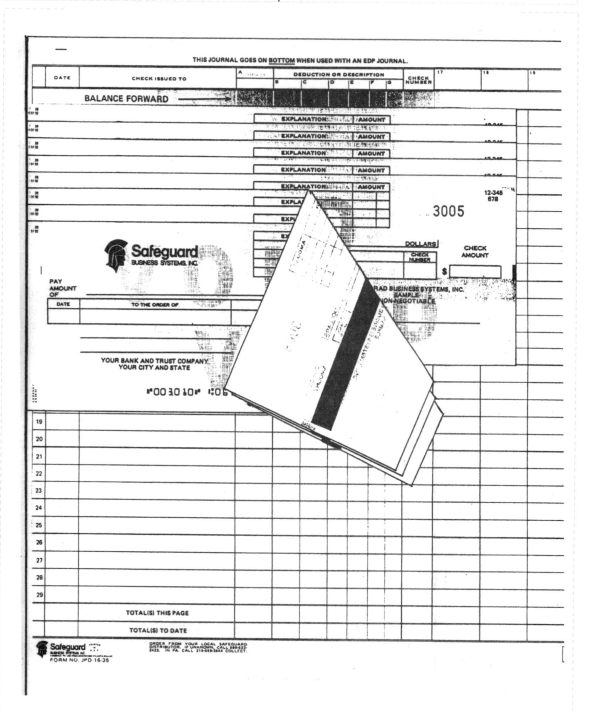

disbursement sheet and enter each expense amount in its appropriate column.

A one-write system is a big time-saver, since all of the information about each check is entered only once (when the check is written). People who write a lot of checks will find this very helpful. One-write systems also help you avoid the situation of writing a check for $58.90 and entering it in your check register as $59.80.

These systems are available with other optional modules, such as client account cards. As you record each deposit, the carbon on the back of the deposit slip copies the amount received on to each client's individual card, allowing you to keep an ongoing record of the balance owed by that client.

One disadvantage of using a one-write system is that it's considerably more expensive than buying a box of checks. Also, some people find it inconvenient to carry around because the one-write checkbook is generally quite large and won't easily fit into your purse or pocket. Another potential problem is that you may find it hard to remember to record expenses paid by cash or credit card, since the one-write system focuses primarily on expenses paid by check.

DOING YOUR
RECORDKEEPING
ON A COMPUTER

11

More and more people are doing their recordkeeping on a computer. While it may not be appropriate to buy a computer just to run a book-keeping program, if you already have one, you will probably find that your financial chores can be handled more quickly with the use of technology.

If you are planning to computerize your recordkeeping, you have several choices of how to do it. The first option is to use a spreadsheet program such as Lotus 1-2-3®, QuatroPro®, or Excel®. Even though some of the programs come with appropriate templates, you will need to set up the spreadsheet yourself, and it will probably look similar to the disbursement sheet shown in Chapter 8. After you insert the appropriate formulas, the columns will automatically total themselves each time you make an entry.

Another option is to use a personal finance or basic accounting program. Quicken®, Microsoft Money®, One-Write Plus®, and Peachtree Accounting®, are among the programs in this category. Quicken® even has a version called Quicken Home and Business®; it includes extra features helpful for small businesses that aren't included in the basic program. These programs are designed for easy use by nonaccountants but are quite adequate for many small businesses.

If, however, you have inventory, need complex reports, have employees, or want to do invoicing as part of your recordkeeping, you may need a more sophisticated finance program such as QuickBooks®, Peachtree Complete Accounting®, M.Y.O.B.® (Mind Your Own Business), or Dac Easy®.

If at all possible, before buying a financial program, try out a friend's copy or a sample copy if offered by the manufacturer. That way you'll see whether the program organizes records in the way you intuitively expect them to be organized. You'll also be able to see whether it has all the features you need without overwhelming you with those you don't need. If one program doesn't meet your needs, try another.

One of the major advantages of most financial programs is that you're able to use the computer to write and print your checks. Although you need to order special checks, the timesaving is great when you use this feature. As you write and print the check, the information on that check (payee, date, etc.) is entered automatically into the appropriate expense category. This is especially helpful for those checks you write month after month (e.g., rent and utilities). Once you've written a check to a particular payee, as soon as you begin the first few letters of that payee's name for a later check, the program will finish the remainder of the name and also fill in the amount of the check. At any time, you can print out a summary of your business income and expenses.

> *When Donna had me prepare her tax return, she was shocked to discover she owed more taxes. She was sure that the number I'd reported for her business income was too high. We reviewed her computer printout together and discovered that she had somehow included her beginning business bank balance of several thousand dollars as business income. Her actual business income was that much less. After correcting her computer records and the tax return, she owed no additional tax after all.*

One major caution: When using computer programs to do your recordkeeping, remember the adage "Garbage in, garbage out." If you don't understand the information you're entering into the program, what comes out may or may not be correct.

It's tempting to conclude that a computer printout must be correct. Just remember that this won't be the case if the data entered is faulty.

FINANCIAL
STATEMENTS

12

At some point you may be asked to provide someone with a financial statement. This might happen when you ask a supplier for credit.

> *Audrey owns a hair salon and uses a linen service to provide her with clean towels each week. She is expected to pay for the towels as they are delivered. When this payment arrangement became more inconvenient, Audrey asked the linen service to bill her and allow her to pay at the end of the month (which is called "extending credit"). The service said it would consider doing that if Audrey would provide a financial statement of her business.*

Also, you may be asked to provide a business financial statement if you apply for a loan to buy a car, computer, house, or any other large purchase. When the lender finds out you are self-employed, often he or she will ask for two or three years of tax returns and a current financial statement.

Financial statements can be useful also in measuring the health of your business. However, since those calculations involve more sophisticated accounting information, they are beyond the scope of this book.

There are two parts to a financial statement. The first is the balance sheet. This is a listing of business assets (things of value that your business owns) and liabilities (what the business owes to others) as of a particular date. The difference between your assets and liabilities is your "equity," or ownership, in the business. A balance sheet is like a photograph of your business finances as of the date of the report. Although not required of sole proprietors, a balance sheet must be included on the annual tax return of corporations, LLCs, and most partnerships. A sample balance sheet follows.

The second part of a financial statement is the profit and loss, or income and expense, statement. It covers a specific period of time, usually from the beginning of one month to the end of another month. The profit and loss statement for Barbara's business for the period from January 1 to December 31 follows.

BALANCE SHEET

BARBARA'S IMPORT JEWELRY COMPANY
Balance Sheet
December 31, 2000

ASSETS

Computer	$ 1,550
Work Table	130
Inventory	1,093
Total Assets	**$ 2,773**

LIABILITIES

Computer Loan Balance	976
Total Liabilities	**$ 976**

OWNER'S EQUITY $ 1,797

PROFIT AND LOSS STATEMENT

BARBARA'S IMPORT JEWELRY COMPANY
Income and Expenses
January 1 - December 31, 2000

INCOME

Jewelry Sales	$ 29,976
Repair Fees	2,643

Total Income $ 32,619

EXPENSES

Rent	$ 4,000
Employee Salaries	2,611
Office Supplies	700
Education Expenses	325
Depreciation	411
Entertainment	56
Interest on Loans	280
Books and Subscriptions	54
Dues	75
Cost of Goods Sold	9,907

Total Expenses $18,419

Net Profit $14,200

Barbara sells and repairs jewelry. Her profit and loss statement (P & L) shows the amount of income that came from customer fees and from sales. Barbara doesn't report here any income she received as an employee (where taxes were taken out of her paychecks) or from any other source. This statement represents solely her business income.

After income, Barbara lists her expenses. Again, these are only business expenses. One line indicates the business rent she paid. This is not for an office-in-home, but rent for an office outside her home. She also lists employee salaries. This is not what she paid herself, because, as a sole proprietor, she's not an employee of her business; this is the amount she paid the employees who work for her. (If Barbara were incorporated, her salary would be listed here, along with those of any other employees.) Barbara lists the amounts she spent on office supplies, education expenses, business entertainment, interest on loans (not the full payment amount, just the interest), books and subscriptions, dues, and so forth. Also, she includes depreciation (an expense discussed in depth in Chapter 22).

Barbara's P & L also includes something called "Cost of goods sold." Cost of goods sold is an expense incurred by businesses that sell products and have an inventory. Inventory and cost of goods sold will be described more fully in the next chapter. The P & L we've been looking at was prepared in the most easily understood format. Normally the cost of goods sold figure is subtracted directly from the income and the resulting figure is called the gross profit. The operating expenses are then subtracted from the gross profit.

After Barbara adds up all her expenses, she subtracts the total from her income. The result is her net profit, sometimes referred to as the bottom line. *What Barbara (and every business owner) pays taxes on is the net profit.*

INVENTORY AND COST OF GOODS SOLD

13

Inventory is what you have on hand to sell to others. This does not include office supplies or office equipment unless you're in the business of selling offices supplies or office equipment to others. Service businesses will generally not have inventories. Because Barbara sells jewelry, she does have an inventory. On January 1, her beginning inventory was zero; she had no jewelry on hand to sell to others. During the year she bought $11,000 worth of jewelry. She bought 3,500 bracelets at $2 each and 4,000 pairs of earrings at $1 per pair. The per item cost is an important figure for her to know. Barbara's inventory is now worth $11,000. Note: This isn't the price at which she will sell the jewelry to others; it's her cost of purchasing the inventory.

INVENTORY

BARBARA'S IMPORT JEWELRY COMPANY

January 1			No inventory
January 6	Purchases: 3,500 bracelets @ $2	=	$7,000
May 23	Purchases: 4,000 pairs of earrings @ $1	=	$4,000
December 31	Remaining Inventory		
	500 bracelets @ $2	=	$1,000
	93 pairs of earrings @ $1=		93
	Total year-end inventory		$1,093

As Barbara sells each item of jewelry, she looks up the original amount she paid for it so that she can reduce her inventory figure accordingly. At the end of the year, Barbara will need to count what's left of her inventory. The total dollar value of the physical inventory should match closely the inventory tally Barbara has kept throughout the year as she sold her jewelry.

No doubt you've noticed stores that are closed temporarily for inventory. Once a year, at least, every business that sells goods needs to do a physical inventory. This means they need to do a hands-on count of what is left of the items they bought to resell to others.

At the end of the year, when Barbara counts what's left of her jewelry, she has 500 bracelets and 93 pairs of earrings. She knows that each bracelet cost her $2, and each pair of earrings cost her $1, which means her ending inventory is $1,093. She subtracts her ending inventory from the earlier $11,000 inventory and finds that her cost of goods sold is $9,907. This figure represents the cost of the goods that were sold—in this case, the cost of the jewelry that sold during the year.

CALCULATING COST OF GOODS SOLD

BARBARA'S IMPORT JEWELRY COMPANY

Beginning of year inventory	0	
Inventory purchases	+ $11,000	
End of year inventory	− 1,093	
Cost of Goods Sold	$ 9,907	

TO CHECK FIGURES:
Bought 3,500 bracelets @ $2

500 are left, so 3,000 must have sold	3,000 x $2	=	$ 6,000

Bought 4,000 pairs of earrings @ $1

93 pairs are left, so 3,907 must have sold	3,907 x $1	=	3,907

Cost of Goods Sold	**$9,907**

Since Barbara originally had 3,500 bracelets and has 500 left, she must have sold 3,000. Since she had 4,000 pairs of earrings and now has 93 pairs left, she must have sold 3,907 pairs. When Barbara multiplies the number of bracelets and pairs of earrings she has sold by the amount they cost her, she should again come out with the $9,907 cost of goods sold figure. What Barbara can deduct on her tax return is the $9,907 cost of the items that sold, not the $11,000 she spent to buy all the bracelets and earrings originally.

If Barbara had bought all her jewelry inventory on December 31 and not sold any of it, she would not be able to deduct any of the $11,000 purchase cost for that year because none had been sold. In that case, the $11,000 becomes the beginning inventory figure for the following year. In the above example, the $1,093 worth of remaining bracelets and earrings becomes Barbara's beginning inventory for next year. As she sells them during that year, she will then be able to deduct their purchase cost.

In addition to keeping track of the cost of each item and the number left at the end of the year, anyone who has inventory needs to keep a record of any inventory removed for personal use. For example, if you sell cosmetics and you keep a supply on hand to sell to customers, you cannot deduct as a business expense (cost of goods sold) any cosmetics you use personally. Anything personal taken out of the business is draw, a concept discussed more fully in the next chapter.

WHAT IS DRAW? 14

When we looked at Barbara's profit and loss statement in Chapter 12 , you may have noticed that draw (the amount of personal money taken from the business) is not listed at all. Remember, if you pay yourself $500 a week from your business or if you pay for groceries from your business checking account, that is draw. Anything personal paid by the business is draw. Draw is not a deductible expense. Neither is it included as income. In fact, for sole proprietors, *draw is not recorded anywhere on a tax return.*

In partnerships, the amount of draw taken by each partner is reported on the tax return. However, this is for information only and isn't part of calculating the net profit. Owners of corporations do not take draw because they are paid as employees.

In Barbara's case, she is taxed on $14,200, which is her net profit after paying business expenses. If you were Barbara, what is the maximum amount of draw that you could take out of your business? You can't take out all the income you bring in; if you did, you wouldn't be able to pay your business expenses. The amount of the net profit (in this case, $14,200) is the most you can take out for yourself and still be able to cover your business expenses.

The IRS doesn't care what you do with the net profit—whether you take it out as a draw or leave it in the business bank account. That's why there is no place on the tax return for you to indicate whether you took out the whole amount, took part of it, or kept it all in the bank account. It doesn't matter. The net profit is what you pay tax on; the IRS doesn't care how you spend it.

People sometimes have trouble understanding how you can take money out of your business and not report it. But if you report the draw as you take it out, you will be paying tax on the same money twice. You're already paying tax on it as your net profit; what you do with it is no one's business but yours.

Could I try to make my net profit zero by taking more draw?

No, draw is not a deductible expense, so it doesn't affect your net profit at all. The only way you can reduce your net profit is to have more deductible expenses or less income. If you take all your profit out as draw, you may not have any money left in your bank account, but you will still have a net profit to report and pay taxes on.

SECTION 3
Employees and Independent Contractors

Twenty Common-Law Rules for Determining the Status of Employees and Independent Contractors

Common-law rules.— To help you determine whether an individual is an employee under the common-law rules, the IRS has identified 20 factors that are used as guidelines to determine whether sufficient control is present to establish an employer-employee relationship.

These factors should be considered guidelines. Not every factor is applicable in every situation, and the degree of importance of each factor varies depending on the type of work and individual circumstances. However, all relevant factors are considered in making a determination, and no one factor is decisive.

It does not matter that a written agreement may take a position with regard to any factors or state that certain factors do not apply, if the facts indicate otherwise. If an employer treats an employee as an independent contractor and the relief provisions discussed earlier do not apply, the person responsible for the collection and payment of withholding taxes may be held personally liable for an amount equal to the taxes that should have been withheld.

The 20 factors indicating whether an individual is an employee or an independent contractor follow.

1) *Instructions.* An employee must comply with instructions about when, where, and how to work. Even if no instructions are given, the control factor is present if the employer has the right to control how the work results are achieved.

2) *Training.* An employee may be trained to perform services in a particular manner. Independent contractors ordinarily use their own methods and receive no training from the purchasers of their services.

3) *Integration.* An employee's services are usually integrated into the business operations because the services are important to the success or continuation of the business. This shows that the employee is subject to direction and control.

4) *Services rendered personally.* An employee renders services personally. This shows that the employer is interested in the methods as well as the results.

5) *Hiring assistants.* An employee works for an employer who hires, supervises, and pays workers. An independent contractor can hire, supervise, and pay assistants under a contract that requires him or her to provide materials and labor and to be responsible only for the result.

6) *Continuing relationship.* An employee generally has a continuing relationship with an employer. A continuing relationship may exist even if work is performed at recurring although irregular intervals.

7) *Set hours of work.* An employee usually has set hours of work established by an employer. An independent contractor generally can set his or her own work hours.

8) *Full-time required.* An employee may be required to work or be available full-time. This indicates control by the employer. An independent contractor can work when and for whom he or she chooses.

9) *Work done on premises.* An employee usually works on the premises of an employer, or works on a route or at a location designated by an employer.

10) *Order or sequence set.* An employee may be required to perform services in the order or sequence set by an employer. This shows that the employee is subject to direction and control.

11) *Reports.* An employee may be required to submit reports to an employer. This shows that the employer maintains a degree of control.

12) *Payments.* An employee is generally paid by the hour, week, or month. An independent contractor is usually paid by the job or on a straight commission.

13) *Expenses.* An employee's business and travel expenses are generally paid by an employer. This shows that the employee is subject to regulation and control.

14) *Tools and materials.* An employee is normally furnished significant tools, materials, and other equipment by an employer.

15) *Investment.* An independent contractor has a significant investment in the facilities he or she uses in performing services for someone else.

16) *Profit or loss.* An independent contractor can make a profit or suffer a loss.

17) *Works for more than one person or firm.* An independent contractor is generally free to provide his or her services to two or more unrelated persons or firms at the same time.

18) *Offers services to general public.* An independent contractor makes his or her services available to the general public.

19) *Right to fire.* An employee can be fired by an employer. An independent contractor cannot be fired so long as he or she produces a result that meets the specifications of the contract.

20) *Right to quit.* An employee can quit his or her job at any time without incurring liability. An independent contractor usually agrees to complete a specific job and is responsible for its satisfactory completion, or is legally obligated to make good for failure to complete it.

From IRS Publication 154

EMPLOYEE OR AN INDEPENDENT CONTRACTOR?

15

Employees are individuals who work for someone else and have social security and income taxes withheld from each paycheck. Independent contractors are people who work for someone else and do not have taxes withheld from the money they are paid.

Chapter 17 explains which taxes and benefits an employer needs to pay when she has employees. For most states, this includes workers' compensation insurance, unemployment insurance, and the employer's share of social security (and in Hawaii, health insurance).

Rather than taking on the extra cost of having employees, many employers have chosen to hire workers as independent contractors or freelancers. The IRS and state taxing agencies are very aware of this and are unwilling to let it continue. As a result, "misclassified employees" is a hot audit focus.

WHO CAN BE CORRECTLY CLASSIFIED AS AN INDEPENDENT CONTRACTOR?

Many people think that if they hire a student or someone who works only occasionally or part-time, it is appropriate to classify that person as an independent contractor. In reality, those are not the factors that determine whether it's correct for the person to be treated as an independent contractor. *There are two key questions in determining whether someone is an employee or an independent contractor: Who has control over the working arrangement? and How independent is the person performing the services?*

For many years, the IRS relied on a guide they called *Twenty Common-Law Rules* in determining whether an individual had been correctly classified as an independent contractor. More recently the IRS has boiled the rules down to three major categories:

- Behavioral control
- Financial control
- Type of relationship

Behavioral control covers such issues as whether the worker already has the skills necessary to do the job or whether she is provided with instructions and/or training. The IRS also looks at whether the worker has control over when and where to work. Most important in determining the true work relationship is whether the worker is told how to do the work or only what end result is desired.

Financial control includes such areas as the extent of the worker's investment in the work. Could the worker have a loss from the work that she's doing, or will she always make a profit? Whose tools and equipment are used? Also looked at is whether the worker makes her services available to the general public or works only for this one company.

Type of relationship covers such factors as whether the business provides the worker with employee-type benefits, such as insurance, a pension plan, vacation pay, or sick pay. Also looked at is how temporary or permanent the work is and whether there is a written contract between the business and the worker. Employee status is also determined by examining the extent to which services performed by the worker are a key aspect of the regular business of the company. If the work is integral to the business, the assumption is that the worker has less control over how it is performed.

Generally, no single one of these factors indicates who should be classified as an employee and who as an independent contractor; the determination is made by looking at the total work arrangement.

Some companies require independent contractors to have an employer ID number. They're hoping, by having this number, that independent contractors will be considered an entity separate from them and that there will be less of a question about whether they're truly independent contractors. But just having that number isn't enough to make someone an independent contractor if other factors point to her being an employee.

Written agreements are not always sufficient to prove independent contractor status. If an independent contractor should have been hired as an employee, an agreement won't be sufficient to keep her from being reclassified if the IRS investigates. However, if you hire someone who really does qualify for independent contractor status, be sure to have her sign a written agreement that includes a statement specifying that she is responsible for paying all of her own taxes.

The penalties are severe for an employer who is caught hiring someone as an independent contractor when that person should have been hired as an employee. The additional taxes owed, plus penalties, equal about 50% of the amount the employee was paid. An employer will be provided with a "safe harbor" (will not be penalized) in classifying an individual as an independent contractor if the following requirements are met:

- The employer has always treated the worker as an independent contractor.
- The employer has filed all required 1099 Forms for this worker.

- The employer has a reasonable basis for treating the worker as an independent contractor.

Reasonable basis applies if the employer relied on a past audit in which the employment status of the worker was allowed to remain as that of an independent contractor. It also applies if a significant segment (at least 25%) of the employer's industry treats workers in a similar way.

FORM SS-8

Form SS-8 is used to ask the IRS to determine whether a worker should be classified as an employee or an independent contractor. Although workers may be tempted, they should not submit this form unless they believe they've been incorrectly classified as independent contractors and don't care whether they lose their jobs. In almost all cases in which the IRS makes an SS-8 determination, independent contractors will be reclassified as employees. But being under the scrutiny of the IRS will not make your employer happy, which is why you should be ready to look for another job if you file an SS-8 form.

If you aren't sure whether the person you're hiring should be considered an independent contractor or an employee, consult with an accountant or attorney who specializes in small business tax issues. The fee you pay for that information may save you a great deal in penalties later.

A cautionary note: Obviously this whole area is one in which you need to be very careful if you're planning to have people help you in your business. As more and more businesses are audited on this matter, some employers have become afraid to hire people as independent contractors. However, there are still many companies that illegally continue to misclassify workers, particularly in the construction industry and the computer field.

DIFFER FROM INDEPENDENT CONTRACTORS AND SELF-EMPLOYED PEOPLE

16

As mentioned in Chapter 15, employees work for someone else and have taxes withheld from their paychecks. Independent contractors work for someone else and don't have taxes withheld from the money they're paid. Self-employed people are business owners who work for themselves and generally offer their services and/or products to more than one customer.

When the term *self-employed* is used in this book, it refers to sole proprietor and partnership business owners as well as independent contractors. The tax implications for these three groups are identical. On the other hand, as discussed in Chapter 3, corporation shareholder/employees are taxed in the same way as are all other employees.

This chapter discusses some of the differences between employees and self-employed people. Because each state has different employer and employee responsibilities, this book covers these regulations in generalities only.

DISABILITY INSURANCE
In some states, the premium for disability insurance is paid by the employee; in other states, the premium is paid by the employer; and in many states, disability insurance is not an offered benefit. When disability insurance coverage is offered, an employee who is unable to work because of a medical problem is eligible to collect disability benefits.

As a self-employed person (or independent contractor), you have no coverage for disability insurance unless you buy a policy yourself. You can buy a private policy through an insurance company or, in some states, you can get elective coverage through the State Human Resources or Employment Development Department. Private disability insurance can be quite costly and is not generally available (or has severe restrictions) to those with existing medical conditions. If you don't have disability insurance, however, an illness or injury that keeps you from working could be catastrophic. For that reason, it is important to purchase disability insurance in addition to health insurance.

WORKERS' COMPENSATION
Workers' compensation is another type of insurance available to employees, but generally not to self-employed people. Most states

require employers to purchase this insurance policy; it provides benefits to any employee injured on the job. Rates for coverage vary
according to the risk involved in the job responsibilities. In some
states, the business owner who has a workers' compensation policy
for employees can include herself in the coverage. Self-employed
people with no employees or residing in states that don't allow the
business owner to be included will have no coverage if they are
injured while working.

UNEMPLOYMENT INSURANCE

Employees also are eligible for unemployment insurance. The
employee and/or her employer (depending on state requirements) pay
somewhere between 1% and 6% of the employee's gross wages
(depending on the state and the employer's experience rating) into the
unemployment insurance fund for the employee. If the employee's job
ends, she is eligible to collect unemployment. If a self-employed person
has a slow period or closes her business, she will not be eligible for
unemployment insurance benefits.

SOCIAL SECURITY AND SELF-EMPLOYMENT TAX

Another difference between employees and self-employed people is
social security, or FICA. When you're an employee, 7.65% of your
wages is withheld from your paycheck and deposited into your social
security account. Your employer adds another 7.65% to your social
security account, for a total contribution of 15.3% of your wages.

When you're self-employed, no one else is contributing for you, so you
are responsible for the entire 15.3%. For self-employed people, social
security tax is called self-employment tax. All self-employment tax you
pay is credited to your social security account. Self-employment tax is
owed any time net self-employment income for the year exceeds $399.

Because self-employed people are required to pay such a large amount
into social security, a calculation is done to reduce the amount on which
the social security tax is calculated. An example of how this tax is calculated for a self-employed person follows.

First, the net income from self-employment is calculated. Remember,
net income is the amount left after business expenses have been deducted.

In an effort to partially equalize the social security liability of
employees and self-employed people, Congress has exempted the first
7.65% of a self-employed person's net income from social security tax. So,
the next step is to multiply your net income by 7.65%. In the example, you
can see that multiplying your net income by 7.65% and then subtracting
that amount from your net income is the same as multiplying your net
income by 92.35%. Self-employed people pay social security tax on
92.35% of their net earnings from self-employment.

CALCULATING SOCIAL SECURITY (SELF-EMPLOYMENT) TAX

$ 12,000	(net self-employment income)
× 7.65%	(percentage of income exempt from self-employment tax)
$ 918	(amount not subject to self-employment tax)

$ 12,000		$ 12,000
− $918	is the same as	× 92.35%
$ 11,082		$ 11,082

$ 11,082	(amount subject to self-employment tax)
× 15.3%	(self-employment tax rate)
$ 1,696	(self-employment tax on $12,000 net profit)

The social security tax rate for self-employed people is 15.3%. The next step is to multiply the 92.35% of your net self-employment income by the 15.3% social security tax rate. The result is the social security tax you will owe on your self-employment income. In this example, the amount owed is $1,696. This is separate from and in addition to the federal and state (where applicable) income tax, which is paid whether you are an employee or self-employed.

Later in this book, when tax forms are discussed, you will see that there is a line on the front page of the 1040 Form (page 116) on which a self-employed person is able to deduct from her total income half of the self-employment tax she pays. Why didn't Congress set it up so that instead of paying 15.3% and requiring these computations, self-employed people would pay something like 13% into social security? I can't answer that. Unfortunately, you'll need to do all this calculating to compute your self-employment tax.

There is a limit to the amount of annual income on which social security or self-employment tax must be paid. The maximum amount is increased each year. For 1999, the maximum income you have to pay social security or self-employment tax on is $72,600. For 2000, the maximum is $76,200.

$ 50,000	wages with social security tax already withheld
+ 26,750	net self-employment income
$ 76,750	total earned income
- 72,600	maximum social security income amount for 1999
$ 4,100	excess earnings
$ 26,750	net self-employment income
- 4,100	excess earnings
$ 22,650	amount of self-employment income subject to self-employment tax

The example above is of Heidi; she had a job as an employee where she earned $50,000 and also a net self-employment income of $26,700. Combined, her two sources of income exceed the maximum income subject to social security or self-employment tax.

Heidi has already had social security tax withheld on the paychecks from her job as an employee, so the adjustment is made on her self-employment income. She needs to pay self-employment tax on only $22,650 of her self-employment income, rather than on the whole $26,750.

A clarification about social security tax: The 7.65% that an employee has withheld from her paycheck for social security and the 7.65% that an employer pays into social security on behalf of the employee are actually made up of two taxes—6.20% for social security and 1.45% for Medicare. The 15.3% self-employment tax paid by self-employed people is actually 12.4% social security and 2.9% Medicare. Social security tax is paid on the first $72,600 of income; Medicare tax is paid on all earned income, no matter how much it totals. In Heidi's case, she will pay the social security portion of self-employment tax on $22,650 of her self-employment income and the Medicare portion on all $26,750 of her net self-employment income.

Social security and Medicare taxes must be paid by employees and self-employed people of all ages. Even those who are collecting social security benefits are required to pay into these two funds if they are earning wages or have a business net profit of $400 or more.

EVALUATE YOUR ALTERNATIVES

Although you won't often have the choice, if you take a job where you are not certain whether it would be more beneficial to be an employee or an independent contractor, you need to calculate the advantages of one over the other. For example, figure how much social security tax you would pay as an employee. Also, bear in mind that as an employee, you are covered for unemployment and workers' compensation and possibly will be provided with other benefits such as health insurance or retirement plans. Then, calculate how much self-employment tax you would pay as an independent contractor. Remember that you won't be covered for unemployment and workers' compensation, but you will be able to deduct expenses that may not be deductible for an employee. To make up for the benefits and taxes you'll be paying on your own, your payment as an independent contractor should be more than what you typically would be paid as an employee. Also, don't forget to consider the nontax benefits of one status over another (e.g., having a regular paycheck as an employee versus being able to choose which hours to work as an independent contractor).

EMPLOYEE PAYROLL
AND
WITHHOLDING

17

Hiring workers as independent contractors may save a business money. Additionally, employers prefer hiring people as independent contractors because they're able to avoid the paperwork and hassles of having employees. However, as pointed out in Chapter 15, the desire to avoid becoming an employer is not sufficient justification for hiring workers as independent contractors.

If you have employees working for you or you are an employee of your incorporated business, it is important that you be fully aware of the requirements for withholding and remitting payroll taxes. Each employee must fill out a W-4 form, indicating how many exemptions she wishes to claim. As the employer, you use that information to withhold from each paycheck the proper amount of federal and state (if applicable) income tax, along with the employee's share of social security and Medicare tax. You need a copy of IRS Circular E to help you do this correctly. Depending on your state regulations, unemployment, disability, or health insurance deductions may also need to be taken from each paycheck.

Once these taxes have been withheld from the employee's paycheck, they must be turned over to the federal and state taxing authorities. Depending on the total amount withheld, the IRS requires that deposits of federal payroll taxes be made quarterly, monthly, or biweekly. IRS payroll deposit coupons are used to deposit this money. State taxing agencies have their own deposit requirements.

At the end of each quarter, employers need to fill out federal and state quarterly payroll tax reports, showing the amount of payroll tax owed and the amount already deposited during the quarter. The federal form is Form 941. After the year ends, a W-2 Form must be sent to each employee reporting how much she earned during the previous year and the amount of taxes that were withheld from her wages.

Employers also are responsible for filing a Form 940, the Federal Unemployment Tax (FUTA) report. The FUTA tax is .8% of the first $7,000 earned by each employee. This amount is reduced by the amount of state unemployment tax paid during the year.

The IRS has no tolerance for incorrectly withheld and remitted payroll taxes. One of the worst tax mistakes you can make is to withhold payroll taxes and then not send them to the IRS in a timely manner. The amount you've withheld belongs to the employee, so you are treated as though you had stolen the money if it is not remitted to the IRS as required. The only time the IRS relaxes this requirement a bit is in the first quarter you have employees. Recently enacted tax legislation allows the IRS to waive payroll tax late payment penalties for new employers who don't correctly make tax deposits during the first quarter. This applies only if the payroll tax is late but paid in full sometime during that first quarter.

Other than this one exception, you can expect large penalties for not making payroll tax deposits as required. It's very tempting to use withheld tax moneys to pay rent or other necessary business expenses. Don't do it. If you can't keep your hands off the withheld tax, keep it in a separate bank account until it's time to send the money to the IRS and the state.

The outline here of your responsibilities as an employer is purposely brief. This is to ensure that you will seek proper guidance once you're ready to hire employees. Here are some suggestions for avoiding problems in this area:

- Attend IRS classes on how to withhold and deposit taxes.
- Meet with a knowledgeable bookkeeper, accountant, or tax preparer. Have that person either handle the payroll responsibilities or provide you with the information you need to do the job yourself.
- Hire a payroll service to handle all the withholding, deposits, and paperwork. It may be well worth the cost, even if you have only one or two employees. Banks provide payroll services, as do private payroll companies.
- Consider leasing employees. Some temporary agencies have arrangements whereby you can lease employees, and the agency handles all the payroll requirements. You may be able to lease an employee or independent contractor who is already working for you and thereby reduce your administrative headaches.

1099 FORMS:
RECEIVING THEM
AND ISSUING THEM

18

Each January, as an employee, you'll be given a W-2 Form by your employer. This form indicates the amount earned during the previous year and the taxes withheld from your wages. As a self-employed person or independent contractor, by January 31 you should receive a 1099 Form from those who, in the course of their business, paid you $600 or more for your services during the previous year. The 1099 Forms are about the same size as W-2 Form.

RECEIVING 1099 FORMS

The purpose of 1099 Forms is to help the taxing authorities find the underground economy—those people who aren't reporting and paying taxes on the money they earn. The payer who issues the 1099 Form will send the IRS (and possibly the state) a copy of the form they send to you. When you file your tax return, the IRS will check to see whether you've included the reported income.

Because no taxes have been withheld from the income reported on a 1099, the only figure listed will be the amount you were paid during the year. You will be given only one or two copies of the 1099 Form because, unlike W-2s, the 1099 Form does not get attached to your federal income tax return. Some states require that you attach a copy of your 1099 Forms to your state return.

As mentioned at the beginning of this chapter, you should receive a 1099 Form from any persons or companies who, *in the course of their business*, paid you $600 or more for your services during the year. If you are a painter and you painted someone's house, you won't receive a 1099 Form for that work, even if you were paid more than $600 because the money wasn't paid as a business expense. But if you paint someone's office, it's an expense that person had in running her business, so she should send you a 1099 Form.

Will you get a 1099 Form from everyone who should give you one? No. A lot of people don't know they're supposed to give them, and it's not your responsibility to chase after the 1099 Forms. Since you don't need to attach the form to your tax return, if you don't get one, it's not your problem. *But you still must report the income on your tax return whether or not you receive a 1099 Form.* This is also true if you don't receive a 1099 because the amount you were paid was less than $600. Some people mistakenly believe that you are not required to report income unless it's over a certain amount. That is not true. All earned income should be included on your tax return.

It's important to keep accurate records of your income so that you're not dependent on the 1099 Forms to tell you what your income was. Occasionally, you will receive a 1099 with an amount on it that differs from your records. This can happen for a number of reasons. Maybe the business wrote you a check on December 29 that you didn't get until January 2, but the check amount was included on your 1099 Form for the year in which the check was written. Or perhaps you were reimbursed for expenses during the year, and the business included on the 1099 Form the amount you were reimbursed, along with the amount you were paid for services. If you don't keep your own records of income earned, you may not know whether the amount reported on the 1099 is accurate and whether it includes amounts paid as reimbursements.

If you receive 1099s that include reimbursements for travel or other expenses, you need to include on your tax return the total amount of income shown on the 1099 Forms; then, in order to make your net income accurate, deduct the travel or other expenses as if they were your own business expenses. Some of your clients will include the reimbursement amount on the 1099, and some will not; it won't be consistent.

You may get one or more 1099 Forms late. You are supposed to receive them by January 31, but often persons who should send out the form are not aware of this requirement. When they have their taxes done in March and their accountants realize the 1099s were never issued, you may be sent one at that time. Meanwhile, you may have already prepared your tax return. This is another reason to keep complete records of your income, rather than depending on the 1099s to tell you how much you've been paid.

As you receive the 1099s, make sure they're accurate. If you do receive an incorrect form, contact the person who gave it to you and ask her to send you a corrected copy. Most important, insist that a corrected copy be sent to the IRS.

It's critical that you make sure that the amount of self-employment income you report on your tax return is equal to or greater than the total of your 1099 Forms, since the IRS can easily check whether you have reported all the income for which you received a 1099. If you don't earn much of your income from other businesses and won't be receiving many 1099 Forms, it is not as important that the forms you receive be correct down to the penny. In that situation, you will be including on your tax return much more income than is reported on the 1099s, so each separate 1099 Form won't be distinguishable.

Earline works as a consultant for three different clients. This is the only self-employment income she received during the year. Earline should check carefully the 1099s from the three clients to make sure the amounts are correct. She also should make sure that the amount listed as self-employment income on her tax return equals the total of the 1099 Forms.

Leslie is a divorce attorney with her own practice. She also teaches a class for which she is paid as an independent contractor. Since Leslie's clients are not paying her in the course of their business, she will not receive 1099 Forms from them, even if they pay her $600 or more during the year. Leslie will receive a 1099 Form for teaching the class. However, since the total self-employment income shown on her tax return is so much greater than the amount on the 1099, Leslie need not be concerned if the amount shown on the form doesn't exactly match her records.

ISSUING 1099 FORMS

You need to issue a 1099 Form to anyone to whom you paid $600 or more for services in the course of your business. This does not include wages paid to employees, since you'll be giving them W-2 forms. The 1099 Forms are for people who are not your employees. This might include subcontractors, a bookkeeper, or a colleague who handled part of a job for you. Also, you need to give a 1099 to anyone to whom you paid rent in the course of your business. This includes subletting or renting an office or studio outside your home. It does not apply to rent you pay for your personal home or for your home office.

You do not give a 1099 to vendors such as the telephone company or the office supply store. You don't need to issue 1099s to corporations either. Unless a business name ends with "Inc.," there is no way to know whether the subcontractor you hired or the person to whom you pay your business rent is incorporated; the only way to know for sure is to ask.

Blank 1099 Forms are available from the IRS and at stationery stores. They come three forms to a page (the IRS asks that you not separate the top copy, which is the one you'll be sending to them). If you look at the 1099 Forms on page 61, you can see

What if the person I paid refuses to give me her social security number?

You can avoid this situation in the future by getting the necessary information when the person begins working for you. At that time, you can give her a W-9 form (available from the IRS), which asks for her social security number. If she doesn't return the form to you, you must withhold 20% federal tax from each payment you make to her. To avoid having this tax withheld, most people will give you their social security number.

If this is a current problem (i.e., you're trying to fill out a 1099 form and can't get the social security number), tell the person that you'll issue the 1099 anyway with her name and address and that in the area where her social security number should be listed, you'll put "refused to give." Most people will quickly relent and provide you with their number. If not, send the IRS the 1099 form with "refused to give" written in the box provided for the social security number.

A SHEET OF 1099 FORMS

Form 1 of 3

9595 ☐ VOID ☐ CORRECTED

PAYER'S name, street address, city, state, ZIP code, and telephone no.		1 Rents $	OMB No. 1545-0115	Miscellaneous Income
		2 Royalties $		
		3 Other income $	Form **1099-MISC**	
PAYER'S Federal identification number	RECIPIENT'S identification number	4 Federal income tax withheld $	5 Fishing boat proceeds $	**Copy A** **For** **Internal Revenue** **Service Center**
RECIPIENT'S name		6 Medical and health care payments $	7 Nonemployee compensation $	
Street address (including apt. no.)		8 Substitute payments in lieu of dividends or interest $	9 Payer made direct sales of $5,000 or more of consumer products to a buyer (recipient) for resale ▶ ☐	**File with Form 1096.** For Paperwork Reduction Act Notice and instructions for completing this form,
City, state, and ZIP code		10 Crop insurance proceeds $	11 State income tax withheld $	see **Instructions for Forms 1099, 1098,**
Account number (optional)	2nd TIN Not. ☐	12 State/Payer's state number	13 $	**5498, and W-2G.**

Form **1099-MISC**   Cat. No. 14425J   Department of the Treasury - Internal Revenue Service

Form 2 of 3

9595 ☐ VOID ☐ CORRECTED

PAYER'S name, street address, city, state, ZIP code, and telephone no.		1 Rents $	OMB No. 1545-0115	Miscellaneous Income
		2 Royalties $		
		3 Other income $	Form **1099-MISC**	
PAYER'S Federal identification number	RECIPIENT'S identification number	4 Federal income tax withheld $	5 Fishing boat proceeds $	**Copy A** **For** **Internal Revenue** **Service Center**
RECIPIENT'S name		6 Medical and health care payments $	7 Nonemployee compensation $	
Street address (including apt. no.)		8 Substitute payments in lieu of dividends or interest $	9 Payer made direct sales of $5,000 or more of consumer products to a buyer (recipient) for resale ▶ ☐	**File with Form 1096.** For Paperwork Reduction Act Notice and instructions for completing this form,
City, state, and ZIP code		10 Crop insurance proceeds $	11 State income tax withheld $	see **Instructions for Forms 1099, 1098,**
Account number (optional)	2nd TIN Not. ☐	12 State/Payer's state number	13 $	**5498, and W-2G.**

Form **1099-MISC**   Cat. No. 14425J   Department of the Treasury - Internal Revenue Service

Form 3 of 3

9595 ☐ VOID ☐ CORRECTED

PAYER'S name, street address, city, state, ZIP code, and telephone no.		1 Rents $	OMB No. 1545-0115	Miscellaneous Income
		2 Royalties $		
		3 Other income $	Form **1099-MISC**	
PAYER'S Federal identification number	RECIPIENT'S identification number	4 Federal income tax withheld $	5 Fishing boat proceeds $	**Copy A** **For** **Internal Revenue** **Service Center**
RECIPIENT'S name		6 Medical and health care payments $	7 Nonemployee compensation $	
Street address (including apt. no.)		8 Substitute payments in lieu of dividends or interest $	9 Payer made direct sales of $5,000 or more of consumer products to a buyer (recipient) for resale ▶ ☐	**File with Form 1096.** For Paperwork Reduction Act Notice and instructions for completing this form,
City, state, and ZIP code		10 Crop insurance proceeds $	11 State income tax withheld $	see **Instructions for Forms 1099, 1098,**
Account number (optional)	2nd TIN Not. ☐	12 State/Payer's state number	13 $	**5498, and W-2G.**

Form **1099-MISC**   Cat. No. 14425J   Department of the Treasury - Internal Revenue Service what information is needed to fill them out. You are asked for your name, address, and social security number, as well as the name, address, and social security number of the person you paid. That information should be gathered when you hire the person or rent the office, not at the end of January, when you're trying to get the forms out. If you wait to get this information until the forms are due, you may find that the person is on vacation or has left the country. Or she might have thought you were paying her under the table because you weren't withholding taxes, and now she refuses to give you the necessary information.

Box 7 of the 1099 Form says, "Nonemployee compensation." Generally it is here that you indicate the amount you paid the person or company. If applicable, box 1 is where you report the amount of rent you paid in the course of your business.

Each 1099 is a five-part form. In the bottom corner it tells you where to send that copy. The first part goes to the IRS. The next copy goes to the state if your state requires it (many don't). The next two copies go to the recipient (the person you paid). Recipients are given two copies because some states require them to attach a copy to their tax return. The final copy is for your records.

THE 1096 FORM

DO NOT STAPLE   6969

Form **1096** Department of the Treasury Internal Revenue Service	**Annual Summary and Transmittal of U.S. Information Returns**	OMB No. 1545-0108

ATTACH IRS LABEL HERE

FILER'S name

Street address (including room or suite number)

City, state, and ZIP code

If you are not using a preprinted label, enter in box 1 or 2 below the identification number you used as the filer on the information returns being transmitted. Do not fill in both boxes 1 and 2.	Name of person to contact if the IRS needs more information Telephone number ( )	**For Official Use Only**

1 Employer identification number	2 Social security number	3 Total number of forms	4 Federal income tax withheld $	5 Total amount reported with this Form 1096 $

Enter an "X" in only one box below to indicate the type of form being filed.   If this is your FINAL return, enter an "X" here .   . ▶ ☐

W-2G 32	1098 81	1098-E 82	1099-T 83	1099-A 80	1099-B 79	1099-C 85	1099-DIV 91	1099-G 86	1099-INT 92	1099-LTC 93	1099-MISC 95	1099-MSA 94	1099-OID 96
☐	☐	☐	☐	☐	☐	☐	☐	☐	☐	☐	☐	☐	☐

1099-PATR 97	1099-R 98	1099-S 75	5498 28	5498-MSA 27
☐	☐	☐	☐	☐

Please return this entire page to the Internal Revenue Service. Photocopies are NOT acceptable.

Under penalties of perjury, I declare that I have examined this return and accompanying documents, and, to the best of my knowledge and belief, they are true, correct, and complete.

Signature ▶   Title ▶   Date ▶

The copies sent to the IRS need to be accompanied by a 1096 Form (see page 62). The 1096 Form acts as a cover sheet, telling the IRS how many 1099 Forms you're sending them.

The 1099 must be sent to the recipient by January 31. The 1096, along with the federal copy of the 1099, must be sent to the IRS by February 28.

There are penalties for not issuing the 1099s and for issuing them incorrectly or late. The penalty for not sending a 1099 Form to the payee and a copy to the IRS is $50 per 1099, for a total of $100 per recipient. Reduced penalties apply if you don't send out the forms on time but do issue them before August of the year in which the forms are due.

HIRING FAMILY MEMBERS

19

Hiring family members and domestic partners to work in your business can be an effective way of transferring income from one person to another. Here are some examples:

> *Adrienne is earning a good living through her business. Her father is retired and could use some extra income. By hiring and paying her father to do the business bookkeeping, Adrienne is able to provide her father with some income and, at the same time, to reduce her own self-employment profit and taxes.*

> *Marilyn hires her 14-year-old daughter Corinne to clean up around her home office. Corinne receives a salary and gets experience having a job. Marilyn pays less tax, because she can deduct the amount she pays Corinne.*

> *Lisa owns a pet grooming business. Her life partner, Joan, has just been laid off from her job. Until Joan finds a new job, Lisa will need to pay all the household bills. Paying Joan's share of the bills is not a deductible expense for Lisa. However, by hiring Joan to work temporarily in her business, Lisa is able to deduct 100% of the wages she pays Joan (which Joan can use to pay her share of the bills).*

In general, the family member or domestic partner must be paid as an employee rather than as an independent contractor, unless she already has her own business doing the type of work you're hiring her to do. This means you need to issue W-2 forms, register as an employer, withhold taxes, pay into social security, and so on. (See Chapter 17 for information about your tax and withholding responsibilities as an employer.)

HIRING YOUR CHILDREN

A special rule applies if you hire your child. You don't need to withhold social security tax as long as she's under age 18. She won't owe any income tax until her total income for the year is over approximately $4,000 (the exact amount increases each year). Although you do need to issue a W-2 Form, if she'll have less than $4,000 total income, you don't need to withhold income tax from her paycheck.

In the previous example, Marilyn pays Corinne $3,600 during the year. Corinne also has $100 in interest income from a bank account. Her income is under $4,000, so although Corinne must file a tax return, she doesn't owe any tax. Meanwhile, Marilyn deducts as a business expense the $3,600 she paid Corinne, saving approximately $500 in self-employment tax and $1,000 in federal income tax.

Corinne could have a total income of $6,000 and not owe any tax if she contributes $2,000 to an IRA retirement account. While it may be hard to imagine a 14-year-old contributing toward retirement, those who begin saving for retirement at a young age will need to contribute far less and, yet, will have more retirement money than those who start contributing later in life.

Hiring your child is a wonderful way to be able to deduct your children's allowances or college funds. However, the child (or other family member) must actually perform the work she is being paid to do, and her pay must be commensurate with the work she's doing and her age and abilities.

Hiring Your Spouse

Hiring your spouse to work in your business can provide benefits to both of you.

> *Susan hires her husband, Daniel, as a sales rep for her office equipment sales company. Susan provides health insurance for all her employees, including Daniel. Daniel's policy covers his spouse (Susan) and their children. Susan is able to deduct the full cost of the health insurance policy as a business expense.*

Normally, a self-employed person can deduct only 60% of her health insurance premium, and even that amount is not deductible as a business expense (see Chapter 28). Susan is able to deduct 100% of her own health insurance cost as a business expense, since it's part of the policy she provides for Daniel.

Other benefits, such as reimbursement for child care expenses, can be offered to employees of your business. If your spouse is an employee, he can take advantage of the benefits, saving you both money.

If your business is incorporated, you are treated as an employee of the business and will be eligible for most employee benefits offered by the corporation. As a sole proprietor, however, you are not an employee of your business, which means you can

A cautionary note: Any benefits you offer must be available to all employees. If your spouse is currently the only employee but you anticipate hiring additional workers in the future, consider carefully before setting up an employee benefit program.

take advantage of such benefits as child care or medical reimbursement programs only if you offer them to your employees and hire your spouse as an employee of your business.

Obviously there are more than tax ramifications to be considered in deciding whether to hire a family member. You will want to seriously think and talk about the potential personal effect of being in business together. However, with proper planning, hiring family members can be an effective tax savings move.

SECTION 4
DEDUCTIBLE EXPENSES

WHAT MAKES EXPENSES DEDUCTIBLE?

20

The key to reducing your net profit (and thus, your tax liability) is not to have more expenses but rather to make existing expenses legitimately tax deductible.

> *Nancy is a workplace consultant. While passing a newsstand, she sees an article about workplace stress in a weekly news magazine. She buys a copy of the magazine but doesn't think of it as a business expense and forgets to get a receipt.*

> *Karen is going to a business conference near her parents' hometown. By making sure she spends the appropriate percentage of her trip doing business (see Chapter 27), she can deduct the cost of a trip to visit her parents.*

Note that I am not suggesting that you include a trip to visit your parents under "business travel" and hope no one ever notices. What I am saying is that a trip that would have been entirely personal (and, therefore, not deductible), may, with some planning and changes, provide some opportunities for tax deductions.

Get into the mind-set of being a self-employed person. Always ask yourself, "Is there any way I could deduct this expense as a business expense?" or "If I change the time or the way I do this, can I make this expense deductible?" If yes, get a receipt, keep canceled checks, and follow the other recordkeeping suggestions presented in Section 2 of this book.

Deductible expenses are those that are ordinary and necessary. Ordinary means that someone else in the same line of work would have a similar expense. Necessary means that in order to operate your business, it was necessary for you to have this expense. In an audit, the IRS may not ask you these specific questions, but this is what the auditor is looking at when reviewing the expenses you deducted:

- Is the expense helpful to your pursuit of profit?
- Is the expense needed in order for you to make money?
- Is the expense appropriate to your pursuit of business?

In other words, in an audit, the IRS is interested in seeing not only that you have backup materials (e.g., canceled checks and receipts) for expenses you claim but also that there is a legitimate business reason for claiming each expense.

BUSINESS
START-UP
EXPENSES

21

As part of preparing to go into business, you'll probably buy supplies such as stationery and business cards. In addition, you may have other start-up expenses such as advertising, telephone, rent, and/or leasehold improvements.

Purchasing inventory and other assets (e.g., equipment and furnishings) may also be part of your prebusiness preparation. Inventory, as discussed in Chapter 13, can be deducted only as you sell it. Other types of assets are depreciated over a period of years, beginning with the year you start your business (see Chapter 22 for information about depreciation).

If you purchase an existing business, your costs may include such items as franchise fees and customer lists. Most of the purchase costs, other than inventory and equipment, are amortized (deducted) over 60 months, beginning with the month the business starts.

As mentioned in Chapter 2, you are considered to be in business when you have gathered together everything necessary to be in business (e.g., licenses, inventory, and store/office rental, if appropriate) and have let others know that your services or products are available for purchase. If you have start-up expenses in the year before you open your business, you won't be able to deduct those expenses until your business actually begins. At that time, you can start depreciating any equipment you bought, and begin amortizing over 60 months (or more, if you choose) the other prebusiness expenses you've incurred. This means that 1/60 of the start-up costs are deducted each month after your business begins. (See the next chapter for more information about depreciation and amortization.)

What if I don't have any income my first year in business? Where do I deduct the expenses?

Although tax preparers differ in how they feel about this, I rarely will fill out a Schedule C for someone who has only business expenses and no business income, as I think this calls attention to the entire tax return. A real estate agent who has necessary business expenses in the year before the escrow closes on the house she sold would be one of the few Schedule Cs with no income that I'd be comfortable preparing. Otherwise, I would encourage the client to bring in some business income (no matter how small) before the end of the year. If that couldn't happen, I'd treat the first year expenses in the same way I treat start-up expenses; amortize them over 60 months, beginning with the first month there is income.

22

WHAT IS DEPRECIATION?

Depreciation can be a hard concept to understand. It means the loss in value of an asset over the time that item is being used in your business. An asset is a thing of value, such as a computer, a desk, or a building, that will last for more than a year. When you buy an asset for your business, the IRS says the cost must be deducted over a period of years, since the item's useful life is longer than one tax year. Each year, you deduct a portion of the cost of these items. That deduction is called depreciation.

In order to be eligible for depreciation, you must be able to answer yes to the following questions:

- Is the asset owned by you?
- Does it have a useful life of 1 year or more?
- Is it tangible (something you can touch)?
- Can it be used in your business?

Land can never be depreciated because it doesn't wear out. Also, inventory is never depreciated.

If you own an item such as a car that is used both for business and personal purposes, you can depreciate only the business-use portion. It's your responsibility to keep adequate records in order to be able to prove the business-use portion of mixed-use property.

Cars, computers, trucks, copiers, cellular phones, and electronic equipment are among the assets considered to be 5-year property. This means they are depreciated over 5 years. Since the first year is calculated as if you bought the property in the middle of the year, it actually takes 6 years to fully deduct 5-year property. If you look at the first column of the chart on page 71, you will see that in the first year you begin depreciating 5-year property, you deduct 20% of its cost. In the second year, you deduct 32% of its cost, and by the end of the sixth year, you will have deducted the full cost.

Other business equipment and office furniture is considered 7-year property. It gets depreciated, as you can see in the second column of the chart, over a period of 8 years. At the end of 8 years, the total cost of the item will have been deducted.

A different depreciation schedule is used for buildings. Depending on when you begin using the building in your business, it will generally be

DEPRECIATION USING MACRS (MODIFIED ACCELERATED COST RECOVERY SYSTEM) DEPRECIATION (FOR ASSETS PURCHASED IN 1987 AND LATER)

	5-Year Property (cars, computers, trucks, copiers, cellular phones)	7-Year Property (office furniture and other business equipment)	Cars and other 5-year property used less than 51% for business
1	20.00 %	14.29 %	10 %
2	32.00 %	24.49 %	20 %
3	19.20 %	17.49 %	20 %
4	11.52 %	12.49 %	20 %
5	11.52 %	8.93 %	20 %
6	5.76 %	8.93 %	10 %
7		8.93 %	
8		4.46 %	

depreciated over 39 years. Buildings "placed in service" after December 31, 1986, and before May 13, 1993, are depreciated over 31½ years.

CALCULATING DEPRECIATION

The amount of depreciation allowed depends on the basis of the item. The basis is generally the original cost of the item including sales tax, shipping, and installation (if applicable). The cost of any improvements made to the property is added to the basis. If the asset is used less than 100% for business, the basis for depreciation is the cost and improvements multiplied by the percentage that the item is used for business. The basis for real estate (buildings) used in business always excludes the value of the land.

The date you place an item into service is the date you begin using it in your business. When you stop using an asset in your business, you stop depreciating it. If you sell the item, you may have a taxable gain due to the depreciation you took on that item (see Marisa's example later in this chapter).

If you bought an item and used it in your business in a previous year and didn't deduct the depreciation on it, you're considered to have

Does everything have to be depreciated?

IRS regulations say that if an item will last more than a year, it needs to be depreciated. I once met with a new client whose prior year tax return included a waste basket she'd bought for $30. It was being depreciated over 7 years. Technically that was correct, but let's be reasonable! If you're an electrician who buys screwdrivers and other small hand tools or a beautician who buys scissors and magazine racks, you can include these low-cost items in categories such as small tools, office supplies, or small furnishings.

taken the depreciation anyway. If you begin claiming depreciation on the item this year, you use the percentage that applies to the number of years since the item was placed into service. For example, if you began using the item in your business 3 years ago, even if you have never depreciated it before, count this as year 3 in calculating the depreciation for the current year.

ASSETS OWNED BEFORE YOU WENT INTO BUSINESS

If you owned an asset before you went into business and you're a sole proprietor, you can't sell the item to your business when you begin using it for business. However, you can begin depreciating it as of the date you place it into service. The year you place it into service is year 1 on the depreciation chart, and you continue to depreciate the property over 5, 7, or 39 years, just as you would if it were an item bought originally for business use. However, the basis used for depreciation is not the original cost of the item but rather its value as of the date it was placed into service. If for some reason (e.g., real estate increasing in value) the original cost is less than fair market value when you begin using a personal asset for business, the basis used is the lesser of cost or fair market value.

What if someone gave me something that I'm using in my business?

You can depreciate it. Its basis (the amount you depreciate) is whatever the cost or basis was for the person who gave it to you.

Theresa bought a computer last year. She started her business this year and uses the computer in her work. When she placed her computer into service, Theresa looked at the classified ads in a newspaper and a computer magazine, and she contacted a used computer store. She learned that the computer she bought last year for $3,000 now has a fair market value of $2,000. Since she uses the computer exclusively for her business, $2,000 is the basis Theresa will use in depreciating it. The first year she's in business, Theresa's depreciation deduction is 20% of the basis of the computer ($400).

LISTED PROPERTY

Certain types of property are called listed property. This means that there are further restrictions on how the property is depreciated. Listed property includes automobiles, cellular telephones, computers, and related peripheral equipment that is not used exclusively at a business establishment or qualified in-home office. Property used for entertainment or recreation, such as cameras, VCRs, and camcorders, is also considered listed property.

If you have listed property that is used less than 51% for business, you must use the depreciation schedule shown in the fourth column of the chart on page 71. As mentioned previously, it is your responsibility to keep records that prove what percentage the property is used for business. If listed property is used 100% for business and is kept at a business location (including a deductible home office), no records of business use need to be kept.

Cars, in addition to being considered listed property, have further restrictions on how they are depreciated each year. These limitations are shown in the chart on page 71. The maximum depreciation you can deduct for a car in the first year you place it into service, if that year is after 1998, is $3,160. You can deduct the full $3,160 only if you use the car 100% for business. Since most cars are used less than 100% for business, the actual amount of deprecation for the first year is $3,160 multiplied by the percentage you use the car for business. (Calculating the business percentage of car use is discussed in Chapter 25.)

SECTION 179 DEPRECIATION

The first part of this chapter discusses regular MACRS depreciation. Another method for depreciating property is to use the Section 179 election. Section 179 refers to a section in the IRS code that says that when you buy something that normally would be depreciated over a period of years, you may choose instead to fully depreciate it in the year you purchase it. Up to $19,000 ($20,000 in 2000) worth of items you purchase each year are eligible for the accelerated treatment. The maximum eligible for Section 179 treatment will increase each year until 2003, when it will be $25,000. The maximum applies to both single persons and married couples, even if each spouse owns a business.

Section 179 is further limited by the total earned income reported on the tax return. The maximum deduction that can be claimed is the amount of total earned income, including wages, or $19,000 ($20,000 in 2000), whichever is less.

> *Louise is married to Jerry. They each started a new business in 2000. Jerry had a profit of $10,000 in his business, and Louise had a loss of $3,000 in hers. Louise also earned $5,000 in wages this year. Jerry bought $10,000 worth of new equipment for his business, and Louise bought $12,000 for hers.*
>
> *Louise and Jerry have two limitations on the amount of Section 179 deduction they can take. Although between them they bought $22,000 worth of qualifying equipment, they are limited to a maximum $20,000 Section 179 deduction. The remainder can be deducted using regular depreciation.*

> *Also, Louise and Jerry are limited by their earned income, which totals $12,000 ($10,000 for Jerry, -$3,000 for Louise's business, and $5,000 in wages). Based on their earned income, they are limited to a $12,000 maximum Section 179 deduction. The remaining $8,000 ($20,000 minus $12,000) can be carried over to next year and be deducted in full then.*

As you can see, assuming your earned income is large enough, Section 179 allows you to buy, for example, a $5,000 computer system and $6,000 worth of office equipment and deduct the entire $11,000 in the year you make the purchase. It's important to understand that Section 179 is still a type of depreciation; thus, the depreciation form, Form 4562, must be included with your tax return even though you're deducting the full cost of the items.

You can't use Section 179 for property you've converted from personal to business use because Section 179 can be used only in the year you originally buy the asset. Also, you can't use Section 179 for listed property used less than 51% for business. Nor can real estate be depreciated using Section 179. Cars remain limited to the figures shown in the chart on page 71, even if you use Section 179 to deduct the maximum allowed in the year you purchase the vehicle.

DECIDING WHEN TO USE SECTION 179

In most cases, when allowed, you will choose to use Section 179. There are a couple of situations, however, when instead you might choose to use regular MACRS depreciation. Probably you would not choose the Section 179 option in a year in which you made very little money in your business. As long as your wages (if any) plus your net self-employment income exceed the amount of the Section 179 deduction you want to take, you're allowed to use Section 179. However, it may not be effective tax planning to depreciate in this way if you have only a small amount of business income.

> *Marisa bought a $2,000 computer to use exclusively in her business. Her wages were $20,000. Her gross self-employment income (before expenses) was $1,500. In addition to buying the computer, Marisa spent $200 on office supplies. If she deducts the computer in full (uses Section 179), her self-employment loss will be $700 ($1,500 − $200 − $2000). The $700 loss will offset $700 of her wages so that her total taxed income will be $19,300. Deducting the computer in full will reduce Marisa's income tax. Since she's in the 15% tax bracket, the $2,000 she spent on the computer will save her $300 in federal income tax.*

If instead Marisa had taken regular MACRS depreciation on the computer this year, she would have been able to deduct 20% ($400) of the cost in the first year. Subtracting that amount, plus the office supplies, from her self-employment income, Marisa would have a net profit of $900 ($1,500 − $200 − $400). The $400 computer depreciation deduction saves Marisa $60 in federal income tax ($400 × 15%) and $57 in self-employment tax ($400 × 92.35% × 15.3%) in the first year. Assuming that she remains in the 15% federal tax bracket for the remaining 5 years she's depreciating the computer, Marisa will save a total of $240 in federal tax ($1,600 × 15%) and $226 in self-employment tax ($1,600 × 92.35% × 15.3%) over that period of time. Using regular MACRS depreciation saves Marisa a total of $583 in tax ($300 in federal income tax plus $283 in self-employment tax) over the 6 years versus the $300 she saves if she deducts the full cost of the computer in the year she buys it. This is because by depreciating the computer over a period of years, Marisa ends up with a net profit from her business, so the deduction saves her both income tax and self-employment tax.

On the other hand, by taking the Section 179 deduction for the full price in the year she buys the computer, Marisa gets a larger deduction in the first year than she would if she used regular MACRS depreciation. If she needs the refund money or hasn't paid enough in estimated tax payments, she may choose the $300 tax savings she could get in 1 year over the $583 savings she would get over the 6-year period. Also, Marisa needs to consider whether she'll still be in business and using the same computer in 6 years.

If Marisa takes Section 179 and deducts the full amount of the computer the year she buys it and then decides to sell it the next year, she may regret her depreciation decision. She bought the computer for $2,000. Using Section 179, she deducts the full $2,000 in the first year. In year two, she sells the computer for $1,500. Because she took Section 179 (fully deducted the $2,000 cost) in year one, her basis in the computer when she sells it is considered to be zero. Therefore, the $1,500 she gets from selling it is fully taxable to her.

As you can see from this example, there's no wrong or right answer about when to use Section 179. Before deciding which method of depreciation is best for you to use, tax planning is necessary to consider your taxes both for the year you purchase the item and for future years.

It needn't be an all-or-nothing choice. You can use Section 179 on some items bought in a year and use regular MACRS depreciation for other items. You also can use Section 179 for part of the cost of the item and regular depreciation for the remainder of the cost.

FORM 4562

A copy of Form 4562, the form used to report the items you're depreciating, is found on pages 77–78. Part I is where you list the items you want to depreciate using Section 179. If the items are considered listed property, you include them in Part V, then carry the total back to Part I.

In Part II, list the items you bought this year that you are depreciating using regular MACRS depreciation. All 5-year items are combined, all 7-year items are combined, and so on. Part III is used to show this year's depreciation amount for items bought in previous years. That amount is entered on line 17.

Line 19 is for listing depreciation on items using a method other than MACRS. MACRS has been the method of depreciation used since 1987. If your business started prior to that date, you may be using either the ACRS or straight-line method of depreciation. Whichever method you begin using on an asset when you place it into service is the method you continue using as long as that asset is used in your business.

Part VI is used to list items to be amortized. Amortization is similar to depreciation but is used for intangible items such as franchise fees, trademarks, and closing costs on real estate purchases. This is the area in which you list the start-up costs you had before your business opened. They are amortized over 60 months, beginning with the month your business starts.

THE FRONT OF FORM 4562

Form **4562**	**Depreciation and Amortization**	OMB No. 1545-0172
Department of the Treasury Internal Revenue Service (99)	**(Including Information on Listed Property)** ▶ See separate instructions. ▶ Attach this form to your return.	19**99** Attachment Sequence No. **67**

Name(s) shown on return	Business or activity to which this form relates	Identifying number

Part I **Election To Expense Certain Tangible Property (Section 179)** (Note: *If you have any "listed property," complete Part V before you complete Part I.*)

1	Maximum dollar limitation. If an enterprise zone business, see page 2 of the instructions . .	**1**	$19,000
2	Total cost of section 179 property placed in service. See page 2 of the instructions	**2**	
3	Threshold cost of section 179 property before reduction in limitation	**3**	$200,000
4	Reduction in limitation. Subtract line 3 from line 2. If zero or less, enter -0-	**4**	
5	Dollar limitation for tax year. Subtract line 4 from line 1. If zero or less, enter -0-. If married filing separately, see page 2 of the instructions	**5**	

(a) Description of property	**(b)** Cost (business use only)	**(c)** Elected cost	
6			

7	Listed property. Enter amount from line 27. . . . . **7**		
8	Total elected cost of section 179 property. Add amounts in column (c), lines 6 and 7 . . .	**8**	
9	Tentative deduction. Enter the smaller of line 5 or line 8	**9**	
10	Carryover of disallowed deduction from 1998. See page 2 of the instructions	**10**	
11	Business income limitation. Enter the smaller of business income (not less than zero) or line 5 (see instructions)	**11**	
12	Section 179 expense deduction. Add lines 9 and 10, but do not enter more than line 11 . .	**12**	
13	Carryover of disallowed deduction to 2000. Add lines 9 and 10, less line 12 ▶ **13**		

Note: *Do not use Part II or Part III below for listed property (automobiles, certain other vehicles, cellular telephones, certain computers, or property used for entertainment, recreation, or amusement). Instead, use Part V for listed property.*

Part II **MACRS Depreciation for Assets Placed in Service ONLY During Your 1999 Tax Year (Do Not Include Listed Property.)**

Section A—General Asset Account Election

14	If you are making the election under section 168(i)(4) to group any assets placed in service during the tax year into one or more general asset accounts, check this box. See page 3 of the instructions . . . . ▶ ☐

Section B—General Depreciation System (GDS) (See page 3 of the instructions.)

(a) Classification of property	**(b)** Month and year placed in service	**(c)** Basis for depreciation (business/investment use only—see instructions)	**(d)** Recovery period	**(e)** Convention	**(f)** Method	**(g)** Depreciation deduction
15a 3-year property						
b 5-year property						
c 7-year property						
d 10-year property						
e 15-year property						
f 20-year property						
g 25-year property			25 yrs.		S/L	
h Residential rental property			27.5 yrs.	MM	S/L	
			27.5 yrs.	MM	S/L	
i Nonresidential real property			39 yrs.	MM	S/L	
				MM	S/L	

Section C—Alternative Depreciation System (ADS) (See page 5 of the instructions.)

16a Class life					S/L	
b 12-year			12 yrs.		S/L	
c 40-year			40 yrs.	MM	S/L	

Part III **Other Depreciation (Do Not Include Listed Property.)** (See page 5 of the instructions.)

17	GDS and ADS deductions for assets placed in service in tax years beginning before 1999 . .	**17**	
18	Property subject to section 168(f)(1) election	**18**	
19	ACRS and other depreciation	**19**	

Part IV **Summary** (See page 6 of the instructions.)

20	Listed property. Enter amount from line 26.	**20**	
21	**Total.** Add deductions on line 12, lines 15 and 16 in column (g), and lines 17 through 20. Enter here and on the appropriate lines of your return. Partnerships and S corporations—see instructions . .	**21**	
22	For assets shown above and placed in service during the current year, enter the portion of the basis attributable to section 263A costs . . **22**		

For Paperwork Reduction Act Notice, see page 9 of the instructions.   Cat. No. 12906N   Form **4562** (1999)

THE BACK OF FORM 4562

Part V	Listed Property—Automobiles, Certain Other Vehicles, Cellular Telephones, Certain Computers, and Property Used for Entertainment, Recreation, or Amusement

Note: *For any vehicle for which you are using the standard mileage rate or deducting lease expense, complete only 23a, 23b, columns (a) through (c) of Section A, all of Section B, and Section C if applicable.*

Section A—Depreciation and Other Information (Caution: *See page 7 of the instructions for limits for passenger automobiles.*)

23a Do you have evidence to support the business/investment use claimed? ☐ Yes ☐ No   **23b** If "Yes," is the evidence written? ☐ Yes ☐ No

(a) Type of property (list vehicles first)	(b) Date placed in service	(c) Business/ investment use percentage	(d) Cost or other basis	(e) Basis for depreciation (business/investment use only)	(f) Recovery period	(g) Method/ Convention	(h) Depreciation deduction	(i) Elected section 179 cost
24 Property used more than 50% in a qualified business use (See page 6 of the instructions.):								
		%						
		%						
		%						
25 Property used 50% or less in a qualified business use (See page 6 of the instructions.):								
		%				S/L –		
		%				S/L –		
		%				S/L –		
26 Add amounts in column (h). Enter the total here and on line 20, page 1						**26**		
27 Add amounts in column (i). Enter the total here and on line 7, page 1							**27**	

Section B—Information on Use of Vehicles

Complete this section for vehicles used by a sole proprietor, partner, or other "more than 5% owner," or related person.
If you provided vehicles to your employees, first answer the questions in Section C to see if you meet an exception to completing this section for those vehicles.

		(a) Vehicle 1		(b) Vehicle 2		(c) Vehicle 3		(d) Vehicle 4		(e) Vehicle 5		(f) Vehicle 6	
28	Total business/investment miles driven during the year (DO NOT include commuting miles—see page 1 of the instructions)												
29	Total commuting miles driven during the year												
30	Total other personal (noncommuting) miles driven												
31	Total miles driven during the year. Add lines 28 through 30												
		Yes	No	Yes	No	Yes	No	Yes	No	Yes	No	Yes	No
32	Was the vehicle available for personal use during off-duty hours?												
33	Was the vehicle used primarily by a more than 5% owner or related person?												
34	Is another vehicle available for personal use?												

Section C—Questions for Employers Who Provide Vehicles for Use by Their Employees

*Answer these questions to determine if you meet an exception to completing Section B for vehicles used by employees who **are not** more than 5% owners or related persons.*

		Yes	No
35	Do you maintain a written policy statement that prohibits all personal use of vehicles, including commuting, by your employees?		
36	Do you maintain a written policy statement that prohibits personal use of vehicles, except commuting, by your employees? See page 8 of the instructions for vehicles used by corporate officers, directors, or 1% or more owners		
37	Do you treat all use of vehicles by employees as personal use?		
38	Do you provide more than five vehicles to your employees, obtain information from your employees about the use of the vehicles, and retain the information received?		
39	Do you meet the requirements concerning qualified automobile demonstration use? See page 8 of the instructions . .		

Note: *If your answer to 35, 36, 37, 38, or 39 is "Yes," you need not complete Section B for the covered vehicles.*

Part VI	Amortization

(a) Description of costs	(b) Date amortization begins	(c) Amortizable amount	(d) Code section	(e) Amortization period or percentage	(f) Amortization for this year
40 Amortization of costs that begins during your 1999 tax year:					
41 Amortization of costs that began before 1999				**41**	
42 **Total.** Enter here and on "Other Deductions" or "Other Expenses" line of your return . . .				**42**	

CAN YOU DEDUCT YOUR HOME OFFICE? 23

Until 1999, strict rules for claiming a home office meant that many self-employed people didn't qualify for this deduction. In order to claim an office-in-home, the work space had to be either the primary place of work for this business; a place where you met with clients or customers; a separate structure not connected to the house; or the sole place business inventory or product samples were stored. Whether the office qualified as the primary place of work was measured by the amount of time spent or money earned in that location.

Beginning with 1999 tax returns, the definition of primary place of work has been expanded. Your home will now qualify as your principal place of business if you use it exclusively and regularly for administrative or management activities of your business and you have no other fixed location where you spend substantial time on these tasks.

> *Rebecca works 30 hours a week as an employee. She also has a small business teaching piano lessons in her home. She added a studio to her home and uses it solely for the lessons. She qualifies for the home office deduction because students come to her home studio. Also, this is the primary place of work for this business, although it isn't the primary place Rebecca spends her time during the week.*

> *Lisa Ann is a management consultant who provides training to corporations. She spends most of each week either conducting training sessions or traveling for business. She prepares for her training sessions in her home office, and that's also where she does her invoicing for current clients and marketing for potential new clients. Under the old rules, she would not have been able to deduct her home office, since it wasn't considered her primary place of work. Under the new rules, because it is the place she performs the administrative tasks for her business and she has nowhere else that she does that, her home office qualifies.*

This change in the definition of primary place of business means that many more people will qualify for the deduction. It doesn't mean, however, that everyone will qualify. As in the past, you can have a home office, but that doesn't necessarily mean you have a deductible office-in-home.

The basic rule for a deductible home office is that the work space must be used regularly and exclusively for your work. "Exclusively" means that nothing else happens in that space. A home office does not need to be a separate room, but it must be a clearly definable space. If you have a desk and computer in your bedroom and meet all the qualifications for a deductible home office, you can claim that portion of your bedroom as your office-in-home. If you work on the dining room table, you can claim a 3-by-6-foot (or whatever the size of your table) office-in-home. However, you cannot also use the dining room table as the place you serve Thanksgiving dinner (or any other meal).

In addition to the regulations already mentioned, there is yet another hurdle to overcome in order to deduct your home office expense. You cannot deduct an office-in-home if you have a loss from your business or if the home office deduction would create a loss. The maximum expense you can deduct for your home office is the amount of net profit from your business, not including the office-in-home.

If your net profit is, for example, $2,000, the most you can deduct for an office-in-home is $2,000. If your home office expenses are $2,000, your net profit will be zero. If your home office expenses are $3,000, you'll be able to deduct $2,000 of them and will still have a net profit of zero. Your net profit can be no lower than zero and still include a deduction for a home office.

If your business has a loss this year, you can't deduct your home office, even if it qualifies, but you can carry the unused expense over to next year's return and deduct it then. The only exception to this is for expenses that would be deductible even without the business, that is, mortgage interest and real estate tax. These expenses can be deducted even if you have a business loss.

CALCULATING THE HOME OFFICE DEDUCTION

Once you've decided that you qualify for the home office deduction, you then need to calculate the percentage of your home used for business. The most accurate way to do this is to measure the total number of square feet in your home and the number of square feet used for business. If the rooms in your home are approximately the same size, you may base your office-in-home percentage on the number of rooms used for business versus the total number of rooms in the house. You can use either of these methods to determine what percentage of your home is used for business. (An example of the home office calculation is shown on page 81.) As you do the measuring, consider creating a diagram of your home office. This, along with photographs of the work space, can be extremely helpful if you're audited and questioned about your home office space.

Be careful when filling out the personal itemized deduction form (Schedule A) that you include only the portion of mortgage interest and real estate tax that you haven't claimed for business. In other words, don't claim the same deduction twice.

After you've calculated the home office percentage, add together your total rent or mortgage interest, all your utilities, the amount of maintenance done on the entire home, and your total real estate taxes and insurance. Once you've combined these expenses, multiply the total by the percentage of the home that's used for business. To that figure, add maintenance on the part of your home that is used exclusively for business, such as painting your office room. The last figure to be added in is the depreciation on the business part of your home. (For more information on depreciation, see Chapter 22.) The portion of your home used for business is depreciated over 39 years, so you get only a small deduction each year. Once all the figures are added together, you'll have your total allowable office-in-home expense.

Since I can already deduct my mortgage interest and real estate taxes as a personal expense, what is the benefit of deducting a home office?

There are three benefits. First, when you deduct those expenses as business expenses, they not only reduce your income tax but also lessen your self-employment tax. Second, by deducting a home office, you're able to deduct utilities, insurance, and depreciation expenses that can't be taken as personal itemized deductions. The third benefit is that having a deductible home office allows you to deduct more of your car mileage expense (discussed in Chapter 25).

CALCULATING THE OFFICE-IN-HOME EXPENSE

Total square feet in home	1000 square feet
Total square feet used for business	200 square feet
Percentage of home used for business	20%
Business net profit (not including deduction for office in home)	$ 3,000
Total rent or mortgage interest	$ 3,600
Add total utilities	350
Add total real estate taxes & insurance	1,000
	$ 4,950
	× 20%
	$ 990
Add maintenance on part of home used exclusively for business	250
Add depreciation on business part of home (using MACRS 39-year method)	700
Total allowable office-in-home expense	**$1,940**

THE 8829 FORM

Form **8829**	**Expenses for Business Use of Your Home**	OMB No. 1545-1266

Form **8829**

Department of the Treasury
Internal Revenue Service   (99)

Expenses for Business Use of Your Home

▶ File only with Schedule C (Form 1040). Use a separate Form 8829 for each home you used for business during the year.

▶ See separate instructions.

OMB No. 1545-1266

19**99**

Attachment
Sequence No. **66**

Name(s) of proprietor(s) | Your social security number

Part I — Part of Your Home Used for Business

1	Area used regularly and exclusively for business, regularly for day care, or for storage of inventory or product samples. See instructions	**1**	
2	Total area of home	**2**	
3	Divide line 1 by line 2. Enter the result as a percentage	**3**	%

- For day-care facilities not used exclusively for business, also complete lines 4–6.
- All others, skip lines 4–6 and enter the amount from line 3 on line 7.

4	Multiply days used for day care during year by hours used per day .	**4**		hr.
5	Total hours available for use during the year (365 days × 24 hours). See instructions	**5**	8,760	hr.
6	Divide line 4 by line 5. Enter the result as a decimal amount . . .	**6**	.	
7	Business percentage. For day-care facilities not used exclusively for business, multiply line 6 by line 3 (enter the result as a percentage). All others, enter the amount from line 3 . . . . . ▶	**7**		%

Part II — Figure Your Allowable Deduction

		(a) Direct expenses	(b) Indirect expenses	
8	Enter the amount from Schedule C, line 29, **plus** any net gain or (loss) derived from the business use of your home and shown on Schedule D or Form 4797. If more than one place of business, see instructions			**8**
	See instructions for columns (a) and (b) before completing lines 9–20.			
9	Casualty losses. See instructions	**9**		
10	Deductible mortgage interest. See instructions .	**10**		
11	Real estate taxes. See instructions	**11**		
12	Add lines 9, 10, and 11	**12**		
13	Multiply line 12, column (b) by line 7	**13**		
14	Add line 12, column (a) and line 13		**14**	
15	Subtract line 14 from line 8. If zero or less, enter -0- .		**15**	
16	Excess mortgage interest. See instructions . .	**16**		
17	Insurance	**17**		
18	Repairs and maintenance	**18**		
19	Utilities	**19**		
20	Other expenses. See instructions	**20**		
21	Add lines 16 through 20	**21**		
22	Multiply line 21, column (b) by line 7	**22**		
23	Carryover of operating expenses from 1998 Form 8829, line 41 . .	**23**		
24	Add line 21 in column (a), line 22, and line 23		**24**	
25	Allowable operating expenses. Enter the **smaller** of line 15 or line 24		**25**	
26	Limit on excess casualty losses and depreciation. Subtract line 25 from line 15		**26**	
27	Excess casualty losses. See instructions	**27**		
28	Depreciation of your home from Part III below	**28**		
29	Carryover of excess casualty losses and depreciation from 1998 Form 8829, line 42	**29**		
30	Add lines 27 through 29		**30**	
31	Allowable excess casualty losses and depreciation. Enter the **smaller** of line 26 or line 30 . .		**31**	
32	Add lines 14, 25, and 31		**32**	
33	Casualty loss portion, if any, from lines 14 and 31. Carry amount to **Form 4684**, Section B . .		**33**	
34	Allowable expenses for business use of your home. Subtract line 33 from line 32. Enter here and on Schedule C, line 30. If your home was used for more than one business, see instructions ▶		**34**	

Part III — Depreciation of Your Home

35	Enter the **smaller** of your home's adjusted basis or its fair market value. See instructions . .	**35**	
36	Value of land included on line 35	**36**	
37	Basis of building. Subtract line 36 from line 35	**37**	
38	Business basis of building. Multiply line 37 by line 7	**38**	
39	Depreciation percentage. See instructions	**39**	%
40	Depreciation allowable. Multiply line 38 by line 39. Enter here and on line 28 above. See instructions	**40**	

Part IV — Carryover of Unallowed Expenses to 2000

41	Operating expenses. Subtract line 25 from line 24. If less than zero, enter -0-	**41**	
42	Excess casualty losses and depreciation. Subtract line 31 from line 30. If less than zero, enter -0- .	**42**	

For Paperwork Reduction Act Notice, see page 4 of separate instructions.   Cat. No. 13232M   Form **8829** (1999)

Where the office-in-home expense is listed on your tax return will depend on whether you're a sole proprietor, a partner, or a corporation shareholder/employee. A sole proprietor includes the expense on Schedule C (see page 119). If the office-in-home expense has not been reported on the partnership return, a partner will list it on Schedule E and use it to offset partnership income. A corporation shareholder/employee, like any other employee, includes the expense on Schedule A as a personal itemized deduction, deductible only if all work-related expenses exceed 2% of her income. Sole proprietors and corporation shareholder/employees must fill out Form 8829 in order to deduct the home office.

FORM 8829

Form 8829 (see page 82) is actually just a more official version of the home office calculation shown on page 81. It asks how much of your home is used regularly and exclusively for business and what the total area of your home is. Then it asks you to list your home office expenses as either direct or indirect. Indirect expenses include mortgage interest, real estate tax, rent, and other expenses you have for the whole house. Direct expenses are those that apply only to the space claimed as the home office. There is no line on the form for rent paid, so if you rent your home, list the rent amount under "other expenses" on line 20. Write "rent" next to that figure.

I heard that if you claim an office-in-home, it has a negative effect when you sell your house.

This can be true. Under new tax law, if you've lived in your home for 2 of the 5 years before you sell it and have a profit on the sale of less than $250,000 ($500,000 if married), you owe no tax on the gain. However, if you use part of your residence as your deductible home office, that portion of your home stops being your personal residence and becomes instead business property. When you sell your home, you may not owe tax on the gain from the sale of the personal portion, but that isn't true of the gain on the business portion. The tax on that gain will be due the year you sell the property. However, if you stop using your home office for at least two of the five years before you sell the house, the property reverts back to personal residence property and, to the extent that the gain is less than $250,000 ($500,000 if married), it is not taxable. Assuming you're still operating your business, to "stop using your home office" means either that your home office no longer qualifies to be deducted (e.g., it's no longer exclusively used for business) or that you have rented office space outside your home. It isn't enough to simply stop claiming the home office deduction on your tax return. One caution: Even if the property reverts back to personal use, the depreciation you've claimed on the home office will be taxed when you sell the house. It's best to consult with your tax professional to see whether taking the deduction now is a wise move.

Part III of the form is used to calculate the depreciation on your home. Only buildings can be depreciated, not the land on which the building sits. Although you can still deduct your home office even if you rent, you can depreciate your home only if you own it.

At the bottom of Form 8829 is a section called "Carryover of Unallowed Expenses to [the next year]." This section is used when you otherwise qualify for the home office deduction but are unable to claim it because you have a loss from your business or your business profit is less than your home office expense. The amount you aren't able to use on this year's return is carried over to next year and can be deducted then (assuming you have enough profit next year to deduct it). In order to carry the expense forward to the next year, you need to fill out Form 8829 and include it in this year's return.

As you can see, there are lots of hoops to jump through in claiming the office-in-home deduction. Many people don't claim this expense, even though they qualify for it, because they've heard that it increases the chance of an audit. My experience as a tax preparer does not support this belief. I've prepared nearly eight thousand tax returns, approximately half of which include an office-in-home deduction. Only two or three of the returns claiming a home office have been audited. While I don't recommend that you take the office-in-home expense without making sure you qualify for it and that it's a wise move for your situation, it can be a valuable deduction for those who claim it.

TELEPHONE
AND OTHER
UTILITY EXPENSES 24

If you qualify to deduct a home office, usually the same percentage used to calculate the deductible rent or mortgage interest is used to calculate the deductible utility expenses. Utilities include gas and electricity, as well as garbage, water, and sewer charges.

The following example illustrates why, occasionally, it will be appropriate to use a different calculation for one or more of the utilities rather than basing the deduction on the percentage of the house used for business:

> *Laurie provides therapeutic massages in her home. She has a room set aside for this business, and the space is 15% of Laurie's total home. Although Laurie deducts 15% of her rent, water, and garbage expense, she deducts 50% of her electricity cost as a business expense. Laurie has found that since she's been doing massages at home, her electricity costs have greatly increased because she uses small electric heaters to keep the massage space warm. To calculate what percentage of the electricity to deduct for the business, Laurie compared her utility bills before she began doing massages in her home to her current bills. She found that the electricity cost had doubled since she began her home business, so she's deducting 50% of the electricity cost as a business expense.*

As in Laurie's case, your home business may use a disproportionate percentage of your home utilities. Computers, laser printers, and copy machines use large amounts of electricity. Photographers may use a lot of water in their darkrooms. Woodworkers usually fill more than the normal number of garbage cans. If your utility bills have increased since you began working in your home, be sure to include the increased amount when you calculate your home office deduction.

Unlike utilities, business telephone expenses can be deducted whether or not you claim a home office. Since there is not a separate line on Schedule C to list telephone expenses, some people include them with the utilities expense. With modems, cellular phones, faxes, and multiple phone lines common in many businesses, phone bills can be high. For that reason, I prefer to list the telephone expense on its own line in the "other expenses" section of Schedule C (see page 119).

If you have a deductible home office, your telephone expenses won't be deducted in the same proportion as other utilities. If you don't have a deductible home office, you can still deduct the business portion of your home phone. In either case, you cannot deduct the telephone base rate or monthly service charge if you have only one phone line going into your home. The IRS believes that you would have had that one line anyway, and deductible expenses are only the additional expenses incurred because you have a business.

Even if you have only one line in your home, you can still deduct any business-related long distance calls. Local business calls are also deductible, but only if there are extra charges for those calls. Also, a deduction can be taken for extra features, such as call waiting or call forwarding, that were added because of the business.

If you have a separate phone line that's used exclusively for your business, the costs for that line are 100% deductible. This is true even if it isn't registered with the phone company as a business line. If you have a second line coming into your home and it's used partially for business, you can deduct a portion of the monthly fees, plus the specific business calls.

Cellular phone costs are deducted in the same way as other telephone expenses. Usually a cellular phone is used less than 100% for business. This is true even if it's used only occasionally to tell your spouse or partner you're on the way home. If the phone is used 95% for business, 95% of the monthly charge can be deducted, plus 100% of the identified business calls. In this example, 95% of the cost of the phone itself would be depreciated.

USING YOUR CAR IN YOUR BUSINESS

25

In order to deduct car expenses, you need to know how much you used your car for business. In fact, the most crucial part of the automobile deduction is the recordkeeping. If you are being audited for any other part of your Schedule C, the auditor will almost always examine any car expenses you've deducted. This is because auditors know that most people don't keep adequate records of car use. When they ask to see your log and you say, "What log?" the auditors are then able to quickly disallow what could have been a substantial deduction.

When asked how many miles their cars were used for business in the prior year, many taxpayers stare at the ceiling as if the answer's written up there. Some tax preparers call this the PFTA ("Plucked From The Air") approach to recordkeeping. It will not stand up in an audit.

Business owners sometimes claim that they use their car 100% for business. If you have a deductible office-in-home, 100% business car use is possible if you have another car available for personal transportation. If you don't have a deductible office-in-home, your car generally won't be used 100% for business because you have at least some commuting miles. Often the business car is also used for a vacation trip or to pick up groceries. True 100% business use is so rare for a passenger vehicle that it stands out if claimed as such on your tax return.

In any case, you can't just make a guess about your car mileage. You need to know how many total miles the car was driven this year and how many of those miles were for business.

A business mile is a mile from one business stop to another business stop. If you have a deductible office-in-home, deductible miles would include driving from your home office to see a client, going to lunch with a colleague, and picking up business supplies. If you do not have a deductible office-in-home, business mileage doesn't start until you get to your first stop of the day. From home to the first stop of the day and from the last stop of the day to home is considered commuting, just as though you were working for someone else.

If you don't have a deductible office-in-home, you may want to consider ways of reducing your commuting or nondeductible mileage. Would it be appropriate for you to have a post office box for your business? If so, open one near your home and use it as your primary business address. Can you buy from a supplier near your home? If so, do it. From home to the

WHEN ARE LOCAL TRANSPORTATION EXPENSES DEDUCTIBLE?

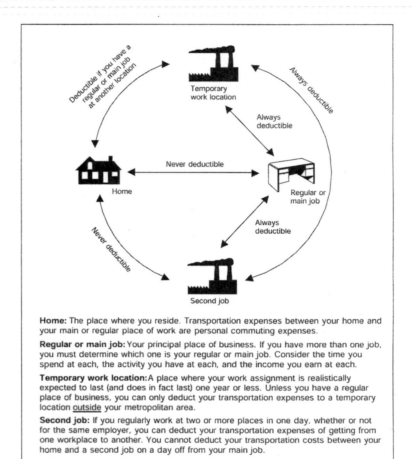

Home: The place where you reside. Transportation expenses between your home and your main or regular place of work are personal commuting expenses.

Regular or main job: Your principal place of business. If you have more than one job, you must determine which one is your regular or main job. Consider the time you spend at each, the activity you have at each, and the income you earn at each.

Temporary work location: A place where your work assignment is realistically expected to last (and does in fact last) one year or less. Unless you have a regular place of business, you can only deduct your transportation expenses to a temporary location <u>outside</u> your metropolitan area.

Second job: If you regularly work at two or more places in one day, whether or not for the same employer, you can deduct your transportation expenses of getting from one workplace to another. You cannot deduct your transportation costs between your home and a second job on a day off from your main job.

post office or supplier will still be commuting, but from that point on, you have deductible business miles. Of course, you might have a hard time explaining in an audit why you also stopped at the post office box or supplier on your way home. If this really isn't reasonable, your trip home will consist of nondeductible miles.

If you travel to a business location outside your tax home, you can include the miles from your home and back to your home as business miles even if you don't have a deductible home office. Your tax home is the approximately 40-mile perimeter around your main place of business. This exception to the general business mile rules will be helpful to those who travel great distances for their business but don't have a deductible home office.

Another helpful exception is for those who have a regular place of business but commute to a temporary work location. You can deduct the round-trip from your home to the temporary location, even if you don't have a deductible office-in-home. To be considered temporary, the work at that location must be irregular or short term.

KEEPING RECORDS

The key to deducting business miles is having good records. Keeping track of the total miles you drive your car each year is easy; just write down the odometer reading each January 1. If you don't have that figure for this year, repair bills (which usually include the odometer reading) may help.

Keeping track of the business miles is harder. Ideally, you'll keep a log (available at any office supply store) or notebook in your car. Write down either the beginning and ending odometer reading for each business trip, or note how many business miles you drive each day. In either case, also note what business locations you visited.

Although it's easy once you get into the habit, many people don't want to keep a car log. If you're one of those people, see if one of the following methods works better for you:

- Write down in your appointment book each day how many business miles you drove that day; the calendar notations will indicate what business locations you visited.
- If you go on the same route or to the same location regularly, measure the distance once and count the number of times you made the trip during the year.
- If you use your vehicle primarily for business, instead of keeping track of the business miles, keep track of the number of personal miles you drive.
- If your business driving is similar throughout the year, keep detailed records for only 1 month each quarter or for 1 week of each month. This will give you enough information that you can fairly accurately calculate your annual business mileage.

CALCULATING THE DEDUCTION

Whichever way you keep your records, once you know the total number of miles the car was driven for the year and how many of those were for business, there are two possible ways of deducting your car expenses. The first is called the actual expense method. In this method, you add together your expenses for gas, oil, repairs, insurance, auto club membership, car license, and loan interest or lease payments. Then multiply the total by the percentage you use the car for business. Add to this figure the car's depreciation (leased cars do not get depreciated), along with your business parking and tolls. The end result is your total business car expense.

MAXIMUM DEPRECIATION LIMITS FOR CARS*

Placed in Service		Depreciation First Year**	Depreciation Later Years	
After	Before			
1986	1989	$2,560	$4,100	2nd yr.
			2,450	3rd yr.
			1,475†	
1988	1991	$2,660	$4,200	2nd yr.
			2,550	3rd yr.
			1,475†	
1990	1992	$2,660	$4,300	2nd yr.
			2,550	3rd yr.
			1,575†	
1991	1993	$2,760	$4,400	2nd yr.
			2,650	3rd yr.
			1,575†	
1992	1994	$2,860	$4,600	2nd yr.
			2,750	3rd yr.
			1,675†	
1993	1995	$2,960	$4,700	2nd yr.
			2,850	3rd yr.
			1,675†	
1994	1997	$3,060	$4,900	2nd yr.
			2,950	3rd yr.
			1,775†	
1996	1998	$3,160	$5,000	2nd yr.
			3,050	3rd yr.
			1,775†	
1997	1999	$3,160	$5,000	2nd yr.
			2,950	3rd yr.
			1,775†	
1998		$3,060	$5,000	2nd yr.
			2,950	3rd yr.
			1,775†	

* All amounts must be reduced if the car is used less than 100% for business purposes.
** This is the maximum amount of your Section 179 deduction and depreciation allowed for the tax year the car is placed in service.
† This amount is also the limit on deductions taken in years after the recovery period.

Depreciation is calculated differently for cars than it is for other assets (see Chapter 22 for general depreciation rules). There are yearly limitations on the amount of depreciation that can be taken for vehicles weighing less than 6,000 pounds. The table on page 90 shows the maximum depreciation that can be taken each year for a car. This figure is assuming 100% business use, so it must be multiplied by the true business percentage before being included on your tax return. For example, a $16,430 car bought in 1999 and used 80% for business in 2000 will have a deprecation deduction in 2000 (year two) of $4,000 ($5,000 × 80%). Vehicles weighing more than 6,000 pounds or designed for a purpose other than regular passenger transport (e.g., flat bed trucks, ambulances, taxis) are not subject to the yearly limitations shown above. Note that some sport utility vehicles (SUVs) exceed 6,000 pounds.

The second method of deducting your car expenses is called the mileage rate or standard method. To use this method, multiply the number of business miles you drove during the year by a cents-per-mile figure. For mileage that occurred between January and March of 1999, 32.5¢ a mile is allowed. Mileage for the remainder of 1999 is deducted at 31¢ a mile. 1999 was an unusual year; usually the same mileage rate figure is used for the entire year. For 2000, the mileage rate figure is 32.5¢ for the entire year. The only expenses you can add to the 32.5¢/31¢ a mile is the business percentage of your car loan interest, the business percentage of your car registration, and your business parking and tolls (parking tickets are never deductible). All other expense are considered to be covered by the 32.5¢/31¢-a-mile deduction.

Page 92 shows an example of both methods of deducting car expenses. In the example, the mileage rate method resulted in a much larger deduction than the actual expense method. This won't always be true. Often, the deduction for the mileage rate method will be greater when you drive a lot of business miles. The actual expense method will usually be larger when a high percentage of your driving during the year is for business.

You can change methods from year to year as long as you use the standard or mileage rate method the first year you buy the car or place it into service. If you use the standard

I've been advised to lease a car for business rather than buy one. Is that a good idea?

A lot of the advertisements encouraging you to lease a car state that you'll be able to deduct the entire lease payment as a business expense. This isn't true. You can deduct only the business percentage of the lease cost, just as you can only deduct the business percentage of other expenses you have for the car. In many cases, the decision about whether to buy or lease a car is a financial decision based on nontax issues. For example, do you want to drive a new car every few years? Do you have enough money for the down payment on a car purchase? Would you rather not tie up your money with large monthly loan payments?

If you do lease a car, you need to make sure that what you have is truly a lease rather than a sales contract. Although it may be called a lease, the intent of the parties involved (you and the lessor) and the conditions of the contract determine whether it's really a lease. If part of your payments are building up equity in the car so that you can purchase it for a relatively small amount at the end of the lease period, you probably have a sales contract rather than a lease. In this case, you depreciate the car rather than deduct the lease payments.

Q

A

method the first year, you can use whichever method is more advantageous in subsequent years. If you don't use the standard method the first year you begin using the car in your business, you'll have to continue to use the actual expense method for as long as you own this car.

CALCULATING BUSINESS CAR EXPENSE

Total miles car was driven this year	20,000
Number of business miles car was driven	12,000
Percentage of miles driven for business	60%

ACTUAL EXPENSE METHOD		MILEAGE RATE (STANDARD) METHOD	
gas, oil, lube	$ 650	5,000 miles @ 32.5¢	$ 1,625
tires	100	(January-March 1999)	
repairs	400		
insurance	600	7,000 miles @ 31¢	2,170
AAA membership	26	(April-December 1999)	
interest on car loan	424	business % of	254
(or lease payment)		car loan interest	
car registration	50	business % of	30
	$ 2,250	car registration	
	× 60%		$ 4,079
	$ 1,350		
depreciation	+ 1,440		
(on business part only)			
Business parking		Business parking	
& tolls	+ 100	& tolls	+ 100
Total car expense	**$ 2,890**	**Total car expense**	**$ 4,179**

MEALS AND ENTERTAINMENT

26

Meal and entertainment expenses are also among the most highly audited expenses. As with car expenses, this is at least in part because many people don't keep adequate records and are unable to prove the deductibility of the receipts they have.

There are only two types of deductible meals. One is when you're away from home overnight. Those meals are the only ones you can deduct whether eating alone or with others. The second type of deductible meals are those in which you meet with someone for a meal and have a reasonable expectation of receiving income or some other business benefit as a result. The "business benefit" might be getting a new client, a referral to a new client, or continuing business from an existing client. Meeting with a colleague to discuss better ways of running your business is another example of a meal with a business benefit. In some way, the discussion you have before, during, or after the meal must provide some immediate or expected benefit to your business. These meals are deductible whether you pay only for your own meal or you also pay for the meals of those with you.

Some meals that would seem to be deductible aren't really. For example, Melanie is working with a client and the client says, "I need you to work late tonight; go out and grab a bite to eat." That meal is not deductible. Even though Melanie was at work before and after she ate, unless she ate with her client and discussed business, it is not a deductible meal.

In order to deduct the expense of these two types of meals, you must keep good records. For each meal, you need to record the following (preferably on the back of the receipt):

- The cost of the meal (don't forget tips)
- The time and date of the meal (your appointment book helps to verify this information)
- The location of the meeting, if not indicated on the receipt
- The name of the person you ate with, her title, and your business relationship

Most importantly, you also need to record the business purpose of the meal, including what was discussed. The deductibility is least likely to be questioned if you ate with a client or a prospective client.

Although this seems like a great deal of information to keep track of, a client of mine had thousands of dollars worth of meal expenses disallowed at an audit. Although she'd included the other required information, she hadn't recorded the business purpose of the meal on each of her receipts. Also, the auditor noted that the same names showed up over and over on the receipts and concluded that my client and her colleagues took turns picking up the check for their meals together (another no-no).

Fortunately, my client was saved from paying hundreds more in taxes when I suggested to the auditor that we use the per diem rate to replace the amounts of the disallowed meals that had taken place while my client was out of town. As a self-employed person, you can use a per diem rate of between $30 and $46 (depending on the city in which you're traveling) instead of actual meal expenses for each day you're away from home overnight. IRS Publication 1542 lists the per diem rate allowed for individual cities within the U.S. If you choose the per diem rate, you must use it consistently for all trips taken during that year. Even if you use the per diem rate, you must have records showing the dates you were traveling (your appointment book is sufficient) and the cities to which you traveled.

Whether you use the actual or per diem expense method, all meals, whether at home or out of town, are only 50% deductible. Keep track of the whole cost of the meal, including tips, but deduct only 50%.

Q *I thought you said earlier that we didn't have to have receipts if the expense was less than $75. Most of my business meals are less than $75.*

A You are right. I said in Chapter 7 that receipts aren't required for business expenses costing less than $75. However, as I said in that chapter, you still need to record the amount spent, where and when it was spent, and what it was spent on. Additionally, for meal expenses, you need to list the business purpose and business relationship of the person with whom you ate.

Q *If I take a client to the theater or a ball game, can I deduct the cost of the tickets as business entertainment?*

A In order to deduct meals or entertainment, a business discussion must take place before, during, or after the meal or entertainment. Also, the meal or entertainment must take place in a location that's conducive (i.e., quiet enough) for a business discussion. However, if you buy theater or ball game tickets and give them to a client but don't accompany her to the event, the tickets may be deductible as a business gift (see Chapter 30).

DEDUCTIBLE TRAVEL 27

Travel is another highly audited expense, which means it requires good recordkeeping. I recommend that you make calendar entries or keep a log for each day of a business trip so that you can prove the deductibility of your travel by showing what you did each day.

Domestic travel is an either/or situation. Either it's primarily a business trip, in which case the airfare is 100% deductible, or it's primarily a personal trip, in which case the airfare is not deductible at all. The airfare is not prorated for domestic travel. Whether a trip is primarily for business is generally, but not always, measured by the amount of time you spend on business compared to the total amount of time you're away. For example, if you are gone for 10 days and you spend 8 of them on business, you are on a primarily business trip. You can deduct all your airfare and all of the expenses for the 8 days you spent on business and none of the expenses for the 2 days not spent on business. If the trip is primarily a personal trip, you can't deduct any of the airfare, but you can deduct the expenses (e.g., hotel, car rental) you had on the days you were doing business.

Emma, who lives in Chicago, is the keynote speaker at a conference for health professionals in Florida. She'll spend 1 day at the conference and then travel to North Carolina for 3 days to visit a childhood friend. Emma can deduct the cost of airfare from Chicago to Florida and back to Chicago. She also can deduct all of her expenses in Florida. She cannot deduct any of her expenses in North Carolina or her airfare from Florida to North Carolina. This is an example of an instance when a "primarily business" trip is not measured by the percentage of days spent on business. Emma would have had to pay anyway for the trip to Florida to give the speech, so that airfare is deductible no matter what she does during the remainder of her time away.

Sara, a health professional, lives in Oregon and will travel to Florida to attend the conference at which Emma is speaking. She'll be at the conference for 4 days and then travel to New York to visit her family for 6 days. Sara's airfare isn't at all deductible, but her hotel, meal, and car rental in Florida are deductible. She may read this book before she goes and decide to sufficiently reduce the

*number of days she spends with her family to make this a "pri-
marily business trip" and, thus, be able to deduct the airfare from
Oregon to Florida and back to Oregon.*

Expenses you can deduct while traveling include airfare, airport
shuttle, taxis, tips, laundry, bus, rental car, and so on. Travel is 100%
deductible, but travel meals are only 50% deductible, so you need to
record your meals separately from the other travel expenses.

Foreign travel—travel outside North America—is handled a bit differently than domestic travel. For foreign travel, you can deduct a percentage of the entire trip based on the number of days you spend on
business versus the total number of days you're away. However, if you are
outside North America for less than 8 days or if less than 25% of your trip
is for personal purposes, no allocation needs to be made, and the full cost
can be deducted.

*JoAnn travels from New York to France to work with a client.
While in France, she spends 8 days with her client and 5 days
relaxing in the French countryside. She also spends 2 days in travel
between New York and France, for a total of 15 days away. JoAnn
can deduct $^{10}/_{15}$ or ($^2/_3$) of her total trip expenses, since the travel
days are counted as work days.*

Travel expenses for your spouse are deductible only if your spouse is
a bona fide employee of your business or if you co-own the business with
him. This is true for both foreign and domestic travel. If one of your goals
is to combine vacations with business trips and you want your spouse to
accompany you, the potentially deductible travel should be considered in
deciding whether you and your spouse or domestic partner should work
together.

INSURANCE DEDUCTIONS

28

Only some types of insurance are deductible. Life insurance premiums are not deductible anywhere on your tax return. Disability insurance premiums are not deductible either (but, if your state requires you to provide disability insurance for your employees, that amount is deductible). If you ever become disabled and begin collecting benefits, the money you receive is not taxable.

Business insurance of any type is deductible. This includes malpractice insurance, business overhead insurance, workers' compensation policies for your employees, and liability insurance. If you have an office-in-home and buy a special policy to protect the business computers you have at home, those premiums are fully deductible.

Car insurance and homeowners or renters insurance are deductible to the extent that you use the car or home for business. A portion of the premiums are deductible along with other car and home expenses (see Chapters 25 and 23).

Health insurance premiums are 60% deductible on the 1040 Form for sole proprietors, partners, and S-corporation shareholders who own more than 2% of the corporation's stock. Note that this deduction is not taken as a business expense except for the portion paid to buy insurance for employees of the business, if any. In 2002, the deduction increases to 70%, and in 2003, self-employed people will be able to deduct 100% of their health insurance premiums.

Deductible health insurance premiums are those that the self-employed person paid for herself, her spouse (if married), and any dependents. If the self-employed person or her spouse is covered by a health insurance plan paid for by an employer, the health insurance deduction cannot be taken for any months in which either spouse was eligible for the employer-subsidized plan.

Long-term care insurance premiums are combined with health insurance premiums to be 60% deductible (45% in 1998) on the 1040 Form.

Another medical deduction opportunity is available through Medical Savings Accounts (MSAs). MSAs are available nationally to only 750,000 taxpayers, as this is a pilot program. Self-employed people and employees

What happens to the other 40% of my health and long-term care insurance premiums?

If you have enough expenses to be able to itemize your personal deductions and if your medical expenses are more than 7.5% of your income, the remainder goes on Schedule A of your tax return (the form for personal itemized deductions).

97

who work for a business that has no more than fifty employees are the groups targeted for this program. To be eligible, the individual must have a "high-deductible" health plan. This means that before medical expenses are covered by insurance, the insured is responsible for an amount between $1,500 and $2,250 ($3,000 to $4,000 for a family).

The MSA enables taxpayers to set aside money to pay for medical expenses that aren't covered by their insurance policy, as well as expenses incurred before they meet the insurance's deductible amount. As with contributions to an IRA, money put into an MSA is deducted from your income, and interest or dividends earned on the account are not included in taxable income. If the money in the account is used for anything other than medical expenses, the distribution is taxable, and there is a 15% penalty.

If interested in establishing an MSA, check first with your health insurance provider to make sure that your plan meets the requirements. Then contact a bank, brokerage house, or insurance company about setting up the MSA portion. Because the program is relatively new, you may need to make several calls before finding a company that offers Medical Savings Accounts.

EDUCATION EXPENSES

29

Education expenses are not particularly prone to audit but still must meet certain requirements. In order to deduct educational expenses, you need to be able to answer no to both of these questions:

- Did you need this education to meet the basic requirements of your profession? In other words, were you unable to begin work in this field unless you took this class?
- Will this study qualify you for a new business or profession?

The IRS does not allow you to deduct the costs of preparing to go into a new field of work. Once you're earning money in an occupation, you can deduct any classes that increase your skills and knowledge in that line of work. This includes all required continuing education classes.

Although education in preparation for a new career cannot be deducted as a business expense, it may be eligible for the lifetime learning credit. This credit is available for courses that are taken at eligible institutions and help you acquire or improve your job skills. Courses that train you for a new field of work also are eligible. The credit is not related to being self-employed and can't be taken if the education expense can be deducted as a business expense. The lifetime learning credit has income restrictions; a phaseout of the amount allowed begins when your adjusted gross income exceeds $40,000 ($80,000 if married). No credit is allowed if your income is over $50,000 ($100,000 if married). If you are eligible, the credit is 20% of the first $5,000 you spend on tuition and fees. Unlike a deduction, which is subtracted from your income before the tax is calculated, a credit is subtracted directly from your income tax. As you can tell, a credit saves you more money than a deduction of the same amount would.

If paying for education is a problem, it may be helpful to know that money can be taken out of an IRA without penalty if it is used to pay for qualified higher education expenses for you, your spouse, or your dependents. The money withdrawn, however, is taxable.

30

OTHER DEDUCTIBLE BUSINESS EXPENSES

As explained in Chapter 20, all ordinary and necessary business expenses are deductible. A list of some common deductible expenses follows. This is not an exhaustive list, and no one business will have all these expenses. You are the person who is most familiar with the expenses of your business.

Most of the expenses listed are self-explanatory, but a few need further clarification:

- Bank service charges and credit card fees are 100% deductible if you have a separate business account, but these must be prorated if you have only one account.
- Client consultation and supervision fees are expenses that psychotherapists and some other health professionals have in meeting with supervisors and consultants to discuss and review their work.
- Contract labor or subcontractor expenses are less likely to be audited if listed on your tax return under the type of work provided (e.g., computer consultant or landscaping services). Reread Chapter 15 to ensure that you're correctly classifying these people as independent contractors rather than employees.
- Dues for professional organizations are deductible. Dues for health clubs or country clubs are not, even if that is where you sometimes meet or entertain clients.
- Gifts are deductible up to a maximum of $25 per person per year. You can spend more on the gift but can deduct only $25 of the total cost. For purposes of this expense, a "person" also means a married couple and so would include a gift given to either spouse.
- Interest is 100% deductible if it is paid on business loans or on credit cards used solely for business purchases. With the exception of home mortgages and home equity loans, interest paid on personal loans and credit cards is not at all deductible. Make sure that money you borrow to pay for business expenses (whether it is actually called a business loan or not),

COMMON BUSINESS EXPENSES

Note: Probably no business will have all these expenses. Your business may have different categories of expenses. Don't agonize over which category an expense belongs in.

Advertising

Accounting/bookkeeping fees

Bank service charges

Car and truck expenses

Client consultation and supervision fees (for therapists)

Contract labor (outside services, subcontractors, etc.)

Credit card fees

Depreciation on assets used in the business

Dues

Education

Entertainment/business meals

Freight

Gifts

Insurance

Interest on business credit cards and loans

Inventory/merchandise purchases (items the business has available for sale to others)

Legal and professional fees

Magazines and books

Maintenance and repairs

Office supplies

Online fees

Payroll taxes (only for businesses with employees and only the employer's share of taxes—not the amount deducted from the employee's paycheck)

Postage

Printing and copying

Rent/office-in-home expense

Sales or excise tax (only for businesses that collect this tax)

Small furnishings and equipment

Telephone (including pager and answering service)

Travel (outside normal business location)

Utilities

Wages (this refers to what is paid to employees, not to yourself or to independent contractors) is used only for that purpose. If you use some of the money for personal living expenses, you will lose the interest deduction on that portion of the loan. A loan or credit card doesn't need to be in the name of your business in order to be deductible. How the loan is used or what expenses are paid by the credit card determines whether the interest is considered business or personal.

- Auto loan interest is deductible only for the percentage that you use the car in your business. School loan interest is deductible as a business expense only if the education was a deductible expense (see Chapter 29 for information about deductible education). School loan interest that doesn't qualify as a business expense can, under certain conditions, be deducted as an adjustment to income on the front of the 1040 Form (see page 116).

- Interest on money borrowed to pay income taxes or set up a retirement plan is not deductible, as these are considered personal expenses. If a home equity loan is used to pay these costs, the interest is claimed as a personal deduction on Schedule A.

- Legal and professional fees include the portion of your accounting and tax preparation costs that involve the preparation of your business tax return. Usually it's clear what portion of the bill is for preparing a corporate or partnership tax return.Schedule C, however, is done as part of your total personal return, so you'll need to ask your preparer how to allocate the costs.

- Magazines and books are deductible if they are expenses you wouldn't have incurred if you hadn't been in business. In other words, if you've always subscribed to the daily paper, you can't deduct the cost for your business. Other general circulation papers and magazines (e.g., *Newsweek®*, *Money®*, or the *New York Times®*) are generally nondeductible unless purchased for your client waiting room. More specialized magazines and journals are deductible.

- Maintenance and repairs are the costs involved in keeping an asset in good working order. For example, a roof repair is a deductible repair expense (assuming the roof is on a building used in your business). An improvement, unlike a repair, increases the value or prolongs the life of an asset. A new roof is an improvement and must be depreciated rather than deducted all in 1 year.

- Online costs are the hourly fees for Internet or online services, such as CompuServe or America Online. If you use the service for both business and personal purposes, you should prorate the expense accordingly.

- Payroll tax expense is the portion of taxes you pay on behalf of your employees. This includes the employer's share of social security and Medicare taxes. Depending on the state, payroll tax expense may also include unemployment or disability insurance paid for employees. Any tax you withhold from an employee's paycheck (i.e., federal or state income tax) is not a payroll tax expense, as it is money withheld from the employee, not paid by you.
- Sales or excise tax paid should be deducted only if the amount you have collected is also included in your gross income figure on line 1 of Schedule C.
- Estimated tax payments and the balance paid (if any) with your tax return are not deductible if you're a sole proprietor, S-corporation, or partnership. Only C-corporations can deduct the income taxes paid for the business.
- Small equipment and furnishings are items that either are very low in price or will last for less than a year. Any assets that will last for more than a year need to be depreciated (see Chapter 22).
- Wages refers to the amount you pay your employees, not the amount you pay yourself, unless you're incorporated (and, thus, are an employee of your corporation). Fees paid to independent contractors are not wages.

To shift income among partners or to ensure that a partner will be paid for services performed, sometimes partnerships will pay guaranteed payments to partners instead of or in addition to draws. A guaranteed payment means that no matter how much or how little the partnership makes, the partner will receive a guaranteed amount. Because partners can't be employees of the partnership, this payment is not salary and no taxes are withheld from it. Unlike draws, however, guaranteed payments are subtracted from the partnership's income to determine the net profit for the business. Also unlike draws, guaranteed payments are reported on the partner's tax return and are subject to self-employment tax. Whether or not a partnership will make guaranteed payments to partners is a tax-planning issue.

A generally nondeductible expense is clothes. Often clients tell me that if they didn't have this business, they wouldn't have bought a good suit because they wouldn't have needed it. It seems that the suit should qualify as a deductible business expense under the "ordinary and necessary" deduction rules, but it doesn't. Even though you normally wear blue jeans, you cannot deduct the new suit because anything that is commonly worn on the street or could be worn on the street is not deductible. A costume worn for work is deductible. Uniforms are deductible, as are special clothes such as steel-toed boots. Jackets with the name of your company are also deductible (as advertising).

Charitable contributions are not a business deduction for sole proprietors, S-corporations, or partnerships. Any money given from your business to charitable organizations is a personal and not a business expense. If you itemize your personal deductions, you can deduct charitable contributions on Schedule A. C-corporations are the only entities that can deduct charitable contributions as a business expense.

The value of the time you donate to a charitable organization is never deductible. This means you cannot deduct the value of donating an hour of your services to a charity's raffle.

Don't spend too much time worrying about the category in which to put an expense. For example, if you have business brochures printed, don't worry over whether to list the expense as advertising or printing. It really doesn't matter; neither printing nor advertising is a highly audited expense category. When appropriate, choose the category least likely to be audited (e.g., put hotel telephone calls under telephone rather than travel), and break down expenses into smaller categories to avoid large amounts in any one expense category.

CHILD CARE EXPENSES

31

Child care, although not a business expense, can be taken as a credit by self-employed people, as well as employees, when the following conditions are met:

- Care is for a dependent under age 13, a disabled spouse, or a dependent of any age who is unable to care for herself or himself.
- You and your dependent or disabled spouse live in the same home.
- The services were provided so that you and your spouse (if married) could work or look for work. The expenses are also deductible if one spouse (when filing a joint return) is a full-time student and the other spouse works.
- The person who provided the care was not your spouse or your dependent.
- You include Form 2441 (Child and Dependent Care Expenses) with your tax return, and on it you list the name, address, and social security or federal ID number of the person(s) or organization(s) that provided the care.

You cannot deduct child care expenses if you are filing as single or head of household and had no earned income (i.e., wages or net profit from self-employment). If you're married and filing jointly, you cannot deduct the child care expense if either you or your spouse had no earned income (unless one of you is a full-time student). The child care deduction for a married couple is limited to the amount of income earned during the year by the lower earning spouse.

If you qualify to deduct child care expenses, you can include after-school and summer programs. You cannot include school tuition for a child in the first grade or older, or overnight camp expenses for any child.

The credit is limited to child care expenses of $2,400 per child per year for a maximum of two children. Either $2,400 per child or the full amount spent on child or dependent care (whichever is less) is multiplied by a figure between 20% and 30% to determine your credit. The lower your income, the higher the percentage you can take. Here's an example of how it works:

Ginny is single and provides all the support for her 5-year-old daughter, Frannie, whom she claims as a dependent. Ginny's sole source of income is her small business, which showed a net profit of $25,000 this year. Ginny paid $4,300 for Frannie's child care this year. The applicable child care percentage for a parent with $25,000 income is 22%. Ginny calculates her child care credit by multiplying $2,400 (the lesser of $4,300 or $2,400) by 22% for a total credit of $528.

A credit is not the same as a deduction. A deduction is subtracted from your income before the tax is calculated. A credit, on the other hand, is subtracted from your income tax after it is calculated. As you can tell, a credit saves you more money than would a deduction of the same amount. The child care credit is a nonrefundable credit, which means that if the credit is more than your total income tax liability, you won't get a refund of the excess credit. The credit can't be used to reduce your self-employment tax, only your income tax.

Some companies offer their employees a dependent care program (DCP) or flexible spending account. If you or your spouse works for one of these companies, this is a benefit definitely worth looking into. With a DCP or flexible spending account, you can set aside a specific amount of your wages each year to be used for child care expenses. The amount set aside is not taxed. For example, if instead of being self-employed, Ginny worked as an employee in a company with a DCP, she would ask the company to set aside $4,300 for her daughter's child care. If Ginny's salary is $25,000, her W-2 would show that she earned $20,700 ($25,000 salary minus $4,300 DCP). She would avoid paying tax on the $4,300, and, since she's in the 15% federal tax bracket, that would save her $645 in federal tax ($4,300 x 15%).

Ginny saves more by using the DCP than by taking the child care credit. You can't do both. If you have the option of a DCP, determine which is best for you. Generally, the higher your (and your spouse's) income, the more tax you'll save by participating in the DCP rather than taking the child care credit. One caution to participating in a DCP is that once you've asked to have a certain amount set aside from your paycheck, if you don't use the full amount, you lose it. For example, if Ginny moved Frannie to less expensive child care that cost, say, only $3,800 for the year, she would lose the remainder of the $4,300 that had been set aside for child care but wasn't used.

As a sole proprietorship or partnership, you can set up a DCP for your employees. Since you're not an employee of your business, however, you don't qualify for the benefits. If your spouse works in your business, he is eligible for a DCP offered by your company, but the benefit must be offered to all your other employees as well.

Check with your state taxing agency to see whether there are state child care credits for which you are eligible. In California, for example, an employer who pays for an employee's child care costs receives a credit of up to $360 for each dependent covered. California law currently considers self-employed people to be both employee and employer for purposes of this credit. This means that a self-employed person who pays for child care for her own child can receive up to $360 per child in state tax credit for providing child care for an "employee's" dependent.

CHILD CARE DEDUCTION CHART

If your adjusted gross income is

Over	But not over	The deductible percentage is
$ 0	10,000	30%
10,000	12,000	29%
12,000	14,000	28%
14,000	16,000	27%
16,000	18,000	26%
18,000	20,000	25%
20,000	22,000	24%
22,000	24,000	23%
24,000	26,000	22%
26,000	28,000	21%
28,000	No limit	20%

RETIREMENT
PLANS

32

Tax-deferred retirement plans are valuable because while saving for your retirement you defer paying taxes on money you earn that is contributed to one of these plans. Additionally, the interest and dividends earned on the money in the retirement plan are also tax deferred. Tax deferred means that no taxes are paid on the money until it's taken out of the retirement account. Since you don't pay tax currently on the interest or dividends, more is left in the account to grow.

Theoretically, when you take the money out of the retirement account, you'll be retired or working part-time, which will put you in a lower tax bracket than you were in when you invested the money. As a result, the money you contributed and the earned interest or dividends will be taxed at a lower rate than they would have been if you hadn't put the money in a tax-deferred account and instead had paid tax on it when it was earned.

Due to compounding, the earlier in life you begin contributing to a retirement plan, the less total amount you'll need to put in to accumulate a substantial amount of retirement money. The money you contribute to a retirement plan, however, should be money that you don't expect to need until you're at least 59½ years old. When you take a distribution from your retirement account, you are taxed on that money in the same way as you're taxed on other income. With few exceptions, the IRS also assesses a 10% penalty if money is taken out before you're 59½. Your state may have a similar penalty, which means that if you take the money out prior to reaching the minimum age, you may lose nearly 50% to federal and state taxes and penalties.

TAX-SHELTERED OR TAX-DEFERRED ANNUITIES

If you're working as an employee in addition to being self-employed, you may have a 401(k) or 403(b) tax-sheltered annuity (TSA) or tax-deferred annuity (TDA) retirement plan available to you. These can also be set up for you as the employee of your corporation. There are a number of reasons why it's a good idea to take advantage of these plans if you have one:

- Your W-2 will show that the amount you earned is your wage amount minus the amount contributed to the tax-deferred plan. As a result, you pay tax on a lower amount of wage income.

- You may not be eligible to deduct an IRA contribution (explained later).
- Your employer may match your contributions to the retirement plan. (If this is the case and you're not participating in the retirement plan, you're throwing money away.)
- Your plan may allow you to borrow against it in the event of emergency or to buy a house.
- It is relatively painless to have a deduction taken from your paycheck and put into your retirement account.

If you do not work as an employee or your employee job doesn't offer a tax-deferred retirement plan, you will want to consider one of the other types of retirement plans available to you.

TRADITIONAL IRAs

Traditional Individual Retirement Arrangements (IRAs) are available to anyone with earned income (i.e., wages or self-employment income). The maximum allowable contribution to an IRA account is the lesser of your compensation or $2,000 per year. If you are single and have a loss from your business and no other earned income for the year, your compensation amount is less than zero, so you're not eligible for an IRA. A married couple can put up to $2,000 per spouse into an IRA, even if one spouse has no earnings. The couple's combined earned income must be at least as much as the total IRA contribution.

The ability to put money into an IRA doesn't necessarily mean that you'll be able to deduct the contribution. Here are the guidelines:

- If you are single, have adjusted gross income of more than $31,000 ($32,000 for 2000 returns), and have a retirement plan at work, your IRA will be only partially deductible.
- If you are single, have income over $41,000 ($42,000 in 2000), and have a retirement plan at work, your IRA contribution won't be deductible at all.
- If you are married, have joint adjusted gross income over $51,000 ($52,000 in 2000), and have a retirement plan at work, your IRA contribution is only partially deductible.
- If you are married, have joint income over $61,000 ($62,000 in 2000), and have a retirement plan at work, no IRA deduction is allowed.
- If you are married and your spouse has a retirement plan at work but you don't, you can deduct your IRA contribution as

long as your joint income is under $150,000. If it's between $150,000 and $160,000, your IRA is partially deductible. If your joint income is more than $160,000, your IRA contribution isn't deductible.

Having a retirement plan at work refers to any type of retirement plan for which you are eligible at your employee workplace at any time during the year. Having a retirement plan at work also refers to having a SEP-IRA or Keogh, the self-employed retirement accounts discussed later in this chapter. If you had no retirement plan at work at any time during the year, you can fully deduct your IRA contribution if you're single. See restrictions above if you are married and your spouse had a retirement plan.

Liz is single and has income in excess of $41,000. For part of this year, she worked as an employee and had a 401(k) retirement plan at work. She can't deduct her IRA contribution even though she no longer works as an employee.

Arthur and Irma are married and have $80,000 in joint income. Arthur works as an employee where he has no retirement plan. Irma is self-employed and contributes to her Keogh retirement account. Although both can contribute to an IRA, Arthur can deduct his contribution, but Irma can't deduct hers. If their joint income had been over $160,000, neither would have been able to deduct his or her own IRA contribution.

Money taken out of an IRA before age 59½ is subject to a 10% early withdrawal penalty. There are three situations in which the penalty is not assessed, although tax is still due on the distribution. The first situation occurs when money taken out is used to pay medical insurance premiums for someone who has received unemployment compensation during 12 consecutive weeks in the preceding year or the year in which the withdrawal takes place. This also applies to self-employed people who would have received unemployment compensation but weren't eligible because they were self-employed.

The second instance in which the penalty isn't assessed is when the money is used to pay higher education expenses for the taxpayer, her spouse, her children, or her grandchildren.

There also is no penalty when up to $10,000 is taken out to be used in buying a first home for the IRA holder or an eligible relative.

Roth IRAs

Up to $2,000 per year can be contributed to a Roth IRA (less if income exceeds $95,000 if single or $150,000 if married). The contribution is not deductible. However, the contributions made can be taken out at any time without penalty or tax. Once the earnings have been invested for at least 5 years, no taxes will be owed on the amount taken out, as long as the account holder is over 59½ or disabled or the money is spent to buy a first home for the IRA owner or an eligible family member. The advantage of these IRAs is that the earnings (interest or dividends) and any increases in value are taxed neither on a yearly basis nor when withdrawn from the account. The Roth IRA is a flexible savings plan that should be considered when saving for a child's education, a home purchase, and/or retirement. Regular IRAs can be rolled over to Roth IRAs, but tax will be owed on the rollover.

The total that can be contributed to any combination of traditional IRA or Roth IRA is $2,000 per person. As long as you meet the income restrictions, you can have a Roth IRA in addition to a retirement plan at your employee job or a self-employed retirement plan such as a SEP-IRA or Keogh.

KEOGH PLANS

A Keogh (pronounced key oh) plan is one of the retirement vehicles available to self-employed people. There are two types of Keogh plans: defined benefit plans and defined contribution plans.

Contributions to a defined benefit Keogh plan are based on a calculation of how much needs to be contributed each year for the individual to be able to receive a predetermined amount at retirement. You need to use an actuarial table to determine the contribution amount and typically will do this with the help of a financial professional. Therefore, the focus here will be on the other type of Keogh: the defined contribution plan.

There are two types of defined contribution Keoghs: profit-sharing and money-purchase plans. You can contribute up to 13.043% of your net self-employment income to a profit-sharing plan. The contribution amount is actually based on the net profit from your business minus the 50% deduction for self-employment tax. If you don't have a net profit from your business, you won't be able to put money into a Keogh.

If you want to be able to contribute more than 13.043% to a retirement plan, you will want to open a Keogh money-purchase plan also. By having both kinds of Keoghs (commonly referred to as a paired plan), you are able to put aside a total of 20% of your net profit for retirement. A money-purchase plan requires you to commit to contributing a set percentage (1% to 20%) of your self-employment profit each year to your retirement account. A profit-sharing plan, on the other hand, requires no commitment, so you can choose each year how much you want to contribute, if any. By having both types of Keoghs, you can commit to putting 6.957% into your money-purchase plan each year. If you want to put in more, you can contribute up to 13.043% to your profit-sharing plan, for a total of 20%. If you have a slow year, you're committed to only the 6.957%.

A Keogh account can be opened with any bank, brokerage, mutual fund, or other financial institution. You will be told that the maximum contribution you can make if you have both types of Keoghs is 25%, and the maximum amount you can put into the profit-sharing plan is 15%. This is because a complex computation is done to calculate the maximum contribution. If you're interested in the details, review the IRS publication on retirement plans (see Appendix D). For expediency, know that the end result is 20% maximum contribution if you have both types of Keoghs and 13.043% if you have only the profit-sharing plan.

A 5500 Form must be filed with the IRS each July 15 for Keogh accounts with a balance of $100,000 or more. If you have a Keogh and you have employees who are over 21 years old and have worked for you at least 1,000 hours during the year, you must cover them under your Keogh and contribute to their retirement plan when you contribute to your own.

SEP-IRA Accounts

Similar rules for covering employees apply to another type of retirement plan available to self-employed people: the simplified employee pension, or SEP-IRA. All employees over age 20 must be covered as long as they worked for you 3 of the last 5 years and make at least $400 a year.

Many of the other Keogh rules apply to the SEP-IRA as well. You can't borrow against either type of retirement plan. Both have penalties if the money is taken out before age 59½. The SEP-IRA is limited to the same 13.043% contribution as is the profit-sharing Keogh. A maximum of $24,000 annually (or the appropriate percentage, whichever is less) can be contributed to a SEP-IRA, while a combined (money purchase and profit-sharing) Keogh has a $30,000 maximum contribution. Both types of retirement plan contributions are deducted at the bottom of page 1 of the 1040 Form, in the adjustments section (see page 116).

Note that a sole proprietor or partner's contribution to a retirement account is not a business deduction and, therefore, does not reduce your self-employment tax. However, a taxpayer in the 28% federal tax bracket who contributes $1,000 to her retirement plan will save $280 in income tax (more if she also pays a state income tax).

One major advantage of the Keogh and SEP-IRA over a regular IRA is that while the contribution to a regular IRA must be made by April 15, contributions to a SEP and Keogh don't need to be made until the due date of the tax return, including extensions. This means that if you're short on cash, you can file an automatic extension for your tax return, pay any tax you owe when you file your extension on April 15, and have until

August 15 (the due date of your extended return) to fund your retirement plan.

Although you don't need to put the money into your Keogh until April 15 (or later, if on extension), you do need to open the account by December 31 of the year for which you're making the contribution. One of the advantages of the SEP-IRA over the Keogh is that you don't need to open it until April 15 (or later, if on extension). Also, SEP-IRAs are usually easier to set up than Keoghs, have no reporting requirements, and the yearly administrative fee may be less.

SIMPLE Accounts

The SIMPLE (Savings Incentive Match Plan for Employees) is particularly designed for small businesses with employees, but it can also be used effectively by one-person businesses. While Keoghs and SEP-IRAs must, under certain conditions, cover employees, only the employer may make contributions to these plans. A SIMPLE enables employees to contribute to a tax-deferred retirement plan without subjecting the employer to the expense and complex administration of a traditional 401(k) type of retirement plan. Employers with SIMPLEs must either match employee contributions dollar for dollar up to 3% of pay or contribute 2% a year to the account of any employee who earns $5,000 or more during the year and who has received at least this much in any 2 preceding years. The maximum contribution required of the employer is $3,200 per employee.

The employer with a SIMPLE is limited to a yearly contribution of $6,000 for herself. Since SIMPLEs can be set up only when there is no other retirement plan, the employer can't also make contributions to a SEP-IRA or Keogh. Although the maximum that can be contributed is less than the amount allowed for these other plans, a SIMPLE can be a good choice for someone who has no employees and only a small net profit from self-employment. For purposes of the SIMPLE, the self-employed person is considered both employer and employee. As the "employee," she can choose to make a tax-deferred contribution to a SIMPLE of up to 100% of her net profit (not to exceed $6,000). As the "employer," she matches her employee's contributions, including her own.

Jennifer is employed as the manager of a construction company. She has a part-time business making gift baskets. Her net income from self-employment is $5,500 for the year. She wants to save as much as possible for retirement. If she opens a SEP-IRA, she can put aside $667 ($5,500 minus $389, which is half of her self-employment tax, times the SEP-IRA percentage of 13.043%). If she opens a paired money-purchase and profit-sharing Keogh, she can put aside $1,022 ($5,500 minus $389 times the paired Keogh

*percentage of 20%). If Jennifer opens a SIMPLE, she can con-
tribute $5,500 (100% of her net profit, up to $6,000) plus match
that amount with 3% of her net profit ($165) for a total retirement
contribution of $5,665.*

Note that the SIMPLE must be opened by October 1 of the year for
which you want to make contributions and that the administration of a
SIMPLE is (despite the name!) slightly more complex than a SEP-IRA or a
Keogh.

There are many factors to take into consideration when deciding which
retirement plan is best for you. A financial planner or tax preparer can
help you select the most appropriate one for your situation. Whichever
one you choose, it's important to start contributing, even if you begin with
just a small amount each year.

SECTION 5
Tax Forms

THE FRONT OF THE 1040 FORM

Form **1040**

Department of the Treasury—Internal Revenue Service

U.S. Individual Income Tax Return 1999

For the year Jan. 1–Dec. 31, 1999, or other tax year beginning ____ , 1999, ending ____ ,

IRS Use Only—Do not write or staple in this space.

OMB No. 1545-0074

Label
(See instructions on page 18.)

Use the IRS label. Otherwise, please print or type.

L A B E L H E R E

Your first name and initial | Last name | Your social security number

If a joint return, spouse's first name and initial | Last name | Spouse's social security number

Home address (number and street). If you have a P.O. box, see page 18. | Apt. no.

City, town or post office, state, and ZIP code. If you have a foreign address, see page 18.

▲ **IMPORTANT!** ▲
You **must** enter your SSN(s) above.

Presidential Election Campaign
(See page 18.)

Do you want $3 to go to this fund? . . . .
If a joint return, does your spouse want $3 to go to this fund? . . . .

Yes | No | Note. Checking "Yes" will not change your tax or reduce your refund.

Filing Status

Check only one box.

1 ☐ Single
2 ☐ Married filing joint return (even if only one had income)
3 ☐ Married filing separate return. Enter spouse's social security no. above and full name here. ▶ _____
4 ☐ Head of household (with qualifying person). (See page 18.) If the qualifying person is a child but not your dependent, enter this child's name here. ▶ _____
5 ☐ Qualifying widow(er) with dependent child (year spouse died ▶ 19___). (See page 18.)

Exemptions

6a ☐ **Yourself.** If your parent (or someone else) can claim you as a dependent on his or her tax return, **do not** check box 6a. . . . .

b ☐ **Spouse** . . . .

c **Dependents:**

(1) First name Last name	(2) Dependent's social security number	(3) Dependent's relationship to you	(4) ✔ if qualifying child for child tax credit (see page 19)
			☐
			☐
			☐
			☐
			☐
			☐

If more than six dependents, see page 19.

No. of boxes checked on 6a and 6b ____

No. of your children on 6c who:
• lived with you ____
• did not live with you due to divorce or separation (see page 19) ____

Dependents on 6c not entered above ____

Add numbers entered on lines above ▶ ☐

d Total number of exemptions claimed . . . .

Income

Attach Copy B of your Forms W-2 and W-2G here. Also attach Form(s) 1099-R if tax was withheld.

If you did not get a W-2, see page 20.

Enclose, but do not staple, any payment. Also, please use Form 1040-V.

7 Wages, salaries, tips, etc. Attach Form(s) W-2 . . . . | 7
8a **Taxable** interest. Attach Schedule B if required . . . . | 8a
 b **Tax-exempt** interest. DO NOT include on line 8a . . . | 8b |
9 Ordinary dividends. Attach Schedule B if required . . . . | 9
10 Taxable refunds, credits, or offsets of state and local income taxes (see page 21) . . | 10
11 Alimony received . . . . | 11
12 Business income or (loss). Attach Schedule C or C-EZ . . . . | 12
13 Capital gain or (loss). Attach Schedule D if required. If not required, check here ▶ ☐ | 13
14 Other gains or (losses). Attach Form 4797 . . . . | 14
15a Total IRA distributions . | 15a | b Taxable amount (see page 22) | 15b
16a Total pensions and annuities | 16a | b Taxable amount (see page 22) | 16b
17 Rental real estate, royalties, partnerships, S corporations, trusts, etc. Attach Schedule E | 17
18 Farm income or (loss). Attach Schedule F . . . . | 18
19 Unemployment compensation . . . . | 19
20a Social security benefits . | 20a | b Taxable amount (see page 24) | 20b
21 Other income. List type and amount (see page 24) _____ | 21
22 Add the amounts in the far right column for lines 7 through 21. This is your **total income** ▶ | 22

Adjusted Gross Income

23 IRA deduction (see page 26) . . . . | 23
24 Student loan interest deduction (see page 26) . . . . | 24
25 Medical savings account deduction. Attach Form 8853 . | 25
26 Moving expenses. Attach Form 3903 . . . . . . | 26
27 One-half of self-employment tax. Attach Schedule SE . | 27
28 Self-employed health insurance deduction (see page 28) . | 28
29 Keogh and self-employed SEP and SIMPLE plans . . | 29
30 Penalty on early withdrawal of savings . . . . . | 30
31a Alimony paid b Recipient's SSN ▶ _____ | 31a
32 Add lines 23 through 31a . . . . | 32
33 Subtract line 32 from line 22. This is your **adjusted gross income** . . . . . ▶ | 33

For Disclosure, Privacy Act, and Paperwork Reduction Act Notice, see page 54. | Cat. No. 11320B | Form **1040** (1999)

USED BY
SELF-EMPLOYED PEOPLE
33

As an independent contractor or self-employed person, you need to file specific tax forms to tell the IRS and state taxing agency about your business income and expenses. A sole proprietor includes these forms on her individual tax return, along with information about any other sources of income she might have. Business entities other than sole proprietorships must file a business tax return, and, in addition, each partner or shareholder must file a separate individual return.

Tax returns are due on April 15 for sole proprietors and most partnerships. S-corporations have a filing deadline of March 15. The forms are due for C-corporations on the 15th day of the 3rd month following the end of the corporation's tax year. Generally, the tax returns submitted by all entities cover business activity for a 12-month period.

Individuals, including sole proprietors, use a calendar year. Their tax returns include business and nonbusiness activity during the period January 1 to December 31. Usually, S-corporations use a calendar year also, unless there is a business purpose for using a different year. C-corporations can choose the beginning month of their tax year, and partnerships use the same tax year as the majority of their partners.

Because of the complexity of partnership and corporate tax returns, the focus in this book is on the forms filed by sole proprietors. The business expenses discussed in Chapters 20 through 32 will be similar on the tax returns for each of the different entities (with some exceptions), but the information requested on the partnership and corporation returns is more comprehensive than that on the sole proprietor's Schedule C. For more information about partnership and LLC returns, get a copy of the IRS Form 1065 and instructions. For corporations, look at Form 1120 for C-corporations, 1120-S for S-corporations, or 1120-A for small corporations (those with total income and total assets under $500,000).

FORM 1040

As a sole proprietor, you and your business are one and the same, so you report the information about your business income and expenses on your individual tax return. You are required to file your taxes on a 1040 Form. If you're used to filing one of the short forms—a 1040-EZ or 1040-A—owning a business will mean a change in forms. As a self-employed person, you can no longer use a short form because a sole proprietor must attach a Schedule C to her tax return to show business income. You are not allowed to attach any forms to the 1040-A or 1040-EZ forms, so the 1040 Form must be used.

The 1040 Form acts as a cover sheet. It provides the IRS with a summary of your income and expense figures for the past year. The details supporting those summary figures are contained on the schedules that are filled out and attached behind the form.

A copy of the front of a 1040 Form is found on page 116. Those parts of the form that are relevant to self-employed people are discussed in this chapter.

Q

A

> **I don't think I earned enough to have to file a tax return. How do I know?**
>
> As a sole proprietor, you must file a tax return once your self-employment net profit (after expenses have been deducted) equals $400 or more. This is the point at which you become liable for self-employment tax (see Chapter 16), even though you may owe no income tax. If your self-employment net profit is less than $400, you don't need to file a tax return unless your total income from all sources is more than $7,050 if single, or more than $12,700 if married and filing jointly. If you're a dependent of someone else, special rules apply. Those over 65 can have a larger income before they are required to file a tax return. Corporations and partnerships must file a tax return each year, even if there is no income from the business.

Line 7 is the first income line. It says, "Wages, salaries, tips, etc. Attach Form(s) W-2." This is where you report income from those jobs you had as an employee where taxes were taken out of your paycheck. Only report on this line money you earned from employers who gave you a W-2 form. Don't include income reported on 1099 Forms or income received as an independent contractor. If your business operates as a corporation, this is where your wages from the corporation will be reported.

The next lines are for reporting interest and dividends earned and state tax refunds and alimony received. Interest earned on a business bank account is included on the interest line. On line 12, the form says, "Business income or loss. Attach Schedule C or C-EZ." As mentioned previously, Schedule C is the form on which you report the income and expenses of your sole proprietorship. Let's take a look at it now (see page 119).

Schedule C

Notice that the top of the form says, "Schedule C, Profit or Loss from Business (Sole Proprietorship)." It then reminds you that partnerships and other business entities must use a different form. Schedule C asks for your name, type of business, and the name of your business if it's different from your own name. If you own several businesses and they are similar (e.g., teaching and consulting), you can include them on the same Schedule C, identifying yourself as a teacher/consultant. However, if your businesses are not similar (e.g., chiropractor and musician), you need to do a Schedule C for each business. If you are married and your spouse is also self-employed, you need to file a Schedule C for each of you.

THE FRONT OF SCHEDULE C

SCHEDULE C
(Form 1040)

Department of the Treasury
Internal Revenue Service   (99)

Profit or Loss From Business
(Sole Proprietorship)

▶ Partnerships, joint ventures, etc., must file Form 1065 or Form 1065-B.

▶ Attach to Form 1040 or Form 1041.   ▶ See Instructions for Schedule C (Form 1040).

OMB No. 1545-0074

1999

Attachment
Sequence No. **09**

Name of proprietor

Social security number (SSN)

A Principal business or profession, including product or service (see page C-1)

B Enter code from pages C-8 & 9
▶

C Business name. If no separate business name, leave blank.

D Employer ID number (EIN), if any

E Business address (including suite or room no.) ▶ ....
City, town or post office, state, and ZIP code

F Accounting method: **(1)** ☐ Cash   **(2)** ☐ Accrual   **(3)** ☐ Other (specify) ▶ ....

G Did you "materially participate" in the operation of this business during 1999? If "No," see page C-2 for limit on losses . ☐ Yes ☐ No

H If you started or acquired this business during 1999, check here . . . . ▶ ☐

Part I Income

1	Gross receipts or sales. **Caution:** *If this income was reported to you on Form W-2 and the "Statutory employee" box on that form was checked, see page C-2 and check here* . . . . . . ▶ ☐	**1**	
2	Returns and allowances	**2**	
3	Subtract line 2 from line 1	**3**	
4	Cost of goods sold (from line 42 on page 2)	**4**	
5	**Gross profit.** Subtract line 4 from line 3	**5**	
6	Other income, including Federal and state gasoline or fuel tax credit or refund (see page C-3) . . .	**6**	
7	**Gross income.** Add lines 5 and 6 . . . . ▶	**7**	

Part II Expenses. Enter expenses for business use of your home **only** on line 30.

8	Advertising	**8**	**19**	Pension and profit-sharing plans	**19**
9	Bad debts from sales or services (see page C-3) . .	**9**	**20**	Rent or lease (see page C-4):	
			a	Vehicles, machinery, and equipment .	**20a**
10	Car and truck expenses (see page C-3)	**10**	**b**	Other business property . .	**20b**
11	Commissions and fees . .	**11**	**21**	Repairs and maintenance . .	**21**
12	Depletion	**12**	**22**	Supplies (not included in Part III) .	**22**
13	Depreciation and section 179 expense deduction (not included in Part III) (see page C-3) . .	**13**	**23**	Taxes and licenses	**23**
			24	Travel, meals, and entertainment:	
14	Employee benefit programs (other than on line 19) . . .	**14**	**a**	Travel	**24a**
15	Insurance (other than health) .	**15**	**b**	Meals and entertainment .	
16	Interest:		**c**	Enter nondeductible amount included on line 24b (see page C-5) .	
a	Mortgage (paid to banks, etc.) .	**16a**	**d**	Subtract line 24c from line 24b .	**24d**
b	Other	**16b**	**25**	Utilities	**25**
17	Legal and professional services	**17**	**26**	Wages (less employment credits) .	**26**
18	Office expense	**18**	**27**	Other expenses (from line 48 on page 2)	**27**

28	**Total expenses** before expenses for business use of home. Add lines 8 through 27 in columns . ▶	**28**	
29	Tentative profit (loss). Subtract line 28 from line 7	**29**	
30	Expenses for business use of your home. Attach **Form 8829**	**30**	
31	**Net profit or (loss).** Subtract line 30 from line 29.		

- If a profit, enter on **Form 1040, line 12,** and ALSO on **Schedule SE, line 2** (statutory employees, see page C-6). Estates and trusts, enter on Form 1041, line 3.

- If a loss, you MUST go on to line 32.

| **31** | |

32 If you have a loss, check the box that describes your investment in this activity (see page C-6).

- If you checked 32a, enter the loss on **Form 1040, line 12,** and ALSO on **Schedule SE, line 2** (statutory employees, see page C-6). Estates and trusts, enter on Form 1041, line 3.

- If you checked 32b, you MUST attach **Form 6198.**

32a ☐ All investment is at risk.
32b ☐ Some investment is not at risk.

For Paperwork Reduction Act Notice, see Form 1040 instructions.   Cat. No. 11334P   Schedule C (Form 1040) 1999

The Back of Schedule C

Part III   Cost of Goods Sold (see page C-6)

33   Method(s) used to value closing inventory: **a** ☐ Cost   **b** ☐ Lower of cost or market   **c** ☐ Other (attach explanation)

34   Was there any change in determining quantities, costs, or valuations between opening and closing inventory? If "Yes," attach explanation . . . . ☐ Yes   ☐ No

35 Inventory at beginning of year. If different from last year's closing inventory, attach explanation . .	**35**	
36 Purchases less cost of items withdrawn for personal use	**36**	
37 Cost of labor. Do not include any amounts paid to yourself	**37**	
38 Materials and supplies	**38**	
39 Other costs	**39**	
40 Add lines 35 through 39	**40**	
41 Inventory at end of year	**41**	
42 **Cost of goods sold.** Subtract line 41 from line 40. Enter the result here and on page 1, line 4 . .	**42**	

Part IV   Information on Your Vehicle. Complete this part **ONLY** if you are claiming car or truck expenses on line 10 and are not required to file Form 4562 for this business. See the instructions for line 13 on page C-3 to find out if you must file.

43   When did you place your vehicle in service for business purposes? (month, day, year) ▶ _____ / _____ / _____ .

44   Of the total number of miles you drove your vehicle during 1999, enter the number of miles you used your vehicle for:

   a Business _____   **b** Commuting _____   **c** Other _____

45   Do you (or your spouse) have another vehicle available for personal use? . . . . ☐ Yes   ☐ No

46   Was your vehicle available for use during off-duty hours? . . . . ☐ Yes   ☐ No

47a   Do you have evidence to support your deduction? . . . . ☐ Yes   ☐ No

  b If "Yes," is the evidence written? . . . . ☐ Yes   ☐ No

Part V   Other Expenses. List below business expenses not included on lines 8–26 or line 30.

_____		
_____		
_____		
_____		
_____		
_____		
_____		
_____		
_____		
48 **Total other expenses.** Enter here and on page 1, line 27	**48**	

PRINCIPAL BUSINESS OR PROFESSIONAL ACTIVITY CODES

New Principal Business or Professional Activity Codes

These codes for the Principal Business or Professional Activity classify sole proprietorships by the type of activity they are engaged in to facilitate the administration of the Internal Revenue Code. These six-digit codes are based on the new North American Industry Classification System (NAICS) and do not resemble prior year codes.

Select the category that best describes your primary business activity (for example, Real Estate). Then select the activity that best identifies the principal source of your sales or receipts (for example, real estate agent). Now find the six-digit code assigned to this activity and **enter it on line B of Schedule C or C-EZ**

(for example, 531210, the Code for offices of real estate agents and brokers).

Note: *If your principal source of income is from farming activities, you should file* **Schedule F** *(Form 1040), Profit or Loss From Farming.*

Accommodation, Food Services, & Drinking Places

Accommodation
721310	Rooming & boarding houses
721210	RV (recreational vehicle) parks & recreational camps
721100	Travel accommodation (including hotels, motels, & bed & breakfast inns)

Food Services & Drinking Places
722410	Drinking places (alcoholic beverages)
722110	Full-service restaurants
722210	Limited-service eating places
722300	Special food services (including food service contractors & caterers)

Administrative & Support and Waste Management & Remediation Services

Administrative & Support Services
561430	Business service centers (including private mail centers & copy shops)
561740	Carpet & upholstery cleaning services
561440	Collection agencies
561450	Credit bureaus
561410	Document preparation services
561300	Employment services
561710	Exterminating & pest control services
561210	Facilities support (management) services
561600	Investigation & security services
561720	Janitorial services
561730	Landscaping services
561110	Office administrative services
561420	Telephone call centers (including telephone answering services & telemarketing bureaus)
561500	Travel arrangement & reservation services
561490	Other business support services (including repossession services, court reporting, & stenotype services)
561790	Other services to buildings & dwellings
561900	Other support services (including packaging & labeling services, & convention & trade show organizers)

Waste Management & Remediation Services
562000	Waste management & remediation services

Agriculture, Forestry, Hunting, & Fishing
112900	Animal production (including breeding of cats and dogs)
114110	Fishing
113000	Forestry & logging (including forest nurseries & timber tracts)
114210	Hunting & trapping

Support Activities for Agriculture & Forestry
115210	Support activities for animal production (including farriers)
115110	Support activities for crop production (including cotton ginning, soil preparation, planting, & cultivating)
115310	Support activities for forestry

Arts, Entertainment, & Recreation

Amusement, Gambling, & Recreation Industries
713100	Amusement parks & arcades
713200	Gambling industries
713900	Other amusement & recreation services (including golf courses, skiing facilities, marinas, fitness centers, bowling centers, skating rinks, miniature golf courses)

Museums, Historical Sites, & Similar Institutions
712100	Museums, historical sites, & similar institutions

Performing Arts, Spectator Sports, & Related Industries
711410	Agents & managers for artists, athletes, entertainers, & other public figures
711510	Independent artists, writers, & performers
711100	Performing arts companies
711300	Promoters of performing arts, sports, & similar events
711210	Spectator sports (including professional sports clubs & racetrack operations)

Construction
233110	Land subdivision & land development
233300	Nonresidential building construction
233200	Residential building construction

Heavy Construction
234100	Highway, street, bridge, & tunnel construction
234900	Other heavy construction

Special Trade Contractors
235500	Carpentry & floor contractors
235710	Concrete contractors
235310	Electrical contractors
235400	Masonry, drywall, insulation, & tile contractors
235210	Painting & wall covering contractors
235110	Plumbing, heating, & air-conditioning contractors
235610	Roofing, siding, & sheet metal contractors
235810	Water well drilling contractors
235900	Other special trade contractors

Educational Services
611000	Educational services (including schools, colleges, & universities)

Finance & Insurance

Credit Intermediation & Related Activities
522100	Depository credit intermediation (including commercial banking, savings institutions, & credit unions)
522200	Nondepository credit intermediation (including sales financing & consumer lending)
522300	Activities related to credit intermediation (including loan brokers)

Insurance Agents, Brokers, & Related Activities
524210	Insurance agencies & brokerages
524290	Other insurance related activities

Securities, Commodity Contracts, & Other Financial Investments & Related Activities
523140	Commodity contracts brokers
523130	Commodity contracts dealers
523110	Investment bankers & securities dealers
523210	Securities & commodity exchanges
523120	Securities brokers
523900	Other financial investment activities (including investment advice)

Health Care & Social Assistance

Ambulatory Health Care Services
621610	Home health care services
621510	Medical & diagnostic laboratories
621310	Offices of chiropractors
621210	Offices of dentists
621330	Offices of mental health practitioners (except physicians)
621320	Offices of optometrists
621340	Offices of physical, occupational & speech therapists, & audiologists
621111	Offices of physicians (except mental health specialists)
621112	Offices of physicians, mental health specialists
621391	Offices of podiatrists
621399	Offices of all other miscellaneous health practitioners
621400	Outpatient care centers
621900	Other ambulatory health care services (including ambulance services, blood, & organ banks)

Hospitals
622000	Hospitals

Nursing & Residential Care Facilities
623000	Nursing & residential care facilities

Social Assistance
624410	Child day care services
624200	Community food & housing, & emergency & other relief services
624100	Individual & family services
624310	Vocational rehabilitation services

Information
511000	Publishing industries

Broadcasting & Telecommunications
513000	Broadcasting & telecommunications

Information Services & Data Processing Services
514210	Data processing services
514100	Information services (including news syndicates, libraries, & on-line information services)

Motion Picture & Sound Recording
512100	Motion picture & video industries (except video rental)
512200	Sound recording industries

Manufacturing
315000	Apparel mfg.
312000	Beverage & tobacco product mfg.
334000	Computer & electronic product mfg.
335000	Electrical equipment, appliance, & component mfg.
332000	Fabricated metal product mfg.
337000	Furniture & related product mfg.
333000	Machinery mfg.
339110	Medical equipment & supplies mfg.
322000	Paper mfg.
324100	Petroleum & coal products mfg.
326000	Plastics & rubber products mfg.
331000	Primary metal mfg.
323100	Printing & related support activities
313000	Textile mills
314000	Textile product mills
336000	Transportation equipment mfg.
321000	Wood product mfg.
339900	Other miscellaneous mfg.

Chemical Manufacturing
325100	Basic chemical mfg.
325500	Paint, coating, & adhesive mfg.
325300	Pesticide, fertilizer, & other agricultural chemical mfg.
325410	Pharmaceutical & medicine mfg.
325200	Resin, synthetic rubber, & artificial & synthetic fibers & filaments mfg.
325600	Soap, cleaning compound, & toilet preparation mfg.
325900	Other chemical product & preparation mfg.

Food Manufacturing
311110	Animal food mfg.
311800	Bakeries & tortilla mfg.
311500	Dairy product mfg.
311400	Fruit & vegetable preserving & speciality food mfg.
311200	Grain & oilseed milling
311610	Animal slaughtering & processing
311710	Seafood product preparation & packaging
311300	Sugar & confectionery product mfg.
311900	Other food mfg. (including coffee, tea, flavorings, & seasonings)

New Principal Business or Professional Activity Codes *(continued)*

Leather & Allied Product Manufacturing
316210 Footwear mfg. (including leather, rubber, & plastics)
316110 Leather & hide tanning & finishing
316990 Other leather & allied product mfg.

Nonmetallic Mineral Product Manufacturing
327300 Cement & concrete product mfg.
327100 Clay product & refractory mfg.
327210 Glass & glass product mfg.
327400 Lime & gypsum product mfg.
327900 Other nonmetallic mineral product mfg.

Mining
212110 Coal mining
212200 Metal ore mining
212300 Nonmetallic mineral mining & quarrying
211110 Oil & gas extraction
213110 Support activities for mining

Other Services

Personal & Laundry Services
812111 Barber shops
812112 Beauty salons
812220 Cemeteries & crematories
812310 Coin-operated laundries & drycleaners
812320 Drycleaning & laundry services (except coin-operated) (including laundry & drycleaning drop off & pickup sites)
812210 Funeral homes & funeral services
812330 Linen & uniform supply
812113 Nail salons
812930 Parking lots & garages
812910 Pet care (except veterinary) services
812920 Photofinishing
812190 Other personal care services (including diet & weight reducing centers)
812990 All other personal services

Repair & Maintenance
811120 Automotive body, paint, interior, & glass repair
811110 Automotive mechanical & electrical repair & maintenance
811190 Other automotive repair & maintenance (including oil change & lubrication shops & car washes)
811310 Commercial & industrial machinery & equipment (except automotive & electronic) repair & maintenance
811210 Electronic & precision equipment repair & maintenance
811430 Footwear & leather goods repair
811410 Home & garden equipment & appliance repair & maintenance
811420 Reupholstery & furniture repair
811490 Other personal & household goods repair & maintenance

Professional, Scientific, & Technical Services
541100 Legal services
541211 Office of certified public accountants
541214 Payroll services
541213 Tax preparation services
541219 Other accounting services

Architectural, Engineering, & Related Services
541310 Architectural services

541350 Building inspection services
541340 Drafting services
541330 Engineering services
541360 Geophysical surveying & mapping services
541320 Landscape architecture services
541370 Surveying & mapping (except geophysical) services
541380 Testing laboratories

Computer Systems Design & Related Services
541510 Computer systems design & related services

Specialized Design Services
541400 Specialized design services (including interior, industrial, graphic, & fashion design)

Other Professional, Scientific, & Technical Services
541800 Advertising & related services
541600 Management, scientific, & technical consulting services
541910 Market research & public opinion polling
541920 Photographic services
541700 Scientific research & development services
541930 Translation & interpretation services
541940 Veterinary services
541990 All other professional, scientific, & technical services

Real Estate & Rental & Leasing

Real Estate
531100 Lessors of real estate (including miniwarehouses & self-storage units)
531210 Offices of real estate agents & brokers
531320 Offices of real estate appraisers
531310 Real estate property managers
531390 Other activities related to real estate

Rental & Leasing Services
532100 Automotive equipment rental & leasing
532400 Commercial & industrial machinery & equipment rental & leasing
532210 Consumer electronics & appliances rental
532220 Formal wear & costume rental
532310 General rental centers
532230 Video tape & disc rental
532290 Other consumer goods rental

Religious, Grantmaking, Civic, Professional, & Similar Organizations
813000 Religious, grantmaking, civic, professional, & similar organizations

Retail Trade

Building Material & Garden Equipment & Supplies Dealers
444130 Hardware stores
444110 Home centers
444200 Lawn & garden equipment & supplies stores
444120 Paint & wallpaper stores
444190 Other building materials dealers

Clothing & Accessories Stores
448130 Children's & infants' clothing stores
448150 Clothing accessories stores
448140 Family clothing stores
448310 Jewelry stores
448320 Luggage & leather goods stores

448110 Men's clothing stores
448210 Shoe stores
448120 Women's clothing stores
448190 Other clothing stores

Electronic & Appliance Stores
443130 Camera & photographic supplies stores
443120 Computer & software stores
443111 Household appliance stores
443112 Radio, television, & other electronics stores

Food & Beverage Stores
445310 Beer, wine, & liquor stores
445220 Fish & seafood markets
445230 Fruit & vegetable markets
445100 Grocery stores (including supermarkets & convenience stores without gas)
445210 Meat markets
445290 Other specialty food stores

Furniture & Home Furnishing Stores
442110 Furniture stores
442200 Home furnishings stores

Gasoline Stations
447100 Gasoline stations (including convenience stores with gas)

General Merchandise Stores
452000 General merchandise stores

Health & Personal Care Stores
446120 Cosmetics, beauty supplies, & perfume stores
446130 Optical goods stores
446110 Pharmacies & drug stores
446190 Other health & personal care stores

Motor Vehicle & Parts Dealers
441300 Automotive parts, accessories, & tire stores
441222 Boat dealers
441221 Motorcycle dealers
441110 New car dealers
441210 Recreational vehicle dealers (including motor home & travel trailer dealers)
441120 Used car dealers
441229 All other motor vehicle dealers

Sporting Goods, Hobby, Book, & Music Stores
451211 Book stores
451120 Hobby, toy, & game stores
451140 Musical instrument & supplies stores
451212 News dealers & newsstands
451220 Prerecorded tape, compact disc, & record stores
451130 Sewing, needlework, & piece goods stores
451110 Sporting goods stores

Miscellaneous Store Retailers
453920 Art dealers
453110 Florists
453220 Gift, novelty, & souvenir stores
453930 Manufactured (mobile) home dealers
453210 Office supplies & stationery stores
453910 Pet & pet supplies stores
453310 Used merchandise stores
453990 All other miscellaneous store retailers (including tobacco, candle, & trophy shops)

Nonstore Retailers
454110 Electronic shopping & mail-order houses
454310 Fuel dealers
454210 Vending machine operators
454390 Other direct selling establishments (including door-to-door retailing, frozen food plan providers, party plan merchandisers, & coffee-break service providers)

Transportation & Warehousing
481000 Air transportation
485510 Charter bus industry
484110 General freight trucking, local
484120 General freight trucking, long-distance
485210 Interurban & rural bus transportation
486000 Pipeline transportation
482110 Rail transportation
487000 Scenic & sightseeing transportation
485410 School & employee bus transportation
484200 Specialized freight trucking (including household moving vans)
485300 Taxi & limousine service
485110 Urban transit systems
483000 Water transportation
485990 Other transit & ground passenger transportation
488000 Support activities for transportation (including motor vehicle towing)

Couriers & Messengers
492000 Couriers & messengers

Warehousing & Storage Facilities
493100 Warehousing & storage (except lessors of miniwarehouses & self-storage units)

Utilities
221000 Utilities

Wholesale Trade

Wholesale Trade, Durable Goods
421600 Electrical goods
421200 Furniture & home furnishing
421700 Hardware, & plumbing & heating equipment & supplies
421940 Jewelry, watch, precious stone, & precious metals
421300 Lumber & other construction materials
421800 Machinery, equipment, & supplies
421500 Metal & mineral (except petroleum)
421100 Motor vehicle & motor vehicle parts & supplies
421400 Professional & commercial equipment & supplies
421930 Recyclable materials
421910 Sporting & recreational goods & supplies
421920 Toy & hobby goods & supplies
421990 Other miscellaneous durable goods

Wholesale Trade, Nondurable Goods
422300 Apparel, piece goods, & notions
422800 Beer, wine, & distilled alcoholic beverage
422920 Books, periodicals, & newspapers
422600 Chemical & allied products
422210 Drugs & druggists' sundries
422500 Farm product raw materials
422910 Farm supplies
422930 Flower, nursery stock, & florists' supplies
422400 Grocery & related products
422950 Paint, varnish, & supplies
422100 Paper & paper products
422700 Petroleum & petroleum products
422940 Tobacco & tobacco products
422990 Other miscellaneous nondurable goods

999999 **Unclassified establishments (unable to classify)**

Next, Schedule C asks for your business address. This address should be the place where you conduct most of your business. In the top right corner is a space for you to record your social security number. Box B asks for your principal business code. The principal business codes are listed on pages 121–122 of this book. Many small businesses don't easily fit any of the existing business codes. Try to find a code that most closely matches your work. You may find it necessary to use a general code like 541990, "all other professional, scientific, and technical services," or 453990, "all other miscellaneous store retailers," if you can't find a more appropriate category.

After the business code, Schedule C asks for your employer ID number (EIN), if you have one. As discussed in Chapter 4, a sole proprietor is not required to have an employer ID number unless she has a Keogh retirement plan (see Chapter 32) or employees. Although some companies require independent contractors to have an employer ID number, this has nothing to do with IRS regulations.

Accounting Methods

Line F of Schedule C asks which accounting method you use: cash, accrual, or other. If you use the cash method of accounting, you report on this tax return the income that you actually received between January 1 and December 31 of last year. You also report the expenses you paid during that period.

If you use the accrual method of accounting, you report your income not when you receive it but when you earn it. You report your expenses when you accrue them or have them, rather than when you pay them. The accrual method must be used by businesses that have an inventory; however, these businesses may choose to report only their inventory purchases and sales on the accrual method; their other income and expenses can be reported on the cash method. This is what is called a hybrid method.

Some business owners choose to use the accrual method of accounting because they feel it gives them a more accurate picture of their business.

> *Ramona, a graphic artist, has many expenses in doing work for her clients. Her clients generally pay her within 60 days of the date she bills them. Ramona did a large job in December and incurred many expenses. She paid some of those expenses in December and some in January. She received payment for the job in February. If Ramona used the cash method of reporting her income and expenses, her records would look as though she didn't work in December (since no income was received), yet she had a great many expenses. If Ramona used the accrual method, she would list in her December records the income she earned (even though she hadn't*

yet received the payment). She would also list the expenses she had (whether or not she'd paid them). When looking at her financial records, Ramona can more easily match her income to the corresponding expenses. Using the accrual method provides a more accurate assessment of her business finances.

Most small business owners choose to use the cash method because it's the one they're most familiar with. Whichever method you choose the first year you start your business is generally the method you use for as long as you own the business. Any changes in accounting method must be approved by the IRS.

If you are using the cash method, you must include on this year's return any income you constructively received by December 31. This means if a client wrote you a check on December 28, 2000, but you didn't get around to picking it up until January 3, 2001, the income from that check belongs on your 2000 return. You could have had the money in 2000 had you chosen to pick up the check. Also, if you receive a check during the last week of December, you can't delay paying taxes on the income by not depositing the check until January. If you received or could have received the money this year, it needs to be reported on this year's return.

Looking again at Schedule C, line G asks whether you materially participated in the operation of your business during the year. This is simply asking if you were involved in operating the business on a regular and substantial basis. For example, if you had bought an ice cream parlor, hired a manager to run it, and gone to Tahiti to live, and if the ice cream parlor had more expenses than income, you would not be able to deduct the loss. You have to be involved in the operation of a business in order to deduct any loss.

Line H asks you to check the small box if you started or acquired the business during this year. In other words, the IRS wants to know if this is your first year in business. They claim that this information is used for statistical purposes in recording how many new businesses are started each year.

The Income Section of Schedule C

As you look further down Schedule C to Part I, the income section, you see that line 1 asks for the amount of your business's gross receipts or sales. Line 2, "Returns and allowances," is where you subtract refunds given or bounced checks, unless you've already subtracted those amounts before entering the figure on line 1. If you have a service business and don't sell a product, the amount entered on line 3 will be the same as the amount entered on lines 5 and 7.

If you sell a product, you need to fill out the "Cost of Goods Sold" section on the back of Schedule C (see page 120). (You'll notice that this is similar to the example shown in Chapter 13.) The back of Schedule C asks for the amount of inventory at the beginning of the year, purchases made during the year, and inventory left at the end of the year. When the ending inventory is subtracted from the combined total of beginning inventory plus purchases, the resulting figure is the cost of goods sold. That figure is entered on line 4 on the front of Schedule C and is subtracted from the gross receipts figure to calculate your gross profit. In most cases, gross income will be the same as gross profit.

The Expense Section of Schedule C

Part II is the place to list business expenses (see Chapters 20 through 32 for information about deductible expenses). Line 9, "Bad debts from sales or services," needs a special explanation. You probably think of bad debts as what happens when you do work for someone and the person doesn't pay you. However, if you are using the cash method of accounting—that is, you report your income only when you receive it—you can't have a bad debt. As far as the IRS is concerned, your time has no value. If you don't get paid for work you did, you don't have to report it as income. You can deduct any expenses you had, but not the time you spent in doing the work. Generally, you can have a bad debt only if you use the accrual method of accounting.

For example, on last year's tax return, Sandy, who uses the accrual method, reported money she earned but hadn't yet received. This year she learned that the company she did the work for had declared bankruptcy and that she would never be paid. Sandy has a deductible bad debt on this year's tax return. She's deducting this year the income she reported last year but never received.

If Sandy had been using the cash method of accounting, she could have taken a bad debt deduction only if she had received payment from the company and reported the income last year and then the check bounced and she learned, this year, that she would never be able to collect on the bad check.

Some cash method taxpayers include their bounced checks under "bad debts." Technically this is okay as long as the income represented by the checks has not also been subtracted from gross receipts. However, since so many taxpayers erroneously

Should I use the same expense categories as those shown on Schedule C?

Not necessarily. You can use those expense categories if they're appropriate to your business, but there are expense categories on Schedule C that are not applicable for many small businesses. On the back of Schedule C (see page120), there's an area labeled "Other Expenses," which is where you can list your own expense categories. There's no reason to limit yourself to only the categories included on the front of the form. In addition to the "Other Expenses" area, you can include as many extra pages of expense categories as needed. Just make sure that each sheet includes your name and social security number. The more you break down your expense categories, the more you're providing an explanation of your expenses to the IRS. This should lessen your chance of being audited.

report lost income as bad debts, the IRS looks carefully at this line, especially for cash method taxpayers. To avoid calling attention to your return, it's better to subtract any bounced checks from the gross receipts figure before entering it on line 1 or to subtract them as "returns and allowances" on line 2.

It's a common but erroneous misconception that you can deduct the value of services you don't get paid for. Unfortunately, there is no deduction if you don't receive payment.

Between the "Cost of Goods Sold" and the "Other Expenses" sections on the back of Schedule C is an area labeled "Information on Your Vehicle." As explained in Chapter 25, there are two ways of deducting business use of a car or truck—the actual expense method and the standard or mileage rate method. If you use the standard method, you can use this section of Schedule C to provide all the required information on your vehicle. If you use the actual expense method, you'll need to fill out information similar to this on Form 4562, the depreciation form (see page 77).

Once you've listed all your expenses on Schedule C, add up the amounts and enter the total on line 28. Then subtract the total expenses from gross income. The result is your tentative profit or loss. It's called "tentative" because the one expense not yet deducted is your office-in-home. As explained in Chapter 23, that is because that you cannot deduct an office-in-home if you have a loss from your business, nor can the office-in-home deduction create a loss. The IRS wants to see first if you have a profit from your business (line 29). Once you determine that there is a profit, then you can deduct expenses on line 30 for business use of your home. After subtracting line 30 from your tentative profit or loss (line 29), the balance is your net

Should I leave the Schedule C lines totally blank and use only the "other expenses" lines?

No, use the categories that are applicable to your business, but don't force your categories to match Schedule C. For example, there's an expense line labeled "Utilities," but no line called "Telephone expenses." For a lot of people, particularly those with a cellular phone, telephone can be a big expense. If you include your telephone expense on the utilities expense line, along with your gas and electric expenses, you may end up with a large amount in the utilities category. You can reduce the amount in this category by recording your utilities on the utility line and adding another category on the back of the form labeled "Telephone" for those expenses.

Isn't there a limit on the number of years I can have a loss?

You may have heard that you can show a loss only for a certain number of years. What the law actually says is that if you show a profit in 3 out of 5 years, you will be presumed to be a business rather than a hobby. Usually it's desirable to avoid being classified as a hobby; hobby expenses are deductible only to the extent of hobby income and then can be taken as an expense only if you can itemize your personal deductions and if your hobby expenses exceed 2% of your adjusted gross income.

The IRS is saying that if you show a profit in 3 out of 5 years, you won't have to prove that you're really a business and not a hobby. The law doesn't say that if you don't show a profit in 3 out of 5 years, you'll be presumed to be a hobby.

profit or loss. Obviously, if you're not deducting expenses for office-in-home, your tentative profit or loss is going to be the same as your net profit or loss.

Reporting Losses on Schedule C

If you have a loss, be sure to enter the amount in parentheses. A loss means that you have more expenses than income.

Even if you haven't shown a profit in a number of years, you can prove that you are really a business (have a "profit motive") by keeping good records, doing advertising, having the appropriate knowledge and skills to operate your business, spending adequate time on the business, and so forth. In determining whether something is a hobby or a business, the IRS also looks at the personal pleasure involved. They are particularly apt to look carefully at photographers, artists, writers, and others whose work could be considered a pleasurable activity. You need to be able to show that you've done everything you could to be successful and that it's not your fault if you have continued losses.

Schedule C-EZ

If you have a very small business, you may want to consider filing the EZ version of Schedule C (see page 128). There are restrictions about who is eligible to file Schedule C-EZ. You can use it instead of Schedule C if your business expenses are less than $2,500, you have no inventory, you don't have a loss, you have only one business, you haven't had any employees during the year, you haven't bought any equipment or anything else that needs depreciating, and you don't deduct expenses for business use of your home. This form probably won't apply to many people reading this book, but it may be a time-saver for someone who, for example, did a consulting job for which she had few expenses.

MORE ABOUT THE 1040 FORM

Whether you use Schedule C or Schedule C-EZ, once you know what your net profit or loss is (line 31 of Schedule C or line 3 of Schedule C-EZ), that figure is carried to line 12 of the 1040 Form. Remember, if you show a loss on Schedule C, put parentheses around the amount as you note it on line 12.

Looking again at the 1040 Form, you'll notice that there are other lines on which to note capital gains, unemployment insurance, pensions, and other sources of income. Line 17, in addition to being used to report rental income, is used by partners and S-corporation shareholders to report their share of the net profit or loss from their businesses. Partnership and S-corporation tax returns include a page called a K-1 Form (see page 129); it is given to each partner or shareholder, telling them the amount of their share of the profit or loss from the business. The partner or shareholder

SCHEDULE C-EZ (Form 1040) Department of the Treasury Internal Revenue Service (99)	**Net Profit From Business** (Sole Proprietorship) ▶ Partnerships, joint ventures, etc., must file Form 1065 or 1065-B. ▶ Attach to Form 1040 or Form 1041. ▶ See instructions on back.	OMB No. 1545-0074 1999 Attachment Sequence No. 09A

Name of proprietor	Social security number (SSN)

Part I General Information

You May Use Schedule C-EZ Instead of Schedule C Only If You:

➤
- Had business expenses of $2,500 or less.
- Use the cash method of accounting.
- Did not have an inventory at any time during the year.
- Did not have a net loss from your business.
- Had only one business as a sole proprietor.

And You:

➤
- Had no employees during the year.
- Are not required to file **Form 4562**, Depreciation and Amortization, for this business. See the instructions for Schedule C, line 13, on page C-3 to find out if you must file.
- Do not deduct expenses for business use of your home.
- Do not have prior year unallowed passive activity losses from this business.

A Principal business or profession, including product or service

B Enter code from pages C-8 & 9
▶

C Business name. If no separate business name, leave blank.

D Employer ID number (EIN), if any

E Business address (including suite or room no.). Address not required if same as on Form 1040, page 1.

City, town or post office, state, and ZIP code

Part II Figure Your Net Profit

1 Gross receipts. Caution: *If this income was reported to you on Form W-2 and the "Statutory employee" box on that form was checked, see* **Statutory Employees** *in the instructions for Schedule C, line 1, on page C-2 and check here* . . . . ▶ ☐ | **1** |

2 Total expenses. If more than $2,500, you **must** use Schedule C. See instructions . . . . . | **2** |

3 Net profit. Subtract line 2 from line 1. If less than zero, you **must** use Schedule C. Enter on **Form 1040, line 12,** and ALSO on **Schedule SE, line 2.** (Statutory employees **do not** report this amount on Schedule SE, line 2. Estates and trusts, enter on Form 1041, line 3.) . . . . . | **3** |

Part III Information on Your Vehicle. Complete this part **ONLY** if you are claiming car or truck expenses on line 2.

4 When did you place your vehicle in service for business purposes? (month, day, year) ▶ ...... / ...... / ....

5 Of the total number of miles you drove your vehicle during 1999, enter the number of miles you used your vehicle for:

a Business .... **b** Commuting .... **c** Other ....

6 Do you (or your spouse) have another vehicle available for personal use? . . . . ☐ Yes ☐ No

7 Was your vehicle available for use during off-duty hours? . . . . ☐ Yes ☐ No

8a Do you have evidence to support your deduction? . . . . ☐ Yes ☐ No

b If "Yes," is the evidence written? . . . . ☐ Yes ☐ No

For Paperwork Reduction Act Notice, see Form 1040 instructions.   Cat. No. 14374D   Schedule C-EZ (Form 1040) 1999

A Partner's K-1 Form

OMB No. 1545-0099

SCHEDULE K-1
(Form 1065)
Department of the Treasury
Internal Revenue Service

Partner's Share of Income, Credits, Deductions, etc.
▶ See separate instructions.

For calendar year 1998 or tax year beginning _____ , 1998, and ending _____ , 19 ___

Partner's identifying number ▶

Partner's name, address, and ZIP code

Partnership's identifying number ▶

Partnership's name, address, and ZIP code

A This partner is a ☐ general partner ☐ limited partner ☐ limited liability company member

B What type of entity is this partner? ▶ ....

C Is this partner a ☐ domestic or a ☐ foreign partner?

D Enter partner's percentage of:

	(i) Before change or termination	(ii) End of year
Profit sharing	.... %	.... %
Loss sharing	.... %	.... %
Ownership of capital	.... %	.... %

E IRS Center where partnership filed return:

F Partner's share of liabilities (see instructions):

Nonrecourse . . . . $ ....

Qualified nonrecourse financing . $ ....

Other . . . . $ ....

G Tax shelter registration number . ▶ ....

H Check here if this partnership is a publicly traded partnership as defined in section 469(k)(2) . . . . ☐

I Check applicable boxes: (1) ☐ Final K-1 (2) ☐ Amended K-1

J Analysis of partner's capital account:

(a) Capital account at beginning of year	(b) Capital contributed during year	(c) Partner's share of lines 3, 4, and 7, Form 1065, Schedule M-2	(d) Withdrawals and distributions	(e) Capital account at end of year (combine columns (a) through (d))
			( )	

		(a) Distributive share item		(b) Amount	(c) 1040 filers enter the amount in column (b) on:
Income (Loss)	1	Ordinary income (loss) from trade or business activities . . .	1		See page 6 of Partner's Instructions for Schedule K-1 (Form 1065).
	2	Net income (loss) from rental real estate activities	2		
	3	Net income (loss) from other rental activities	3		
	4	Portfolio income (loss):			
	a	Interest	4a		Sch. B, Part I, line 1
	b	Ordinary dividends	4b		Sch. B, Part II, line 5
	c	Royalties	4c		Sch. E, Part I, line 4
	d	Net short-term capital gain (loss)	4d		Sch. D, line 5, col. (f)
	e	Net long-term capital gain (loss):			
		(1) 28% rate gain (loss)	e(1)		Sch. D, line 12, col. (g)
		(2) Total for year.	e(2)		Sch. D, line 12, col. (f)
	f	Other portfolio income (loss) (attach schedule)	4f		Enter on applicable line of your return.
	5	Guaranteed payments to partner	5		See page 6 of Partner's Instructions for Schedule K-1 (Form 1065).
	6	Net section 1231 gain (loss) (other than due to casualty or theft) .	6		
	7	Other income (loss) (attach schedule)	7		Enter on applicable line of your return.
Deductions	8	Charitable contributions (see instructions) (attach schedule) . .	8		Sch. A, line 15 or 16
	9	Section 179 expense deduction	9		See pages 7 and 8 of Partner's Instructions for Schedule K-1 (Form 1065).
	10	Deductions related to portfolio income (attach schedule) . . .	10		
	11	Other deductions (attach schedule)	11		
Credits	12a	Low-income housing credit:			
		(1) From section 42(j)(5) partnerships for property placed in service before 1990	a(1)		Form 8586, line 5
		(2) Other than on line 12a(1) for property placed in service before 1990	a(2)		
		(3) From section 42(j)(5) partnerships for property placed in service after 1989	a(3)		
		(4) Other than on line 12a(3) for property placed in service after 1989	a(4)		
	b	Qualified rehabilitation expenditures related to rental real estate activities	12b		
	c	Credits (other than credits shown on lines 12a and 12b) related to rental real estate activities.	12c		See page 8 of Partner's Instructions for Schedule K-1 (Form 1065).
	d	Credits related to other rental activities	12d		
	13	Other credits.	13		

For Paperwork Reduction Act Notice, see Instructions for Form 1065.   Cat. No. 11394R   **Schedule K-1 (Form 1065)**

THE FRONT OF SCHEDULE E

SCHEDULE E (Form 1040) Department of the Treasury Internal Revenue Service (99)	**Supplemental Income and Loss** (From rental real estate, royalties, partnerships, S corporations, estates, trusts, REMICs, etc.) ▶ Attach to Form 1040 or Form 1041. ▶ See Instructions for Schedule E (Form 1040).	OMB No. 1545-0074 19**99** Attachment Sequence No. **13**

Name(s) shown on return | Your social security number

Part I   **Income or Loss From Rental Real Estate and Royalties**   Note: *Report income and expenses from your business of renting personal property on* **Schedule C** *or* **C-EZ** *(see page E-1). Report farm rental income or loss from* **Form 4835** *on page 2, line 39.*

1 Show the kind and location of each **rental real estate property:**

A ....

B ....

C ....

2 For each rental real estate property listed on line 1, did you or your family use it during the tax year for personal purposes for more than the greater of:
- 14 days, **or**
- 10% of the total days rented at fair rental value?

(See page E-1.)

	Yes	No
A		
B		
C		

Income:		**Properties**			**Totals** (Add columns A, B, and C.)
		A	B	C	
3 Rents received	3				3
4 Royalties received	4				4
Expenses:					
5 Advertising	5				
6 Auto and travel (see page E-2)	6				
7 Cleaning and maintenance	7				
8 Commissions	8				
9 Insurance	9				
10 Legal and other professional fees	10				
11 Management fees	11				
12 Mortgage interest paid to banks, etc. (see page E-2)	12				12
13 Other interest	13				
14 Repairs	14				
15 Supplies	15				
16 Taxes	16				
17 Utilities	17				
18 Other (list) ▶	18				
19 Add lines 5 through 18	19				19
20 Depreciation expense or depletion (see page E-3)	20				20
21 Total expenses. Add lines 19 and 20	21				
22 Income or (loss) from rental real estate or royalty properties. Subtract line 21 from line 3 (rents) or line 4 (royalties). If the result is a (loss), see page E-3 to find out if you must file **Form 6198**	22				
23 Deductible rental real estate loss. **Caution:** *Your rental real estate loss on line 22 may be limited. See page E-3 to find out if you must file* **Form 8582.** *Real estate professionals must complete line 42 on page 2*	23	(	)(	)(	)
24 **Income.** Add positive amounts shown on line 22. **Do not** include any losses				24	
25 **Losses.** Add royalty losses from line 22 and rental real estate losses from line 23. Enter total losses here				25	( )
26 Total rental real estate and royalty income or (loss). Combine lines 24 and 25. Enter the result here. If Parts II, III, IV, and line 39 on page 2 do not apply to you, also enter this amount on Form 1040, line 17. Otherwise, include this amount in the total on line 40 on page 2				26	

For Paperwork Reduction Act Notice, see Form 1040 instructions.   Cat. No. 11344L   **Schedule E (Form 1040) 1999**

The Back of Schedule E

Schedule E (Form 1040) 1999   Attachment Sequence No. **13**   Page **2**

Name(s) shown on return. Do not enter name and social security number if shown on other side. | **Your social security number**

Note: *If you report amounts from farming or fishing on Schedule E, you must enter your gross income from those activities on line 41 below. Real estate professionals must complete line 42 below.*

Part II   Income or Loss From Partnerships and S Corporations

Note: *If you report a loss from an at-risk activity, you MUST check either column (e) or (f) on line 27 to describe your investment in the activity. See page E-5. If you check column (f), you must attach **Form 6198**.*

27	**(a)** Name	**(b)** Enter **P** for partnership, **S** for S corporation	**(c)** Check if foreign partnership	**(d)** Employer identification number	Investment At Risk? **(e)** All is at risk	**(f)** Some is not at risk
A						
B						
C						
D						
E						

	Passive Income and Loss		Nonpassive Income and Loss		
	(g) Passive loss allowed (attach **Form 8582** if required)	**(h)** Passive income from **Schedule K-1**	**(i)** Nonpassive loss from **Schedule K-1**	**(j)** Section 179 expense deduction from **Form 4562**	**(k)** Nonpassive income from **Schedule K-1**
A					
B					
C					
D					
E					
28a Totals					
b Totals					

29	Add columns (h) and (k) of line 28a	29	
30	Add columns (g), (i), and (j) of line 28b	30 (	)
31	Total partnership and S corporation income or (loss). Combine lines 29 and 30. Enter the result here and include in the total on line 40 below	31	

Part III   Income or Loss From Estates and Trusts

32	**(a)** Name	**(b)** Employer identification number
A		
B		

	Passive Income and Loss		Nonpassive Income and Loss	
	(c) Passive deduction or loss allowed (attach **Form 8582** if required)	**(d)** Passive income from **Schedule K-1**	**(e)** Deduction or loss from **Schedule K-1**	**(f)** Other income from **Schedule K-1**
A				
B				
33a Totals				
b Totals				

34	Add columns (d) and (f) of line 33a	34	
35	Add columns (c) and (e) of line 33b	35 (	)
36	Total estate and trust income or (loss). Combine lines 34 and 35. Enter the result here and include in the total on line 40 below	36	

Part IV   Income or Loss From Real Estate Mortgage Investment Conduits (REMICs)—Residual Holder

37	**(a)** Name	**(b)** Employer identification number	**(c)** Excess inclusion from **Schedules Q**, line 2c (see page E-6)	**(d)** Taxable income (net loss) from **Schedules Q**, line 1b	**(e)** Income from **Schedules Q**, line 3b

38	Combine columns (d) and (e) only. Enter the result here and include in the total on line 40 below	38	

Part V   Summary

39	Net farm rental income or (loss) from **Form 4835**. Also, complete line 41 below	39	
40	TOTAL income or (loss). Combine lines 26, 31, 36, 38, and 39. Enter the result here and on Form 1040, line 17 ▶	40	

41	**Reconciliation of Farming and Fishing Income.** Enter your **gross** farming and fishing income reported on Form 4835, line 7; Schedule K-1 (Form 1065), line 15b; Schedule K-1 (Form 1120S), line 23; and Schedule K-1 (Form 1041), line 14 (see page E-6)	41	
42	**Reconciliation for Real Estate Professionals.** If you were a real estate professional (see page E-4), enter the net income or (loss) you reported anywhere on Form 1040 from all rental real estate activities in which you materially participated under the passive activity loss rules . . .	42	

Schedule E (Form 1040) 1999

transfers that information to the back of Schedule E (see page 131). The information from Schedule E is then entered on line 17 of the partner's or shareholder's individual tax return. Again, remember, if you have a loss from your share of the business, be sure to record it in parentheses.

All the income figures on the 1040 Form are added together, and the total is noted on line 22. Self-employment income is just one part of your total income. If you have a loss from self-employment, it will offset some of your income from other sources. For example, if you have a $2,000 loss from self-employment but also have $40,000 in wages, the $2,000 loss will offset $2,000 of the wages, making your total income figure $38,000. If you are married and filing a joint return, your spouse's income is also included in the total income figure.

Below the total income figure on the 1040 Form are some lines on which to show adjustments (subtractions) to your income. The first line is for an IRA deduction—if you contribute to a traditional IRA and qualify to deduct it (which, as you read in Chapter 32, is dependent on your total income and whether you and/or your spouse is covered by a retirement plan at work). The next line is for a deduction of up to $1,500 ($2,000 in 2000) of student loan interest that can't be included as a business expense. Some income restrictions apply to this deduction, and it is allowed only for interest paid within 60 months of the first date that interest payments are required. Next is the line on which you deduct the amount contributed to your Medical Savings Account (see Chapter 28). Line 27 is the place you deduct one half of your self-employment tax (as discussed in Chapter 16). Note that this isn't a business deduction, but it does reduce your taxable income and, thus, your income tax.

What if I total all my income and find that because of the loss from my business, my income is less than zero?

In this case, you have what's called a Net Operating Loss (NOL). NOLs require a complex tax calculation that is beyond the scope of this book. If you have an NOL (which generally happens only when the loss from your business exceeds your income from other sources), be sure to take advantage of it. The loss can be carried back 2 years, and that year's return can be amended so that you receive a refund. The other option is to carry the loss forward, where it's used to offset income earned in the following year. The IRS assumes you'll choose to carry back the loss, so you must include a statement (called an election) on the return with the NOL if you choose, instead, to carry the loss forward.

Line 28 of the 1040 Form is for the self-employed health insurance deduction. On this line, sole proprietors, partners, and S-corporation shareholders can deduct 60% of the health insurance and long-term care premiums (not the medical expenses) they paid for themselves, their spouses (if married), and any dependents. (See Chapter 28 for more information about deductible premiums.)

Below the line for health insurance is the line on which self-employed people deduct contributions to a retirement plan. (See Chapter 32 for more information about Keogh, SEP, and SIMPLE retirement plans.)

All of these adjustments are added together and then subtracted from your total income. The result is your adjusted gross income. That figure is listed on line 33 and is also carried over to the back of the 1040 Form (see page 134).

Personal Itemized Deductions and the Personal Exemption

Several other items can be deducted from your adjusted gross income. These deductions have nothing to do with your self-employment and are available to all taxpayers.

First are your personal itemized deductions. If you own your home or have large medical expenses or large charitable contributions, you will probably be able to itemize your personal deductions. Note that these are personal, not business, deductions. They include mortgage interest, real estate taxes, state income taxes paid or withheld, charitable contributions, medical expenses, and so on.

If you don't have enough of those expenses to be able to itemize, you'll take the standard deduction. For 1999, the standard deduction is $4,300 if single and $7,200 if married and filing jointly. For 2000, the figures are $4,400 if single and $7,350 if married and filing jointly. On line 34 of the return, you subtract out either your personal itemized deductions or the standard deduction.

The other amount deducted from your adjusted gross income is a personal exemption for yourself, your spouse, and each dependent. This also has nothing to do with being self-employed; you get this personal exemption just for being you. For 1999, the exemption amount is $2,750 for each person being claimed on your return. In 2000 the exemption amount increases to $2,800.

One thing to be aware of is that the personal exemption and personal itemized deduction amounts are reduced when your adjusted gross income exceeds about $125,000 (less if married and filing separately, and more if head of household or married and filing jointly). The instructions for the 1040 Form include a worksheet to calculate this "phaseout" if it applies to you.

After the personal deductions and exemptions are subtracted, what's left is your taxable income (line 39). Using the taxable income figure, your income tax is calculated and entered on line 40.

The next section of the 1040 Form lists several credits, including the child care credit, which is discussed in Chapter 31.

Self-Employment Tax

After your credits (if any) are subtracted from your income tax, there's a section on the 1040 Form to report other taxes owed. The other tax that applies to sole proprietors and partners is self-employment tax. Earlier in this chapter, we saw that the net profit or loss figure from Schedule C is

THE BACK OF FORM 1040

Tax and Credits

34	Amount from line 33 (adjusted gross income)	34	
35a	Check if: ☐ **You** were 65 or older, ☐ Blind; ☐ **Spouse** was 65 or older, ☐ Blind. Add the number of boxes checked above and enter the total here . . . . ▶ 35a		
b	If you are married filing separately and your spouse itemizes deductions or you were a dual-status alien, see page 30 and check here . . . . . . ▶ 35b ☐		

Standard Deduction for Most People

Single: $4,300

Head of household: $6,350

Married filing jointly or Qualifying widow(er): $7,200

Married filing separately: $3,600

36	Enter your **itemized deductions** from Schedule A, line 28, **OR standard deduction** shown on the left. **But see** page 30 to find your standard deduction if you checked any box on line 35a or 35b **or** if someone can claim you as a dependent . . .	36	
37	Subtract line 36 from line 34	37	
38	If line 34 is $94,975 or less, multiply $2,750 by the total number of exemptions claimed on line 6d. If line 34 is over $94,975, see the worksheet on page 31 for the amount to enter .	38	
39	**Taxable income.** Subtract line 38 from line 37. If line 38 is more than line 37, enter -0-	39	
40	**Tax** (see page 31). Check if any tax is from **a** ☐ Form(s) 8814 **b** ☐ Form 4972 . . ▶	40	
41	Credit for child and dependent care expenses. Attach Form 2441	41	
42	Credit for the elderly or the disabled. Attach Schedule R . .	42	
43	Child tax credit (see page 33)	43	
44	Education credits. Attach Form 8863	44	
45	Adoption credit. Attach Form 8839	45	
46	Foreign tax credit. Attach Form 1116 if required	46	
47	Other. Check if from **a** ☐ Form 3800 **b** ☐ Form 8396 **c** ☐ Form 8801 **d** ☐ Form (specify)	47	
48	Add lines 41 through 47. These are your **total credits**	48	
49	Subtract line 48 from line 40. If line 48 is more than line 40, enter -0- . . . . . . ▶	49	

Other Taxes

50	Self-employment tax. Attach Schedule SE	50	
51	Alternative minimum tax. Attach Form 6251	51	
52	Social security and Medicare tax on tip income not reported to employer. Attach Form 4137	52	
53	Tax on IRAs, other retirement plans, and MSAs. Attach Form 5329 if required	53	
54	Advance earned income credit payments from Form(s) W-2	54	
55	Household employment taxes. Attach Schedule H	55	
56	Add lines 49 through 55. This is your **total tax** . . . . ▶	56	

Payments

57	Federal income tax withheld from Forms W-2 and 1099 . .	57	
58	1999 estimated tax payments and amount applied from 1998 return .	58	
59a	**Earned income credit.** Attach Sch. EIC if you have a qualifying child		
b	Nontaxable earned income: amount . . ▶ and type ▶	59a	
60	Additional child tax credit. Attach Form 8812	60	
61	Amount paid with request for extension to file (see page 48)	61	
62	Excess social security and RRTA tax withheld (see page 48)	62	
63	Other payments. Check if from **a** ☐ Form 2439 **b** ☐ Form 4136	63	
64	Add lines 57, 58, 59a, and 60 through 63. These are your **total payments** . . . . ▶	64	

Refund

Have it directly deposited! See page 48 and fill in 66b, 66c, and 66d.

65	If line 64 is more than line 56, subtract line 56 from line 64. This is the amount you **OVERPAID**	65	
66a	Amount of line 65 you want **REFUNDED TO YOU.** . . . . ▶	66a	
▶ b	Routing number ☐☐☐☐☐☐☐☐☐ ▶ c Type: ☐ Checking ☐ Savings		
▶ d	Account number ☐☐☐☐☐☐☐☐☐☐☐☐☐☐☐☐☐		
67	Amount of line 65 you want **APPLIED TO YOUR 2000 ESTIMATED TAX** ▶	67	

Amount You Owe

68	If line 56 is more than line 64, subtract line 64 from line 56. This is the **AMOUNT YOU OWE.** For details on how to pay, see page 49 . . . . ▶	68	
69	Estimated tax penalty. Also include on line 68	69	

Sign Here

Joint return? See page 18.

Keep a copy for your records.

Under penalties of perjury, I declare that I have examined this return and accompanying schedules and statements, and to the best of my knowledge and belief, they are true, correct, and complete. Declaration of preparer (other than taxpayer) is based on all information of which preparer has any knowledge.

Your signature	Date	Your occupation	Daytime telephone number (optional) ( )
Spouse's signature. If a joint return, BOTH must sign.	Date	Spouse's occupation	

Paid Preparer's Use Only

Preparer's signature	Date	Check if self-employed ☐	Preparer's SSN or PTIN
Firm's name (or yours if self-employed) and address		EIN	
		ZIP code	

carried to line 12 of the 1040 Form, where business income or loss is reported. That same figure is also carried to Schedule SE, which is the third tax form that all sole proprietors will need to include as part of their individual tax returns. A copy of Schedule SE is on page 136.

Partners in a partnership that has a profit will also need to attach a Schedule SE to their individual tax returns. Schedule SE is used to calculate the amount of self-employment tax owed. Self-employment tax, you'll remember, is social security tax for self-employed people. (Self-employment tax is discussed more fully in Chapter 16.)

Most self-employed people will be able to use the short Schedule SE. Under certain circumstances related to your non-self-employment income, the long Schedule SE will need to be used (see page 137).

The short Schedule SE has only six lines. The first two are used to report your net profit from farming (line 1) or from your Schedule C business (line 2). As explained earlier, each business must have its own Schedule C. However, only one Schedule SE is filled out for each person, and the net profit from all businesses owned by that person are combined on that one Schedule SE.

If a married couple runs a business together as a sole proprietorship, they will file only one Schedule C for the business, but each spouse will need to include a Schedule SE showing his or her share of the self-employment tax on the business income. If a husband and wife each own a business, each must file a Schedule C and also a Schedule SE. The income reported on Schedule SE becomes part of your social security account earnings.

Line 3 of the short Schedule SE is a total of lines 1 and 2. On line 4 your net profit from self-employment is multiplied by 92.35%. (As discussed in Chapter 16, having self-employed people pay self-employment tax on only 92.35% of their net self-employment earnings was Congress's attempt to equalize the amount self-employed people pay into social security with that paid by employees.)

Line 4 says that if 92.35% of your net self-employment income is less than $400, you don't need to file Schedule SE, as no self-employment tax is owed.

Line 5 is used to calculate the self-employment tax at the 15.3% self-employment tax rate.

Line 6 is where you divide your self-employment tax figure in half. As explained earlier, half of the self-employment tax you pay is deductible on line 26 of the 1040 Form not as a business expense but as an adjustment to income.

Once you've filled out the self-employment tax form, go back to line 50 of the 1040 Form and record your self-employment tax amount. Then, add your income tax to your self-employment tax. The result on line 56 is your total tax liability.

SCHEDULE SE (Form 1040) Department of the Treasury Internal Revenue Service (99)	**Self-Employment Tax** ▶ See Instructions for Schedule SE (Form 1040). ▶ Attach to Form 1040.	OMB No. 1545-0074 **1999** Attachment Sequence No. **17**
Name of person with **self-employment** income (as shown on Form 1040)	Social security number of person with **self-employment** income ▶	

Who Must File Schedule SE

You must file Schedule SE if:

- You had net earnings from self-employment from **other than** church employee income (line 4 of Short Schedule SE or line 4c of Long Schedule SE) of $400 or more, **OR**

- You had church employee income of $108.28 or more. Income from services you performed as a minister or a member of a religious order **is not** church employee income. See page SE-1.

Note: *Even if you had a loss or a small amount of income from self-employment, it may be to your benefit to file Schedule SE and use either "optional method" in Part II of Long Schedule SE. See page SE-3.*

Exception. If your only self-employment income was from earnings as a minister, member of a religious order, or Christian Science practitioner **and** you filed Form 4361 and received IRS approval not to be taxed on those earnings, **do not** file Schedule SE. Instead, write "Exempt–Form 4361" on Form 1040, line 50.

May I Use Short Schedule SE or MUST I Use Long Schedule SE?

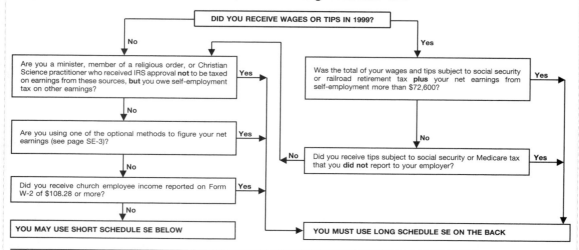

Section A—Short Schedule SE. Caution: *Read above to see if you can use Short Schedule SE.*

1	Net farm profit or (loss) from Schedule F, line 36, and farm partnerships, Schedule K-1 (Form 1065), line 15a	**1**	
2	Net profit or (loss) from Schedule C, line 31; Schedule C-EZ, line 3; Schedule K-1 (Form 1065), line 15a (other than farming); and Schedule K-1 (Form 1065-B), box 9. Ministers and members of religious orders, see page SE-1 for amounts to report on this line. See page SE-2 for other income to report	**2**	
3	Combine lines 1 and 2	**3**	
4	**Net earnings from self-employment.** Multiply line 3 by 92.35% (.9235). If less than $400, **do not** file this schedule; you do not owe self-employment tax . . . . ▶	**4**	
5	**Self-employment tax.** If the amount on line 4 is: • $72,600 or less, multiply line 4 by 15.3% (.153). Enter the result here and on **Form 1040, line 50.** • More than $72,600, multiply line 4 by 2.9% (.029). Then, add $9,002.40 to the result. Enter the total here and on **Form 1040, line 50.**	**5**	
6	**Deduction for one-half of self-employment tax.** Multiply line 5 by 50% (.5). Enter the result here and on **Form 1040, line 27**	**6**	

For Paperwork Reduction Act Notice, see Form 1040 instructions.   Cat. No. 11358Z   **Schedule SE (Form 1040) 1999**

THE BACK OF SCHEDULE SE—THE LONG VERSION

Name of person with **self-employment** income (as shown on Form 1040)	Social security number of person with **self-employment** income ▶		

Section B—Long Schedule SE

Part I   Self-Employment Tax

Note: *If your only income subject to self-employment tax is **church employee income,** skip lines 1 through 4b. Enter -0- on line 4c and go to line 5a. Income from services you performed as a minister or a member of a religious order **is not** church employee income. See page SE-1.*

A   If you are a minister, member of a religious order, or Christian Science practitioner **and** you filed Form 4361, but you had $400 or more of **other** net earnings from self-employment, check here and continue with Part I . . . . . . ▶ ☐

1	Net farm profit or (loss) from Schedule F, line 36, and farm partnerships, Schedule K-1 (Form 1065), line 15a. **Note:** *Skip this line if you use the farm optional method. See page SE-3* . .	**1**		
2	Net profit or (loss) from Schedule C, line 31; Schedule C-EZ, line 3; Schedule K-1 (Form 1065), line 15a (other than farming); and Schedule K-1 (Form 1065-B), box 9. Ministers and members of religious orders, see page SE-1 for amounts to report on this line. See page SE-2 for other income to report. **Note:** *Skip this line if you use the nonfarm optional method. See page SE-3*.	**2**		
3	Combine lines 1 and 2	**3**		
4a	If line 3 is more than zero, multiply line 3 by 92.35% (.9235). Otherwise, enter amount from line 3	**4a**		
b	If you elected one or both of the optional methods, enter the total of lines 15 and 17 here . .	**4b**		
c	Combine lines 4a and 4b. If less than $400, **do not** file this schedule; you do not owe self-employment tax. **Exception.** If less than $400 and you had **church employee income,** enter -0- and continue ▶	**4c**		
5a	Enter your **church employee income** from Form W-2. **Caution:** *See page SE-1 for definition of church employee income* **5a**	**5b**		
b	Multiply line 5a by 92.35% (.9235). If less than $100, enter -0-	**5b**		
6	**Net earnings from self-employment.** Add lines 4c and 5b	**6**		
7	Maximum amount of combined wages and self-employment earnings subject to social security tax or the 6.2% portion of the 7.65% railroad retirement (tier 1) tax for 1999	**7**	72,600	00
8a	Total social security wages and tips (total of boxes 3 and 7 on Form(s) W-2) and railroad retirement (tier 1) compensation **8a**			
b	Unreported tips subject to social security tax (from Form 4137, line 9) **8b**			
c	Add lines 8a and 8b	**8c**		
9	Subtract line 8c from line 7. If zero or less, enter -0- here and on line 10 and go to line 11 . ▶	**9**		
10	Multiply the **smaller** of line 6 or line 9 by 12.4% (.124)	**10**		
11	Multiply line 6 by 2.9% (.029)	**11**		
12	**Self-employment tax.** Add lines 10 and 11. Enter here and on **Form 1040, line 50**	**12**		
13	**Deduction for one-half of self-employment tax.** Multiply line 12 by 50% (.5). Enter the result here and on **Form 1040, line 27** **13**			

Part II   Optional Methods To Figure Net Earnings (See page SE-3.)

Farm Optional Method. You may use this method **only** if:
- Your gross farm income[1] was not more than $2,400, **or**
- Your net farm profits[2] were less than $1,733.

14	Maximum income for optional methods	**14**	1,600	00
15	Enter the **smaller** of: two-thirds (⅔) of gross farm income[1] (not less than zero) **or** $1,600. Also include this amount on line 4b above	**15**		

Nonfarm Optional Method. You may use this method **only** if:
- Your net nonfarm profits[3] were less than $1,733 and also less than 72.189% of your gross nonfarm income,[4] **and**
- You had net earnings from self-employment of at least $400 in 2 of the prior 3 years.

Caution: *You may use this method no more than five times.*

16	Subtract line 15 from line 14	**16**	
17	Enter the **smaller** of: two-thirds (⅔) of gross nonfarm income[4] (not less than zero) **or** the amount on line 16. Also include this amount on line 4b above	**17**	

[1]From Sch. F, line 11, and Sch. K-1 (Form 1065), line 15b.   [3]From Sch. C, line 31; Sch. C-EZ, line 3; Sch. K-1 (Form 1065), line 15a; and Sch. K-1 (Form 1065-B), box 9.
[2]From Sch. F, line 36, and Sch. K-1 (Form 1065), line 15a.   [4]From Sch. C, line 7; Sch. C-EZ, line 1; Sch. K-1 (Form 1065), line 15c; and Sch. K-1 (Form 1065-B), box 9.

Schedule SE (Form 1040) 1999

The Tax Payments Section of the 1040 Form

After you've entered your total tax liability, the next section of the 1040 Form is where you record the payments you've made. How much have you had withheld from your paycheck? How much have you paid in estimated tax payments? How much did you pay with your extension if you filed an extension? On line 64, add up your total payments and compare that figure to your total tax amount on line 56. Either you've overpaid, in which case you can have it refunded to you or applied to your next year's estimated taxes, or you've underpaid, in which case you owe the IRS.

There's a little space at the bottom of form 1040—line 69. This is where you calculate your estimated tax penalty if you haven't sent in enough taxes during the year. (Estimated taxes and related penalties are discussed in Chapter 35.)

> **Q**
>
> *Now that I've seen which expenses can be deducted and how the tax returns should be done, I realize that I made a lot of mistakes on last year's return. Should I do something about that?*
>
> **A**
>
> Form 1040X (and a corresponding form for your state) is used to amend an individual tax return. On the 1040X, you show the figures as they were originally entered on your return; then you show the corrected figures. There is a section on the form to explain why you're amending the return. If you make extensive changes to a form such as Schedule C, also attach a revised version of the form. If the corrections are in your favor, you'll receive a refund plus interest. If the corrections are in the IRS's favor, you'll need to send additional tax payment plus interest with the 1040X form. You have 3 years from the date the original return was filed or 2 years from when you paid the tax (whichever is later) to amend a return.

STATE TAXES? 34

Seven states don't have a state income tax: Alaska, Nevada, Washington, Texas, Florida, South Dakota, and Wyoming. Tennessee and New Hampshire assess income tax only on interest and dividends. All other states and the District of Columbia expect you to file a state return if your income is above the minimum requirement. If you live in one state and work in another, you may have to file a return in both states. Moving from one state to another in the course of a year means that you need to file a return in the state you left and in the state to which you moved, reporting the income earned in each state.

Generally, state tax returns are due the same date as federal returns, April 15, but several states have different due dates for their returns. Hawaii returns are due April 20, Delaware and Iowa returns are due April 30, Virginia returns are due May 1, and Louisiana and Arkansas returns are due May 15.

Some states follow the same tax law as the IRS; others are quite different. Some state tax returns look very similar to the federal return; others look nothing like the 1040 Form. Some state returns use your federal income in the calculation of your state taxes; others ignore totally the federal calculations. Some states allow you to deduct a portion of the federal taxes you pay, but most don't. Rhode Island and Vermont state taxes are calculated as a percentage of the federal tax paid.

In all states, the state tax rate is lower than federal rates. Also, there is no self-employment tax assessed at the state level.

Some cities also assess an income tax that is collected as part of the state return. New York City, for example, has a city income tax as well as an Unincorporated Business Tax (UBT) on income earned by a sole proprietor.

Detailing each state's tax requirements is beyond the scope of this book; therefore, be sure to check with your own state taxing agency to find out what you need to know. A list of phone numbers and a Web site link for state tax agencies can be found in Appendix C.

SECTION 6
Estimated Tax Payments

MAKING
QUARTERLY ESTIMATED
TAX PAYMENTS

35

Our tax system is set up on a pay-as-you-go basis. Taxes are due at the end of the quarter in which money is earned. Your tax return is due on April 15, not your taxes.

When you work as an employee, your employer withholds taxes from your paycheck. By the end of each quarter, your employer has remitted to the IRS and the state all the taxes that were withheld from paychecks during the quarter. As a self-employed person, you also are required to send in payments to the IRS and the state at the end of each quarter.

Corporations are required to make estimated tax payments throughout the year if the corporation's remaining tax liability will be $500 or more. Although the estimated tax information in this book is directed toward sole proprietors, the procedure is similar for corporations. Corporate estimated tax payments are submitted on Form 1120 W and are due on the 15th day of the 4th, 6th, 9th, and 12th months of the corporation's tax year.

Partnerships pay no tax as an entity, but each partner follows the same procedure used by sole proprietors to determine whether estimated tax payments are needed. S-corporations, like partnerships, do not pay taxes at the entity level. If there is a corporate profit after the employee-owners are paid, the shareholders must, like partners, calculate the individual income tax owed on their share of the profit. This tax may need to be paid in quarterly installments.

WHO NEEDS TO MAKE QUARTERLY PAYMENTS?

Any individual or couple (if married and filing jointly) who expects to have a remaining tax liability of $1,000 or more needs to make estimated tax payments. What does "remaining tax liability" mean? The following example helps to explain this term.

Jack and Ellen are married and file jointly. Jack had wages of $40,000 this year. Ellen had self-employment net earnings of $30,000 (remember, net is after business expenses have been deducted). Jack and Ellen have a total income of $70,000 for the year. The full $70,000 minus personal itemized deductions and personal exemptions is subject to federal income tax (which is approximately $10,500 on that amount of income). Only Ellen's self-employment income is subject to self-employment tax.

Remember, the self-employment tax is calculated by multiplying her $30,000 net profit by 92.35%, then by 15.3%, resulting in a tax of $4,239. The total tax liability for Jack and Ellen is $14,739 ($10,500 income tax plus $4,239 self-employment tax). Because Jack worked as an employee, he had $9,000 in federal income tax withheld from his paycheck. That means Jack and Ellen have a remaining tax liability of $5,739 ($14,739 minus the $9,000 withheld). In other words, if they do nothing, on April 15 they'll owe $5,739.

To repeat: If you expect your remaining tax liability, after any withholding, to be $1,000 or more, you must make estimated tax payments. If you (or your spouse) worked part of the year as an employee and had some taxes withheld from your wages, take that amount into consideration in calculating your remaining tax liability. If neither you nor your spouse worked as an employee during the year, your remaining tax liability will be the same as your total tax liability. As explained in Jack and Ellen's example, total tax liability consists of your income tax plus your self-employment tax.

QUARTERLY PAYMENT DUE DATES

If you do expect to have a remaining tax liability of $1,000 or more, estimated payments are due four times during the year. The due dates are as follows:

April 15
June 15
September 15
January 15

The payments are due *on* those dates, not sometime around the dates. The January 15 payment is not the first payment for the new year but rather the final payment for the prior year. For example, the payment made on January 15, 2001, is for the final quarter of 2000, not the first quarter of 2001.

ESTIMATED TAX VOUCHERS

Estimated tax payments are sent in with Form 1040-ES. Form 1040-ES is not a tax return but, instead, serves the same purpose as a bank deposit slip. Examples of 1040-ES forms, which are also called estimated tax vouchers, are found on page 144. Note that the due date is indicated on each voucher. When you send in the voucher with your

THE 1040-ES FORM (ESTIMATED TAX VOUCHERS)

Form **1040-ES**
Department of the Treasury
Internal Revenue Service

Payment Voucher 3

OMB No. 1545-0087

Calendar year—Due Sept. 15, 1999

File only if you are making a payment of estimated tax. Return this voucher with check or money order payable to the **"United States Treasury."** Please write your social security number and "1999 Form 1040-ES" on your check or money order. Do not send cash. Enclose, but do not staple or attach, your payment with this voucher.

Amount of payment	Please type or print	Your first name and initial	Your last name	Your social security number
		If joint payment, complete for spouse		
		Spouse's first name and initial	Spouse's last name	Spouse's social security number
$.............		Address (number, street, and apt. no.)		
		City, state, and ZIP code (If a foreign address, enter city, province or state, postal code, and country.)		

For Privacy Act and Paperwork Reduction Act Notice, see instructions on page 5.

- - - - - - - - - - - - - - - - Tear off here - - - - - - - - - - - - - - - -

---

Form **1040-ES**
Department of the Treasury
Internal Revenue Service

Payment Voucher 2

OMB No. 1545-0087

Calendar year—Due June 15, 1999

File only if you are making a payment of estimated tax. Return this voucher with check or money order payable to the **"United States Treasury."** Please write your social security number and "1999 Form 1040-ES" on your check or money order. Do not send cash. Enclose, but do not staple or attach, your payment with this voucher.

Amount of payment	Please type or print	Your first name and initial	Your last name	Your social security number
		If joint payment, complete for spouse		
		Spouse's first name and initial	Spouse's last name	Spouse's social security number
$.............		Address (number, street, and apt. no.)		
		City, state, and ZIP code (If a foreign address, enter city, province or state, postal code, and country.)		

For Privacy Act and Paperwork Reduction Act Notice, see instructions on page 5.

- - - - - - - - - - - - - - - - Tear off here - - - - - - - - - - - - - - - -

---

Form **1040-ES**
Department of the Treasury
Internal Revenue Service

Payment Voucher 1

OMB No. 1545-0087

Calendar year—Due April 15, 1999

File only if you are making a payment of estimated tax. Return this voucher with check or money order payable to the **"United States Treasury."** Please write your social security number and "1999 Form 1040-ES" on your check or money order. Do not send cash. Enclose, but do not staple or attach, your payment with this voucher.

Amount of payment	Please type or print	Your first name and initial	Your last name	Your social security number
		If joint payment, complete for spouse		
		Spouse's first name and initial	Spouse's last name	Spouse's social security number
$.............		Address (number, street, and apt. no.)		
		City, state, and ZIP code (If a foreign address, enter city, province or state, postal code, and country.)		

For Privacy Act and Paperwork Reduction Act Notice, see instructions on page 5.

payment, in effect you are making a deposit to your tax account. Until you file your tax return for the year, the IRS has no way of knowing why you're making the payments. It's not only self-employed people who are required to send quarterly payments; anyone who expects to owe $1,000 or more when she files a tax return must make these estimated payments.

When the IRS receives your money, they don't know whether you've started a business, sold some stock at a gain, received a pension, or had some other source of taxable income. If you receive any correspondence from the IRS during the year, it won't be related to this year's estimated tax payment because the IRS doesn't know enough about your tax situation for this year to question you about it.

After sending in the voucher, you will not hear from the IRS. You will not get a note asking why you sent the money in or why you didn't send money last quarter. The IRS won't tell you that the payment arrived late or that it was too much or that it wasn't enough. There will be no acknowledgment at all. The only thing you may get from the IRS, after you've sent in a payment for the first time, is a set of preprinted vouchers. The preprinted vouchers will have your name and social security number on them, but they won't indicate how much to send in because, again, the IRS has no way of knowing why you're making estimated payments or the amount of your tax liability.

If you look at the vouchers on page 144, you'll see that the only information asked for is your first and last name (and your spouse's first and last name, if filing jointly), your address, your social security number, and the amount of payment being sent. The vouchers don't ask why you're sending the money or whether you started a business this year. Nor do they ask how much you expect to make this year or how much you'll be sending in estimated tax payments throughout the year. They don't even ask you how much of what you're sending is for income tax and how much for self-employment tax.

If you're married and file your tax return jointly with your spouse, be sure the names on the vouchers are consistent with your tax return. Whichever spouse is listed first on the tax return should also be listed first on the voucher, since the IRS uses the first name and social security number on the tax return as the tax account number for the couple. Even if your spouse isn't self-employed, be sure to list him on the estimated tax voucher so that the money gets credited to the correct tax account.

When calculating the amount to send (instructions are in Chapter 36), those who file a joint return need to look at the total income earned as a couple, not just the amount earned by the self-employed spouse. Similarly, if you have income from wages *and* from self-employment, it will not be accurate to base your estimated payments solely on the self-employment income. The calculation must be based on the total picture, including the entire income you (and your spouse, if married and filing jointly) will have from all sources for the whole year. The reason estimated tax calculations can't accurately be based solely on self-employment income, and only for the portion of the year that's already gone by, is because our tax system is a graduated one with several tax brackets, depending on income.

FEDERAL TAX RATES

A copy of the 1999 federal tax rate schedule is shown below. The schedule changes slightly from year to year, so make sure you're working with the one that applies to the current year. The tax rate schedule is used to calculate your federal income tax liability, which is based on your taxable income. Remember from Chapter 33 that taxable income is the figure arrived at after everything has been deducted, including your personal exemption and personal itemized deductions or the standard deduction.

The tax rate schedule for single people is read like this: If your taxable income is over zero but not over $25,750, your income tax is 15% of the amount over zero. A person with less than $25,750 taxable income is in the 15% tax bracket. If your taxable income is over $25,750 but not over $62,450, according to the tax rate schedule, your tax is 28% of the amount

THE 1999 TAX RATE SCHEDULE

1999 Tax Rate Schedules

Caution: *Do not use these Tax Rate Schedules to figure your 1998 taxes. Use only to figure your 1999 estimated taxes.*

Single—Schedule X

If line 5 is: Over—	But not over—	The tax is:	of the amount over—
$0	$25,750	.........15%	$0
25,750	62,450	$3,862.50 + 28%	25,750
62,450	130,250	14,138.50 + 31%	62,450
130,250	283,150	35,156.50 + 36%	130,250
283,150	....	90,200.50 + 39.6%	283,150

Head of household—Schedule Z

If line 5 is: Over—	But not over—	The tax is:	of the amount over—
$0	$34,550	.........15%	$0
34,550	89,150	$5,182.50 + 28%	34,550
89,150	144,400	20,470.50 + 31%	89,150
144,400	283,150	37,598.00 + 36%	144,400
283,150	....	87,548.00 + 39.6%	283,150

Married filing jointly or Qualifying widow(er)—Schedule Y-1

If line 5 is: Over—	But not over—	The tax is:	of the amount over—
$0	$43,050	.........15%	$0
43,050	104,050	$6,457.50 + 28%	43,050
104,050	158,550	23,537.50 + 31%	104,050
158,550	283,150	40,432.50 + 36%	158,550
283,150	....	85,288.50 + 39.6%	283,150

Married filing separately—Schedule Y-2

If line 5 is: Over—	But not over—	The tax is:	of the amount over—
$0	$21,525	.........15%	$0
21,525	52,025	$3,228.75 + 28%	21,525
52,025	79,275	11,768.75 + 31%	52,025
79,275	141,575	20,216.25 + 36%	79,275
141,575	....	42,644.25 + 39.6%	141,575

over $25,750 plus $3,862.50. That person is in the 28% tax bracket. This doesn't mean that all of her income is taxed at 28%; the first $25,750 of taxable income is taxed at 15%, and the next approximately $35,000 is taxed at 28%. The $3,862.50 figure is 15% of $25,750, since tax is paid at a rate of 15% on the first $25,750 of taxable income.

In calculating the amount of estimated tax due, if you look only at the amount you earned this quarter or only at the self-employed spouse's income, without considering income from all sources for the entire year, the calculations will probably be incorrect.

> *Juanita is a single woman who makes the mistake of calculating her estimated payments based solely on her self-employment income. She earns $10,000 net income from self-employment during the first quarter of the year. She looks at the tax rate schedule and seeing that $10,000 is less than $25,750 sends in 15% of $10,000 to cover her income tax. The next quarter she again has $10,000 net self-employment income. She sends in the same amount as she sent the first quarter. She earns the same amount in the third and fourth quarters and sends in the same payment as in the first and second quarters. Each quarter she has sent in 15% of $10,000. By the end of the year, she has $40,000 of self-employment income and $30,000 in wages, for a total income of $70,000. However, she is not in the 15% tax bracket, and she's possibly not even in the 28% tax bracket but rather in the 31% tax bracket. By considering each quarter of self-employment income by itself without looking at her total income for the year, Juanita has not been sending in nearly enough money.*

To avoid Juanita's situation, you need to make an educated guess about the entire year's income from all sources. These are called "estimated tax payments" because you're estimating what you think your income and taxes are going to be for the year. This is especially hard to do the first year you're in business. If you have no idea what you're going to earn this year, the only thing you can do is calculate your income and tax liability at the end of each quarter and project what the remainder of the year will be like. If you had been in business for 10 years and could see that your earnings and expenses are about the same each year, you would know that if you send in the same amount this year as you did last year, most likely you will cover this year's taxes. But when you are just starting out in business, you don't have those prior years to use as a projection for the current year. You have to estimate what you think the year is going to look like, which can be a very difficult thing to do.

Does the IRS always penalize people who don't do their estimated payments correctly?

Every once in a while someone's under payment is overlooked, but in general you will be penalized if you don't make a payment, send it late, or don't send enough. Because the IRS isn't aware of your tax situation during the year, the penalty won't be assessed until you file your tax return for the year.

PENALTIES

Before showing you how to do the estimated tax calculations, I want to discuss penalties. If you don't send in enough during the year or if you send your payment in late, you will have a penalty. The penalty at the present time is 8% a year on the amount that should have been sent in but wasn't. Since it's actually interest, the rate goes up and down quarterly as interest rates fluctuate. The penalty is calculated on a daily basis, so if you can't send what you owe on the due date, you should send as much as you can as soon as possible rather than wait until the next due date. If a payment was due April 15 and you send it on April 30, you'll have much less penalty than if you include the amount with your June 15 payment.

Remember, federal tax withheld from your (or your spouse's) paycheck as an employee has also been deposited to your tax account. While you may have neglected to send a quarterly estimated tax payment, your withholding for that quarter (if you had any) may be sufficient to protect you from penalties.

AVOIDING PENALTIES

By using one of these three payment methods, you can avoid penalties:

1. Owe less than $1,000 when you file your tax return. If that's your situation, no estimated tax payments are necessary.
2. Each quarter, send one quarter of what your total tax liability was last year.
3. Each quarter, send 90% of the amount you're really going to owe for that quarter.

The first method is self-explanatory. The second and third methods are not as straightforward. As explained earlier, when you add together your income tax and your self-employment tax on the 1040 Form, you get a figure called your total tax liability. Look at the back side of your 1040 Form from last year. Find the line that says "your total tax." The exact line number varies from year to year, but it will be somewhere between lines 50 and 55. If you divide your last year's total tax amount by the four quarters and every quarter send a payment equal to that amount, you will have no penalty when you file your return this year, no matter how much more you owe on April 15. This is the second method of avoiding estimated tax penalties. You don't have to have been self-employed last year in order to use this method of paying the current year's estimated tax payments.

Ali started her own business last year. She didn't make very much money, so her total tax liability for last year (income tax plus self-employment tax) was only $1,000. In order to avoid penalties this year, Ali has to send estimated tax payments of at least $250 per quarter (¼ of $1,000). That amount bears no relation to the actual amount she's earning this year. To avoid penalties, she must send at least that amount each quarter whether or not she has self-employment income during that quarter. She can't wait until January and send the whole amount in then; equal payments must be sent throughout the year in order to use this method of avoiding penalties. By sending $250 each quarter, Ali is protected from penalties no matter how much she earns this year. As it turns out, Ali makes a lot of money this year, and her total tax liability is $10,000. She'll owe $9,000 ($10,000 minus the amount she's already sent in) when she files her return in April, but she'll have no penalties.

The way Ali pays her quarterlies is the method used by many self-employed people to make their estimated tax payments. If your business gets to a very stable point and you earn a similar amount each year, basing the current year's payments on the prior year's tax amount means that you'll be sending in approximately enough to cover this year's tax. In any case, as long as you send in an amount equal to or more than 100% of the prior year's total tax liability, at a minimum you'll be protected from penalties. *Note:* If you expect your adjusted gross income to be more than $150,000 ($75,000 if married and filing separately), your four payments must equal 105% rather than 100% of the prior year's total tax liability.

The negative side of choosing this way of making your estimated payments is that you're only protecting yourself from penalties; it doesn't mean you won't owe any additional tax. You might end up owing a lot more when you file your tax return. When Ali comes for her tax appointment and I tell her that she owes an additional $9,000 on April 15, she whines, "But you told me all I had to do was send in one quarter of last year's tax liability each quarter." Yes, that's true, but as I told her last year, that amount was just enough to protect her from penalties, not to cover this year's tax liability.

Using the prior year's tax liability as the method for determining how much to send for the current year's estimated payments won't make sense if you earned a lot more last year than you're going to earn this year. In that case, you wouldn't want to send in one quarter of what your tax was last year in order to avoid penalties this year. The appropriate method to use in this situation is the next method.

This third method of avoiding penalties is done by estimating your real tax liability for the current year and sending in 90% of it on a quarterly basis. The advantage of sending in estimates based on current income figures is that when you do your taxes at the end of the year, you should owe very little, if any, and you won't be surprised, as Ali was, to learn that you owe a great deal more in taxes. The next chapter will explain how to calculate the tax liability on your current year earnings.

Assuming that you earned less last year than you're going to earn this year, here is the ideal way to make estimated tax payments: Look at last year's total tax liability, send in one fourth of that amount each quarter, but also know how to calculate how much you're actually going to owe for this year and set that extra money aside in an interest-bearing savings account so that it's available to pay on April 15 with your tax return.

The reality is that most people do not have enough discipline to do their estimated payments in that way. They may start out with good intentions of setting aside the money, but an emergency comes up and they end up paying for it with what should be their tax money. The crucial thing is to not be in denial about the taxes you'll owe. If you're not sending in the full amount you owe for each quarter, know that eventually (and no later than April 15 of the following year) you'll have to come up with that money.

If you're using a tax professional to prepare your quarterly estimates, make sure she asks you whether you want to base your estimates on the prior year's tax liability or on what you're actually going to earn this year. If you don't specify, some preparers assume you want to base your payments on the prior year's tax. It's up to you. Remember, if you base it on the prior year's tax, that amount may or may not cover your total tax liability for this year; but, in any case, if all payments are made on time, there will be no penalty.

Q

A

I didn't make my June 15 estimated payment. It's now July 20. Should I send the payment now or include it with my September 15 payment?

Since the penalties for not making a payment or for sending too little are calculated on a daily basis ($1/365$ of the penalty amount each day), it's best to send your payment as soon as possible to reduce the amount you'll be penalized when you file your tax return.

FORM 2210

If you will have penalties for late or insufficient estimated tax payments, Form 2210 (see pages 151–152) is used to calculate those penalties. Form 2210 has another important function for those taxpayers who didn't send four equal estimated tax payments because they didn't have an equal amount of income in each of the four quarters.

As previously mentioned, if you're basing your estimated tax payments on last year's tax liability, you need to send (or have withheld) one-fourth of last year's tax each quarter, no matter how much you actually earn that quarter.

Form **2210**	Underpayment of	OMB No. 1545-0140
	Estimated Tax by Individuals, Estates, and Trusts	19**98**
Department of the Treasury Internal Revenue Service	▶ See separate instructions. ▶ Attach to Form 1040, 1040A, 1040NR, 1040NR-EZ, or 1041.	Attachment Sequence No. **06**

Name(s) shown on tax return	Identifying number

Note: *In most cases, you **do not** need to file Form 2210. The IRS will figure any penalty you owe and send you a bill. File Form 2210 **only** if one or more boxes in Part I apply to you. If you do not need to file Form 2210, you still may use it to figure your penalty. Enter the amount from Part III, line 21, or Part IV, line 35, on the penalty line of your return, but **do not** attach Form 2210.*

Part I **Reasons for Filing**—If 1a, 1b, or 1c below applies to you, you may be able to lower or eliminate your penalty. But you MUST check the boxes that apply and file Form 2210 with your tax return. If 1d below applies to you, check that box and file Form 2210 with your tax return.

1 Check whichever boxes apply (if none apply, see the **Note** above):

a ☐ You request a **waiver.** In certain circumstances, the IRS will waive all or part of the penalty. See **Waiver of Penalty** on page 2 of the instructions.

b ☐ You use the **annualized income installment method.** If your income varied during the year, this method may reduce the amount of one or more required installments. See page 4 of the instructions.

c ☐ You had Federal income tax withheld from wages and, for estimated tax purposes, you treat the withheld tax as paid on the dates it was actually withheld, instead of in equal amounts on the payment due dates. See the instructions for line 23 on page 3.

d ☐ Your required annual payment (line 14 below) is based on your 1997 tax and you filed or are filing a joint return for either 1997 or 1998 but not for both years.

Part II **Required Annual Payment**

2	Enter your 1998 tax after credits (see page 2 of the instructions)	**2**	
3	Other taxes (see page 2 of the instructions)	**3**	
4	Add lines 2 and 3	**4**	
5	Earned income credit **5**		
6	Additional child tax credit **6**		
7	Credit for Federal tax paid on fuels **7**		
8	Add lines 5, 6, and 7	**8**	
9	Current year tax. Subtract line 8 from line 4	**9**	
10	Multiply line 9 by 90% (.90) **10**		
11	Withholding taxes. **Do not** include any estimated tax payments on this line (see page 2 of the instructions)	**11**	
12	Subtract line 11 from line 9. If less than $1,000, stop here; **do not** complete or file this form. You do not owe the penalty	**12**	
13	Enter the tax shown on your 1997 tax return. **Caution:** *See page 2 of the instructions*	**13**	
14	**Required annual payment.** Enter the **smaller** of line 10 or line 13	**14**	

  Note: *If line 11 is equal to or more than line 14, stop here; you do not owe the penalty. Do not file Form 2210 unless you checked box 1d above.*

Part III **Short Method** (**Caution:** *See page 2 of the instructions to find out if you can use the short method. If you checked box **1b** or **1c** in Part I, skip this part and go to Part IV.*)

15	Enter the amount, if any, from line 11 above **15**		
16	Enter the total amount, if any, of estimated tax payments you made **16**		
17	Add lines 15 and 16	**17**	
18	**Total underpayment for year.** Subtract line 17 from line 14. If zero or less, stop here; you do not owe the penalty. Do not file Form 2210 unless you checked box 1d above	**18**	
19	Multiply line 18 by .05043	**19**	
20	● If the amount on line 18 was paid **on or after** 4/15/99, enter -0-.		
	● If the amount on line 18 was paid **before** 4/15/99, make the following computation to find the amount to enter on line 20. $\quad$ Amount on $\quad \times \quad$ Number of days paid $\quad \times \quad$ .00019 ..... line 18 $\qquad$ before 4/15/99	**20**	
21	**PENALTY.** Subtract line 20 from line 19. Enter the result here and on Form 1040, line 69; Form 1040A, line 44; Form 1040NR, line 68; Form 1040NR-EZ, line 27; or Form 1041, line 26 . . ▶	**21**	

For Paperwork Reduction Act Notice, see page 1 of separate instructions. $\qquad$ Cat. No. 11744P $\qquad$ Form **2210** (1998)

Form 2210   Page **3**

Schedule AI—Annualized Income Installment Method (see pages 4 and 5 of the instructions)

Estates and trusts, **do not** use the period ending dates shown to the right. Instead, use the following: 2/28/98, 4/30/98, 7/31/98, and 11/30/98.

		(a) 1/1/98–3/31/98	(b) 1/1/98–5/31/98	(c) 1/1/98–8/31/98	(d) 1/1/98–12/31/98
Part I	**Annualized Income Installments** Caution: *Complete lines 20–26 of one column* **before** *going to the next column.*				
1	Enter your adjusted gross income for each period (see instructions). (Estates and trusts, enter your taxable income without your exemption for each period.) **1**				
2	Annualization amounts. (Estates and trusts, see instructions.) . . **2**	4	2.4	1.5	1
3	Annualized income. Multiply line 1 by line 2 . . . . **3**				
4	Enter your itemized deductions for the period shown in each column. If you do not itemize, enter -0- and skip to line 7. (Estates and trusts, enter -0-, skip to line 9, and enter the amount from line 3 on line 9.) **4**				
5	Annualization amounts **5**	4	2.4	1.5	1
6	Multiply line 4 by line 5 (see instructions if line 3 is more than $62,250) **6**				
7	In each column, enter the full amount of your standard deduction from Form 1040, line 36, or Form 1040A, line 21 (Form 1040NR or 1040NR-EZ filers, enter -0-. **Exception:** Indian students and business apprentices, enter standard deduction from Form 1040NR, line 35 or Form 1040NR-EZ, line 11.) **7**				
8	Enter the **larger** of line 6 or line 7. . . . . **8**				
9	Subtract line 8 from line 3 . . . . **9**				
10	In each column, multiply $2,700 by the total number of exemptions claimed (see instructions if line 3 is more than $93,400). (Estates and trusts and Form 1040NR or 1040NR-EZ filers, enter the exemption amount shown on your tax return.) **10**				
11	Subtract line 10 from line 9 . . . . **11**				
12	Figure your tax on the amount on line 11 (see instructions) . . . **12**				
13	Form 1040 filers only, enter your self-employment tax from line 35 below **13**				
14	Enter other taxes for each payment period (see instructions) . . **14**				
15	Total tax. Add lines 12, 13, and 14 . . . . **15**				
16	For each period, enter the same type of credits as allowed on Form 2210, lines 2, 5, 6, and 7 (see instructions) **16**				
17	Subtract line 16 from line 15. If zero or less, enter -0- **17**				
18	Applicable percentage **18**	22.5%	45%	67.5%	90%
19	Multiply line 17 by line 18 . . . . **19**				
20	Add the amounts in all previous columns of line 26 . . . . . **20**	▓▓▓			
21	Subtract line 20 from line 19. If zero or less, enter -0- **21**				
22	Enter ¼ of line 14 on page 1 of Form 2210 in each column . . . **22**				
23	Enter amount from line 25 of the previous column of this schedule. **23**	▓▓▓			
24	Add lines 22 and 23 and enter the total **24**				
25	Subtract line 21 from line 24. If zero or less, enter -0- **25**				▓▓▓
26	Enter the **smaller** of line 21 or line 24 here and on Form 2210, line 22 . . . . ▶ **26**				
Part II	**Annualized Self-Employment Tax**				
27a	Net earnings from self-employment for the period (see instructions) **27a**				
b	Annualization amounts **27b**	4	2.4	1.5	1
c	Multiply line 27a by line 27b **27c**				
28	Social security tax limit **28**	$68,400	$68,400	$68,400	$68,400
29	Enter actual wages for the period subject to social security tax or the 6.2% portion of the 7.65% railroad retirement (tier 1) tax . . **29**				
30	Annualization amounts **30**	4	2.4	1.5	1
31	Multiply line 29 by line 30 . . . . **31**				
32	Subtract line 31 from line 28. If zero or less, enter -0- **32**				
33	Multiply the smaller of line 27c or line 32 by .124 . . . . . . **33**				
34	Multiply line 27c by .029 . . . . **34**				
35	Add lines 33 and 34. Enter the result here and on line 13 above ▶ **35**				

If you're basing your payments on this year's true income, the IRS assumes that your income is the same each quarter, so they expect you to make four equal quarterly payments. Although you won't be contacted during the year, when you file your tax return, the IRS will be prepared to penalize you if you didn't make identical payments all four quarters.

Form 2210 can be used to show the IRS that varying amounts were earned each quarter and that the amount sent was based on the true amount earned in that quarter. If you didn't start your business until after March 31 (the end of the first quarter), or you had a large amount of income one quarter but not another, or you had a seasonal business such as selling Christmas trees, the only way to let the IRS know that you shouldn't be penalized for uneven payments is to file Form 2210 with your tax return. Be sure to show your actual quarterly income by filling out the Annualized Income Installment Method on page 3 of the 2210 Form (see page 152).

Form 2210 is filed only once a year with your tax return in April. Don't send it with your quarterly payments. Attach it to your return to show the IRS why you shouldn't be penalized or to calculate the penalties for not having sent enough or having sent late payments during the year.

> *Should I send in Form 2210 with my tax return even if I don't have an excuse for not making an estimated tax payment? In other words, should I calculate my own estimated tax penalty?*
>
> Form 2210 is a tedious form to fill out. If a preparer is doing your return or if you're using a computerized tax program, go ahead and fill out the form. Otherwise, unless there's a possibility you can get out of some of the penalty, let the IRS fill it out and bill you for penalties.

STATE ESTIMATED TAX PAYMENTS

The states that have an income tax (see Chapter 34) generally require people who will owe above a certain amount when they file their tax return to make estimated tax payments during the year. Some states require residents to make estimated payments whenever they're required by the IRS. For all states, except Hawaii, the estimated tax payments are due on the same dates as the federal payments. Hawaii's estimated tax payments are due on the 20th rather than the 15th day after the end of the quarter.

COMPUTING ESTIMATED TAX PAYMENTS FOR 2000

These five steps will show you how to compute your estimated tax payments:

STEP 1:

Add together all income you expect to receive from all sources this year. This includes your net self-employment income, any wages, other miscellaneous income, and your spouse's income if married and filing jointly.

STEP 2:

Calculate the self-employment tax on your projected self-employment income by multiplying the projected net self-employment income included in Step 1 by 92.35% and then by 15.3%.

STEP 3:

Starting with the figure in Step 1 (projected total income), subtract out

half of your projected self-employment tax (Step 2 result divided by 2); *and*, $2,800 for yourself, your spouse, and each dependent; *and* your personal itemized deductions or the $4,400 standard deduction ($7,350 if married).

What's left is your projected taxable income for the year.

STEP 4:

Look on the tax rate schedule to find what the income tax is on your projected taxable income. Subtract out the amount of federal income tax that will be withheld from your and your spouse's wages (if any). The figure that's left is the remainder that you'll owe for federal income tax.

STEP 5:

Take the income tax figure from Step 4. Add the projected self-employment tax figure from Step 2. The total of these figures equals your remaining tax liability. This figure is then divided by the number of quarters remaining in the year.

CALCULATING
THE AMOUNT TO
SEND QUARTERLY

36

This chapter describes in detail how to calculate the amount of money to send in or set aside each quarter, based on this year's true tax liability. Whether you choose to actually send it in or to send in only the minimum amount necessary to avoid penalties, this calculation will help avoid the surprise of learning that you owe a great deal more on April 15.

To understand how to do the estimated tax calculation, an overview of the process is shown on page 154. Appendix B includes a step-by-step example of an estimated tax calculation, along with a worksheet for your use. The 2000 personal exemption, standard deduction, and tax rate amounts were not available when this book went to press. They will be slightly different than the 1999 amounts used here.

In calculating the amount to send with your estimated tax vouchers, first add together all income you expect to receive from all sources this year. This is your projected income. It includes your net self-employment income—remember, net is after business expenses have been deducted—any wages, any other miscellaneous income, and your spouse's income, if you're married and filing jointly.

Then, calculate the self-employment tax on the portion of your total income that is from self-employment. Do this by multiplying your projected net self-employment income first by 92.35%, and then by 15.3%.

Next, using the figure in step 1—your projected total income—subtract out the following:

- Half of your projected self-employment tax
- The $2,750 (1999 amount) personal exemption for yourself, your spouse, and each dependent, which you get just for being you
- Your personal itemized deductions, if you itemize your personal deductions, or the standard deduction, which for 1999 is $4,300 if single and $7,200 if married and filing jointly

The remaining figure is your projected taxable income for the year.

Then, using the tax rate schedule (see page 138) determine how much income tax there is on your projected taxable income. From that amount subtract out whatever amount you (or your spouse, if married) expect to have withheld from your paychecks, if any. If you earned money as an employee during part of the year or are continuing to earn money as an employee, look at your paystub to see how much federal income tax will be withheld from each check. After you have subtracted the projected withholding amount (if any), the remainder is the amount you'll owe for federal income tax.

Add that figure to your projected self-employment tax in Step 2, and the total is your remaining tax liability for the year. This is the balance you'll owe on April 15 with your tax return unless you send it in earlier via estimated tax payments or additional withholding.

Remember, this is only a projected or estimated amount. If you have no idea what your income will be this year, you must redo this calculation each quarter before sending in your estimated tax voucher. However, once you understand how to compute this, it won't be difficult to redo each quarter.

If you're still feeling a little lost about how this calculation is done, take a look at the example in Appendix B.

If I'm working as an employee and I'm not going to have that much income as a self-employed person, can I just change my withholding at work and claim zero or even have my employer withhold extra so that I don't have to make estimated payments?

Yes, but you still need to calculate what you think you're going to owe for the year to ensure that your withholding covers the amount due on your self-employment income as well as your wages.

A lot of people don't like having to think about estimated payments; instead they prefer to adjust their (or their spouse's) withholding to cover the amount due. This obviously won't work if you have a lot of self-employment income and not a lot of wages on which to have taxes withheld.

However, this is one way to reduce or eliminate penalties. If you haven't made the estimated payments that you should have made, you can increase your withholding for the remainder of the year. Since the IRS assumes that your income was earned equally throughout the year, they also assume your withholding was done equally throughout the year. You can take advantage of that assumption to have more tax payment credited to the earlier quarters.

SECTION 7
Getting Help

Form **9465**
(Rev. January 1996)
Department of the Treasury
Internal Revenue Service

Installment Agreement Request

▶ See instructions below and on back.

OMB No. 1545-1350

Note: *Do not file this form if you are currently making payments on an installment agreement. You must pay your other Federal tax liabilities in full or you will be in default on your agreement.*

If you can't pay the full amount you owe, you can ask to make monthly installment payments. If we approve your request, you will be charged a $43 fee. **Do not include the fee with this form.** We will deduct the fee from your first payment after we approve your request, unless you choose **Direct Debit** (see the line 13 instructions). We will usually let you know within 30 days after we receive your request whether it is approved or denied. But if this request is for tax due on a return you filed after March 31, it may take us longer than 30 days to reply.

To ask for an installment agreement, complete this form. Attach it to the front of your return when you file. If you have already filed your return or you are filing this form in response to a notice, see **How Do I File Form 9465?** on page 2. If you have any questions about this request, call 1-800-829-1040.

Caution: *A Notice of Federal Tax Lien may be filed to protect the government's interest until you pay in full.*

1	Your first name and initial	Last name	Your social security number
	If a joint return, spouse's first name and initial	Last name	Spouse's social security number
	Your current address (number and street). If you have a P.O. box and no home delivery, show box number.		Apt. number
	City, town or post office, state, and ZIP code. If a foreign address, show city, state or province, postal code, and full name of country.		

2 If this address is new since you filed your last tax return, check here . . . . ▶ ☐

3 ( ) _____ _____
   Your home phone number   Best time for us to call

4 ( ) _____ _____ _____
   Your work phone number   Ext.   Best time for us to call

5 Name of your bank or other financial institution:

6 Your employer's name:

Address

Address

City, state, and ZIP code

City, state, and ZIP code

7 Enter the tax return for which you are making this request (for example, Form 1040). But if you are filing this form in response to a notice, don't complete lines 7 through 9. Instead, attach the bottom section of the notice to this form and go to line 10 . . . . ▶ _____

8 Enter the tax year for which you are making this request (for example, 1995) . . . . ▶ _____

9 Enter the total amount you owe as shown on your tax return . . . . ▶ $ _____

10 Enter the amount of any payment you are making with your tax return (or notice). See instructions . ▶ $ _____

11 Enter the amount you can paym each month. **Make your payments as large as possible to limit interest and penalty charges.** The charges will continue until you pay in full . . . . ▶ $ _____

12 Enter the date you want to make your payment each month. Do not enter a date later than the 28th ▶ _____

13 If you would like to make your monthly payments using **Direct Debit** (automatic withdrawals from your bank account), check here. . . . . ▶ ☐

Your signature	Date	Spouse's signature. If a joint return, BOTH must sign.	Date

Privacy Act and Paperwork Reduction Act Notice.—Our legal right to ask for the information on this form is Internal Revenue Code sections 6001, 6011, 6012(a), 6109, and 6159 and their regulations. We will use the information to process your request for an installment agreement. The reason we need your name and social security number is to secure proper identification. We require this information to gain access to the tax information in our files and properly respond to your request. If you do not enter the information, we may not be able to process your request. We may give this information to the Department of Justice as provided by law. We may also give it to cities, states, and the District of Columbia to carry out their tax laws.

WHAT IF YOU DON'T HAVE ENOUGH MONEY TO PAY YOUR TAXES?

37

One crucial thing to remember about your taxes is that even if you don't have the money to pay them, your return should be filed on time. The penalty for not filing your tax return on time is 5% a month, whereas the penalty for not paying your taxes on time is only ½ of 1% per month. Never delay filing your return because you don't have enough money to pay your taxes.

The late filing and late payment penalties are in addition to any penalties you might have for not making your estimated tax payments on time or not sending in enough each quarter. (For more information on those penalties, see Chapter 35.)

Each year more than five million taxpayers file Form 4868 (see page 160), asking the IRS for an extension. This is an extension of time to file your tax return, not an extension of time to pay any taxes due. As long as you send it in by April 15, Form 4868 is an automatic extension, giving you until August 15 to file your tax return. Anyone can ask for an extension; there's no need to have an excuse for waiting to send in your return. If you need even more time to prepare your return, file Form 2688 by August 15. This is an application for an additional extension of time to file your return. Form 2688 is not an automatic extension; the IRS will give you an additional 2 months to file only if you have a good reason for the delay.

Until recently, the IRS required that any taxes due be paid with your extension form on April 15. Now, if you file an extension on April 15, the IRS asks that you give a good faith estimate of the amount you expect to owe and pay whatever you can at that time. Interest and late payment penalties will be added to any additional amount due.

As emphasized in the chapters on estimated tax payments, you should send as much as you can as soon as you can to avoid or lessen penalties. Nevertheless, at some point you may find yourself unable to pay the remaining tax you owe.

In recent years the IRS has made it easier to pay your taxes by allowing installment payments. Form 9465 should be filled out and included when you file your federal return (see page 158). On this form you'll indicate how much you can afford to send each month. There is a $43 charge to set up the installment plan.

If you're on an installment plan and you're late making any of your monthly payments, the total amount you owe will immediately become due. Even with an installment agreement, interest and penalties (for not paying on time) will continue to accrue until you've paid off your tax liability. The penalty is the same ½% per month mentioned previously; the interest changes from quarter to quarter and is currently 8% per year on the unpaid balance. Beginning in 2000, as long as the tax return is filed on time, the penalty is reduced to ¼% per month for people with installment plans.

If you owe so much that you can't possibly ever pay it off, the IRS may accept an Offer In Compromise, which means that you offer to pay a lesser amount than you owe in order to settle the bill immediately. You need to fill out a complete financial statement and present it with the appropriate paperwork. Your offer will be accepted only if the IRS believes it will not be able to collect the full amount due from you within the near future. Discussion of an Offer In Compromise is beyond the scope of this book. A tax professional will be able to provide you with more information.

THE 4868 FORM

For Privacy Act and Paperwork Reduction Act Notice, see page 4.   Cat. No. 13141W   Form **4868** (1998)

▼ DETACH HERE ▼

Form **4868**
Department of the Treasury
Internal Revenue Service

Application for Automatic Extension of Time To File U.S. Individual Income Tax Return
For calendar year 1998, or other tax year beginning _____ ,1998, ending _____ ,19 ____ .

OMB No. 1545-0188

Identification

1 Your name(s) (see instructions)

Address (see instructions)

City, town or post office, state, and ZIP code

2 Your social security number   3 Spouse's social security no.

Complete ONLY If Filing Gift/GST Tax Return

This form also extends the time for filing a gift or generation-skipping transfer (GST) tax return if you file a calendar (not fiscal) year income tax return. Check below **only** if requesting a gift or GST tax return extension, and enter your tax payment(s) in Part IV:

Yourself ▶ ☐   Spouse ▶ ☐

Individual Income Tax

4 Total tax liability on your income tax return for 1998 $ _____
5 Total 1998 payments . . . . . . _____
6 **Balance.** Subtract 5 from 4 . . . . _____

Gift/GST Tax—If you are **not filing** a gift or GST tax return, go to Part V now. See the instructions.

7 Your gift or GST tax payment. . . $ _____
8 **Your spouse's** gift/GST tax payment . _____

Total

9 **Total liability.** Add lines 6, 7, and 8 $ _____
10 Amount you are paying. . . . . ▶ _____

If line 10 is less than line 9, you may be liable for interest and penalties. See page 3.

RECORDKEEPING
AND TAX RETURNS

38

After reading this book, you may feel a bit overwhelmed and wonder if it's time to consider getting some help.

BOOKKEEPERS

If you feel comfortable with the recordkeeping system you've set up for your business and you seem to have enough time to keep track of your income and expenses, it's probably not necessary for you to hire a bookkeeper. However, if you find that you're spending more time doing your recordkeeping than you want to be or you're spending time on that when you could be spending the time making money, it may be time to hire a part-time bookkeeper.

Talk to colleagues about possible bookkeeper recommendations. When talking to the prospective bookkeeper, ask her in what form she'll want information from you:

- Will she work from your checkbook and piles of receipts, or will she expect you to have entered some information on to a spread-sheet?
- Will she be providing you with regular profit and loss reports?
- Is she willing to train you to do some of the work if you want to be more involved?
- If you'll be entering some of your financial information into a computer program, does the bookkeeper use the same program?
- Do you need to have a minimum number of hours of work for her to do before she's willing to work with you?
- Does she prepare tax returns? If yes, look also at the hints in the next section about selecting a tax preparer; if not, in what form will your financial information be given back to you?

TAX PREPARERS

Similar guidelines regarding when to hire a bookkeeper are used in deciding when to enlist the services of a tax preparer. If you're spending time working on your tax return when you could be using that time more profitably by working on your business, it's time to think about using a tax preparer. Also, if you're not sure you're handling things correctly on your return, it may cost you less to use a preparer than pay penalties on an incorrectly prepared return. A preparer may also save you money by taking deductions you've forgotten to claim.

If you want to be more involved with your tax return preparation, one possibility is to prepare your own return and then have a tax preparer look it over. The preparer won't sign the return, since it was prepared by you, but she should catch any blatant errors or answer questions you have. Not all preparers are willing to do this; but if you look around, you will find one who is.

Having a tax professional review your return is also important if you prepare the return on a computer. The tax preparation programs seem like a good idea and are marketed as containing all the help you need to do your own return. Yet, in most consultations I've done with people who did their returns using one of these programs, there were problems or mistakes with the return. The most common problem area was depreciation. The programs don't seem to give enough information about what depreciation is, who should take it, and how to calculate it. Also, people are surprised at the amount of time involved in learning and using a tax preparation program. The programs appear to be most useful for those who are familiar with computers and already understand what information goes into the tax return and which schedules to use. The programs can also be helpful for those who want to do "what if" scenarios (e.g., what would happen if we got married by December 31 rather than after January 1?).

If you decide you want to hand your tax work over to someone else, find a qualified tax professional. Searching for a tax preparer is best started by asking for recommendations from friends and colleagues. Try to get referral names from someone who has a business or tax situation similar to yours. It's best to look for a tax preparer as early as possible, rather than beginning your search in March or April.

There are different types of tax preparers, and you will need to decide what level of help you need. Probably you're most familiar with the chain operations. Generally, they are conveniently located and relatively inexpensive. The knowledge, experience, and skill level vary greatly among the personnel who work in these offices. Many of the chain operations pay their workers on commission, which means the preparers are anxious to complete your return quickly and move on to the next customer. Typically, you won't find preparers in this setting who will talk with you extensively about your business or help with planning for the future; but the fee for an individual return with a Schedule C will be among the lowest you'll find. If you use a chain service, you may work with a different preparer each year, so if continuity is important to you, this choice may not be your best bet.

Some states require tax preparers to be licensed. A license may indicate a skill or knowledge level or simply that a minimum number of hours of education have been completed. If your state requires preparers to be licensed, be sure to ask the preparers you interview if they have a current license. Using an unlicensed preparer may be no better than having your brother-in-law prepare your return. I always chuckle when I think of the following true story relayed by a fellow tax preparer:

I met a current client originally at a cocktail party. When she found out what I do for a living, she quickly told me that a neighbor does her taxes. She added that he wasn't really a tax professional. "Actually," she said, "he's a carpenter by trade, but he charges a lot less than a real tax preparer would charge.

I pointed out that that was an incredible coincidence, as I am a tax professional who does carpentry on the side! Of course, I never studied carpentry or apprenticed at it; I just taught myself as best as I could. And I make mistakes. I might use the wrong nails or type of wood for some jobs, and I'm always worried that something I build might someday come crashing down on top of a customer. But, of course, I charge a lot less than a real carpenter.

That woman from the cocktail party has been my client for 5 years now.

The types of preparers discussed in the remainder of this section generally don't fall under state tax preparer licensing regulations because they have their own professional licensing requirements. Attorneys and certified public accountants (CPAs) are licensed by their respective states, whereas enrolled agents (EAs) are licensed by the IRS.

CPAs, enrolled agents, and tax attorneys can attend an IRS audit without you and can argue on your behalf. They can also represent you in other IRS-related matters. Other types of tax preparers can represent a taxpayer without her being present, but only for those tax returns they prepared.

Enrolled agents are either former IRS employees or tax preparers who have passed an exhaustive 2-day exam on tax theory and practice given by the IRS. All enrolled agents specialize in tax return preparation and taxpayer representation; some also do bookkeeping and accounting.

CPAs may or may not prepare individual and small business tax returns. Instead, their focus may be on large corporations, internal audits, or other types of financial services. Although many are, don't make the assumption that all CPAs are knowledgeable about or interested in working with small businesses or preparing individual tax returns.

Tax attorneys are tax specialists who provide the most expensive tax help you can get. Generally it is not appropriate to have a tax attorney prepare your 1040 and Schedule C forms. However, if you are having difficult problems with the IRS or are considering a complicated transaction that has tax ramifications, a tax attorney's expertise may be well worth the cost.

Whichever category of preparer you select, you want to find someone who works regularly with and cares about very small (micro) businesses. Also, you want to make sure she's up to date on current tax law (ask when she took her last update class). You want someone who is available year-round in case you get a letter from the IRS or want to discuss changing your estimated tax payments in June or November. Ask for the names of several of her small business clients whom you can talk to as references.

When you talk to or meet with a potential preparer, listen to your intuition. Of course you want to know practical items, such as how much she charges, whether she does tax planning, how she charges for your phone calls during the year, in what format she expects to receive tax information from you, and whether she'll meet with you personally or hand your tax preparation over to someone else in the firm. At the same time, pay attention to whether the preparer seems to care about you and your small business. Do you feel comfortable asking questions of this person, and does she answer them in a way that you understand? Are you two in sync as to how aggressive or cautious to be in the preparation of your tax return? Although tax laws appear to be black and white, there are many ways to interpret them. You want to work with someone who will prepare your return in the way that's most comfortable for you.

No one wants to be the recipient of the dreaded letter (or, sometimes, phone call) saying, "Your return has been selected for review (audit)." In reality, only a small percentage of people are audited each year. Schedule C filers are audited more often than other taxpayers; but even then, the chances of being audited are only 1% to 4%, depending on the amount of income shown on the return and the part of the country in which the taxpayer lives (some areas have higher audit rates than others).

Partnerships and corporations with less than $100,000 gross income are audited at $1/_3$ the rate of unincorporated businesses. For some taxpayers, this is a sufficient reason to choose to operate as one of those entities rather than as a sole proprietor.

The IRS sends out one hundred million letters to taxpayers each year. Don't assume that a letter from the IRS means you're being audited. The majority of IRS correspondence is not related to audits. You may receive a bill with penalties for not making last year's estimated tax payments on time. Or you may receive a questionnaire asking whether you really qualify to claim your child as a dependent on your tax return. The IRS will contact you if the amounts received in estimated tax payments differ from the amount you listed on your tax return as having been paid. You'll also hear from the IRS if the math on your return is incorrect. None of these letters means that the IRS is auditing you or that it has reviewed your return other than in the specific area mentioned in the letter.

A true audit letter will tell you that your return has been selected for examination. If an appointment date is not indicated, you will be asked to schedule an appointment for the audit within 10 days of the date of the letter. The letter will list the areas the IRS is questioning, and there will be a list of items to bring (or have on hand, if it's a field audit). The list will include bank statements, invoices, receipts, and so on. (Chapter 7 discusses more completely the items the IRS expects you to have.) The letter will also ask you to bring your tax return for the years before and after the year being audited. That doesn't mean those years are being audited too; you're asked to bring those returns in case there are items being carried over from one year to another and, also, so that the auditor can see whether items have been handled similarly from year to year. As with everything else you bring to the audit, do not hand the returns to the auditor unless he or she asks for them.

Don't ever assume your income is too low for you to be audited. Since one major focus of IRS audits is unreported income, a small income may be exactly why you were chosen for an audit. While you may be supported by your family, your lover, or school scholarships, none of those sources are reported on your tax return, so the IRS may be wondering how you're managing to pay for food and rent. The auditor may ask you to list your monthly expenses and the sources of the money used to pay those expenses. The IRS is trying to determine if you could have lived on the amount of income you've reported on your tax return.

Currently, the IRS is not doing random audits. That means there is a specific reason if you're chosen for an audit. For example, your expenses may exceed the average amount for similar businesses. Or maybe you listed a very large amount in one expense category, and the IRS wants to make sure you are entitled to take the full deduction. The 1099 Forms submitted to the IRS may indicate that your income was higher than the amount you reported. Sometimes just putting an item of income or expense on the wrong line of your tax return is enough to trigger an audit. Since the IRS only does an audit when they believe they will be able to assess enough additional tax to pay for the staff time involved, you can assume they're looking at something specific on your return.

In some IRS districts, soon after you receive your audit letter, you are sent a preliminary report of proposed changes. The report points out which areas of the return the IRS is investigating, what unreported income they're aware of (if any), and which expenses they're planning to disallow if you can't prove your case. The report will also indicate the additional taxes and penalties you can expect if you don't show up for the audit or don't win your case. You can choose to accept the report as it is and pay the additional amount due, or you can go to the audit (or have a representative go for you) and argue your case.

Generally, the worst thing that can happen in an audit is that an expense will be disallowed or unreported income will be added to your return. In either case, you are assessed penalties, as well as having to pay the additional tax due. The penalty for not reporting income you received is 50% of the additional tax due (75% for fraud). Only in cases where fraud is suspected or where there is a very large amount of unreported income will the Criminal Investigation Division of the IRS get involved. In general, you don't need to fear being sent to jail if a discrepancy is found during the audit. Although careless mistakes may have been responsible for your being audited in the first place, they are not considered to be fraud.

There are two types of audits: field audits and office audits. If you're scheduled for a field audit, the auditor will come to your place of work to do the audit. Business returns are often handled by field auditors. These auditors are usually more experienced and knowledgeable than office auditors. Often, they will spend several days or longer reviewing your records.

Office audits are held at the nearest IRS office. The auditor carefully writes down all information you provide. However, the initial meeting is likely to last a day or less. If there is additional information needed, you can send or bring it in.

The auditor will begin by asking you a number of questions. She'll ask whether you had income other than that shown on the return (e.g., gifts or loans) and whether you participated in barter transactions. She'll want to know how long you've been in business and exactly how your business operates. Then she'll ask to see your bank statements and records of money deposited. If you invoice your clients or customers, she'll want to see copies of those invoices. Business owners who are required to collect a sales or excise tax will be asked to provide those tax returns for comparison with the income reported on their income tax returns. Then, of course, the auditor will want to see the receipts for their expenses.

The auditor looks at your expense receipts not only to make sure you have them but also to determine whether you were entitled to deduct the expenses. Did you pay them? Are they ordinary and necessary expenses for your business?

Some areas looked at closely in an audit are

- Did you report all money you earned?
- Did you write off personal expenses as business expenses?
- Does your reported income match your lifestyle?
- If you have employees, are you filing the appropriate payroll forms?
- If you have independent contractors, have they been misclassified?

You (or your representative) should go to the audit totally organized. If your business expenses are being investigated, bundle together all the receipts and canceled checks for each expense category shown on your return. If possible, attach to the top of the bundle an adding machine tape showing the total expenses for that category. The auditor will be impressed with your thoroughness, and you may be able to shorten the time spent in the audit. After adding up a few of the bundles and finding that her totals are the same as the totals on your tapes, the auditor may decide to accept your figures and forgo adding up all the receipts. If, in the course of preparing for the audit, you discover some expenses you didn't claim, be sure to take the receipts with you to the audit for use in offsetting any expenses that are disallowed.

The tendency for most taxpayers in an audit is to talk too much. People want to explain how they happened to have that expense and why their friend said it would be deductible. They reveal too much information and prolong the audit with unnecessary chatter. Don't fall into that trap. If you go to an audit, speak only when spoken to and answer concisely only the question you're asked. This is not the place to express hostility about the government or the amount of taxes you're required to pay!

Do you need a tax professional to represent you at an audit? It depends on the issues involved. If they're straightforward and the audit appears to be focused on whether you have receipts to back up the expenses you claimed, you can probably represent yourself. On the other hand, if you deducted expenses that were in a gray area and you need to use previous court cases to back up the deductibility of the expense, you'll probably want a tax professional to go and argue your case for you. Even if you choose to represent yourself, a 1-hour consultation with a tax professional prior to the audit will help you prepare correctly.

Generally, it's not a good idea for taxpayers to accompany their tax professional to the audit; either you should go or she should go. An unaccompanied taxpayer is given some leniency by the auditor because she's an amateur at preparing her return and representing herself. A tax preparer is given a certain respect because the auditor knows that this is a professional who is familiar with tax law. If the taxpayer and tax professional go together, the duo doesn't get the advantage that either would get if she went alone. Sometimes, however, the auditor will insist on meeting with the taxpayer before the audit can be wrapped up.

When shopping for a tax professional, make sure that person will be available to represent you in the event of an audit. Most preparers charge extra for audit representation. As discussed in the previous chapter, while anyone can accompany you to an audit and while the preparer of a tax return can represent that return, only attorneys, CPAs, and enrolled agents can represent all returns (whether or not prepared by them) without the taxpayer being there.

At the end of the audit, one of several things will happen. If expenses are disallowed, you (or your representative) will point out any expenses that weren't claimed on the original return. You'll try to negotiate with the auditor ("I understand why you need to disallow that, but I hope you agree with the appropriateness of accepting this"). The auditor may ask you to send additional information before concluding the audit. If possible, try to go to the audit with everything that might be asked for. When you provide missing information later, it can sometimes disappear in the bowels of the IRS (be sure to send copies, not originals, and send the information by certified mail with return receipt requested). Additionally, since you (or your representative) are not there to argue for its acceptance, the new information may be disregarded.

If everything necessary is at the audit, generally the auditor will conclude the audit before you leave. You will be given a final report showing the changes made. You can sign the report and pay any additional taxes and penalties assessed (or agree to the proposed refund). Or you can appeal the audit decision to the auditor's supervisor, the Appeals Office, or Tax Court.

Not all audits result in your owing taxes. Sometimes the IRS owes you after the audit is completed. Sometimes neither of you owes the other because nothing significant was changed on the return. This is called a "no change" audit and is highly desirable. Not only do you not owe the IRS, but also if you're called for an audit about identical issues for either of the 2 years following the audited year, you can tell the audit office that you had a "no change" for those items within the prior 2 years. Sometimes the audit will be called off, although cancellations due to a repetitive audit happen less frequently for Schedule C filers than for other types of returns.

HOW LONG DO YOU NEED TO KEEP RECORDS?

40

Although most audits occur within 24 months of the time you file your return, the IRS actually has 3 years in which to examine your return. The statute of limitations increases to 6 years if the IRS believes that your return involves substantial understatement of income (i.e., more than 25% of your income was not reported). If you didn't file a return, there is no statute of limitations protecting you from an IRS investigation.

Most audits occur at the federal level, and then the IRS notifies the state of the results: this usually takes some time. Because the state also wants to be able to collect from you in cases where, as a result of the audit, more income or fewer expenses are allowed, most states have a statute of limitations that exceeds that of the IRS. In California, for example, the tax department has 4 years in which to contact you about your return.

Obviously, you'll want to hold on to all records (receipts, canceled checks, IRS correspondence, etc.) connected with your tax return until the statute of limitations runs out for all applicable taxing agencies. This will be between 3 and 5 years from the date you filed your return or paid the tax, whichever comes later. After that time, you can dispose of receipts, invoices, and canceled checks for most items related to a particular return.

The receipts for any assets you bought (e.g., computer, car, office furniture) that you're still using should be kept for as long as you own that asset, plus 3 to 5 years. Receipts related to a house you own (whether or not the home is used for business) should be kept for 5 years after it is sold.

Copies of your tax returns should be kept forever. They take up very little space and, if they serve no other purpose, the nostalgia element alone makes them worth holding on to. You never know when you may need something contained on a return from years ago.

> Marny, a self-employed house cleaner, was in an automobile accident last year and was unable to work for 6 months. The other party was at fault. When settling with the other driver's insurance company, Marny needed a way to show how her income had been reduced by not being able to work after the accident. Her tax returns from the previous 5 years provided her with the actual numbers she needed to present to the insurance company.

Each year, for 20 years, Judy contributed money to an IRA account. Many of those years she had no other retirement account, but some years she was covered by an employer's pension plan. In the years she was part of another plan, Judy's IRA contribution wasn't deductible, so when she removes the money, there will be no tax due on those amounts. If Judy hasn't kept her tax returns for all the years she put money into an IRA, she won't know how many of the contributions were deductible and, therefore, how much of her distribution is taxable.

Once you finish preparing a tax return, put all the receipts, canceled checks, and related materials into a box and label it with that year's date. Put it up on a closet shelf, in the basement, or in some other storage place. You don't need to pay any further attention to that box until 4 or 5 years later (when you'll throw most of it out); but it's comforting to know the records are there if you need them.

THE END
(WHICH IS REALLY THE BEGINNING)

41

If you've made it this far in this book, you should have most of the information you need to keep on track with your business finances. I know that sometimes it seems overwhelming, and also there may be times when you wonder if it's really worth being self-employed. Just remember, you've managed to become an expert in your field. Although you're capable of doing so, it may not be imperative that you also become an expert in the tax and recordkeeping field.

I recently met with Lauren to prepare her tax return. Since she was a new client, I asked about her computer consulting business. For half an hour, she talked with enthusiasm and answered my questions about the Internet and the nine online message boards she coordinates. As a neophyte in cyberspace, I understood only a portion of what she was talking about, but her enthusiasm was contagious. Finally, I told Lauren we needed to talk about her taxes. I began asking her questions about various items to be included on her tax return. Little by little, I saw the enthusiasm leave Lauren's face as she realized she didn't know the answers to some of my questions. Perhaps she felt she should have a better knowledge of her finances. Maybe she thought I would think less of her abilities because she didn't understand what I was asking for.

What was apparent to me is that Lauren is an expert in her field and loves her work. I'm also an expert in my field and love my work (most of the time!). Eventually I hope to have a better understanding of the Internet, and I know that one day Lauren will have a better understanding of her business taxes. For either of us to feel stupid for not being experts in each other's fields doesn't make sense.

Not understanding everything we'd like to know doesn't mean we're unable to learn. There is a lot of information in the world; most of us are still in the process of grasping that which we think will be meaningful for us.

When it comes to recordkeeping and taxes, there may be a limit as to how much you want to learn before passing the work on to an expert in the field. Or you may decide that you want to learn enough to be comfortable in preparing your own tax returns. Having reached this point in the book, you're off to a great start.

However you use what you've learned here, may your business prosper!

APPENDICES

HOW TO
RECONCILE A
BANK STATEMENT

Chapter 6 provides general information about balancing your checkbook and reconciling it to your bank statement. The instructions here take you through the process in detail.

Usually the back of the bank statement has an area in which to do the reconciliation. The following steps can be done on the back of the statement or on a separate piece of paper:

1. Make a list of all outstanding checks, including the check number and amount. These are checks that you've written but that don't yet show on the bank statement as having been cashed.

2. Make a list of all outstanding deposits. These are deposits that you have made to your account but that don't yet show up on your bank statement.

3. Begin with the ending bank balance as shown on the bank statement. Subtract from that number the total of the outstanding checks and add to it the total of the outstanding deposits. This will give you an adjusted bank balance.

4. In your check register, enter all the transactions that show up on your bank statement but that have not yet been entered into your own records. These might include unrecorded bank service fees, automatic transfers between bank accounts, interest earned on the account, ATM withdrawals, and automatic bill payments. Be sure to add those that should be added (credits) and to subtract those that should be subtracted (debits).

5. Having made the adjustments in your check register, calculate your new checkbook balance.

6. Compare your adjusted bank balance to your new checkbook balance.

If the two still don't match, try the following:

- Check the addition and subtraction in your checkbook by going back to the last date in which the checkbook balance matched the bank balance. Recalculate all transactions since that date. Be sure you didn't add a transaction when you should have subtracted it, and vice versa.
- See whether the amount of the discrepancy matches a check or a deposit amount.

- Compare, one by one, the amounts of the checks and deposits on the bank statement with the amounts entered in your checkbook. If the difference between the checkbook balance and the bank statement balance can be divided by 9, there is likely a transposition error (the correct numerals are recorded, but they're entered in the wrong order). For example, if your bank statement balance is $101.92 and your checkbook balance is $101.29, the difference is $.63, which can be divided by 9. Most likely a check was entered in the checkbook for a different amount than was actually written on the check. Sometimes the numerical amount on a check is different from the written-out amount (a mistake was made when the check was written). Look at the bank statement to see which amount was used when the check was cashed.
- Review the bank statement for any entries you haven't picked up. Occasionally an amount is subtracted without a check number being listed next to the amount. Make sure you haven't counted the corresponding check as outstanding.
- Compare the amount of the discrepancy to the outstanding checks and deposits on your prior month's bank statement to see whether it matches any of those.
- If you have carbon checks, the amounts on the duplicates are sometimes not very legible. Verify that you subtracted the correct amount from your checkbook balance.

Don't assume that the amount of the discrepancy between the bank statement and your checkbook balance is the amount you need to find. For example, if the balances differ by $204.34, it may be because you didn't record a deposit for one amount and a check for another, which together total $204.34.

If the discrepancy is large, that doesn't mean it will be harder to find. A discrepancy of $650.00 is usually no harder to locate than one of $6.50.

Banks rarely make mistakes that show up on the bank statement, but it is possible. With the use of computers, mistakes in calculations are unlikely. More likely, a bank error occurs when the bank cashes a check for an amount different from the one you wrote. This type of error is caught when you compare the check amounts on the bank statement to those noted in your check register.

If you still can't get the two balances to match, take your bank statement and checkbook to the bank and ask someone to help you. Some banks now charge for this service.

Once you have a reconciled balance, draw a line in your check register and enter the new balance. Next month, if the bank statement and checkbook balances don't match, it will be helpful to know at what point you last had an accurate balance.

HOW TO **CALCULATE ESTIMATED**
TAX PAYMENTS:
A STEP-BY-STEP EXAMPLE

For general information about who needs to make estimated tax payments and how to calculate the amounts due, refer to Chapters 35 and 36. The example here will provide you with specific instructions for performing each step in the estimated tax calculation. There is extra space on these pages for you to fill in your own numbers, and calculate your own estimated tax figures.

First let's look at Erin's situation and her calculation. All the numbers in Erin's calculation have been rounded to the nearest dollar. Also, since year 2000 tax rates were not yet available when this book went to press, 1999 rates have been used in conjunction with personal exemption and standard deduction amounts for 2000.

It's April 13. Erin has an estimated tax payment due on April 15 for income she received during the period from January 1 to March 31. This is her first year of self-employment, she is single, and she does not itemize her personal deductions but instead takes the standard deduction. Erin has no dependents (so is able to take an exemption for only herself), and this year she has no income other than self-employment income. Because she operates a hair salon, Erin receives all income as she earns it. She does her bookkeeping and taxes on a cash basis. Obviously those factors make the following example as simple as possible. If your situation is different from Erin's (e.g., you're married, you have some income from wages or another source, or you itemize your personal deductions), you will need to adjust your figures accordingly.

Erin has been keeping very good records of her income and expenses. When she reviews them, she discovers that she has had $4,000 net profit from her business for the first quarter. Remember, net profit is after business expenses have been deducted. Because she's never been self-employed before, Erin has no idea what she is going to earn this year. Using her first quarter profit as a guide, Erin guesses that she might have a $4,000 profit in each of the following quarters. She multiplies this quarter's $4,000 by four quarters to calculate the amount she expects to earn for the year, thus projecting that her net self-employment income for the year will be $16,000.

To begin figuring her tax liability, Erin first calculates the self-employment tax on her projected $16,000 net profit. To do this, she multiplies the $16,000 by 92.35% and then by the 15.3% self-employment tax rate. The result is a projected self-employment tax of $2,261 for the year.

Next, from Erin's $16,000 projected income, she subtracts her personal exemption of $2,800, her standard deduction of $4,400, and half of her projected self-employment tax. The result is a projected taxable income for the year of $7,670. If you've forgotten what the personal exemption and standard deduction are, review page 133. When Erin looks at the tax rate schedule (page 146), she sees that the 15% tax bracket covers taxable income between zero and $25,750. Since $7,670 is within that range, Erin's projected income tax is 15% of $7,670, or $1,151.

Adding Erin's projected self-employment tax of $2,261 to her projected federal income tax of $1,151 equals a total tax for the year of $3,412. Erin divides the $3,412 into four quarterly payments and sends in one quarter, or $853, on April 15.

On June 15, Erin's second quarterly payment is due. This payment is for income earned during the period from April 1 through May 31. Notice that the second quarter is only a 2-month quarter. The first and third quarters are 3 months each. The second quarter is 2 months, and the fourth quarter is 4 months. Could this be an IRS plot to confuse us even more?

CALCULATIONS ERIN DID THIS QUARTER:

		YOUR CALCULATIONS:
$ 4,000	net profit from self-employment	
× 4	number of quarters in a year	× 4
$ 16,000	projected net profit for the year	
× 92.35%	self-employed people pay self-employment tax on 92.35% of their net self-employment earnings	× 92.35%
$ 14,776		
× 15.3%	this is the self-employment tax rate	× 15.3%
$ 2,261	projected self-employment tax for the year	
$ 16,000	projected net profit for the year	
− $ 2,800	personal exemption, available for each taxpayer, spouse, and dependent	
− $ 4,400	standard deduction for single taxpayers ($7,350 for married taxpayers)	
− $1,130	½ of the projected self-employment tax	
$ 7,670	projected taxable income for the year	
× 15%	federal income tax rate for this amount of income	× (see tax rate schedule)
$ 1,151	projected federal income tax for the year	
$ 2,261	projected self-employment tax for the year	
+ $ 1,151	projected federal income tax for the year	
$ 3,412	total tax liability for the year	
÷ 4	the 4 quarters of the year	÷ 4
$ 853	amount Erin needs to send this quarter	

In calculating the payment due for the second quarter, an extra step is needed because the payment covers only 2 months. In the first quarter, Erin had $4,000 net profit from self-employment. In the second quarter, her profit was $12,000. Erin adds the two quarters together and sees that in 5 months she's earned $16,000. Her $15,000 net income year to date divided by the 5 months that have gone by equals $3,200 per month. Erin needs to project her income for the year based on what she's already earned, so she multiplies the $3,200 monthly net profit by 12 months; the result is projected income for the year of $38,400. This is radically different from the $16,000 annual income she projected when she did this calculation last quarter.

The remaining steps for this quarter's calculation are similar to those done last quarter. Erin next calculates her self-employment tax by multiplying the $38,400 by 92.35%, then by 15.3%. The result is a projected self-employment tax for the year of $5,426. She then subtracts her personal exemption, the standard deduction, and half of her projected self-employment tax from her $38,400 projected income. The result is $28,487 projected taxable income for the year.

As shown on the tax rate schedules, the 15% tax bracket for single people ends at $25,750. Since Erin's projected taxable income is over that amount, most of it will be taxed at 15%, but a small portion of it will be taxed at 28%. After doing the income tax calculation, Erin discovers that her projected income tax for the year is $4,629. She adds this amount to the $5,426 projected self-employment tax, and it now appears that her total tax for the year will be $10,055.

Erin has two choices at this point. She can send in just a quarter's worth of that amount ($2,514) to cover the second quarter. Or she can catch up with the amount she really owes the IRS at this point in time. Since she thought she would be earning so much less this year, her payment last quarter doesn't equal a quarter of what it now appears her total tax liability will be. Erin decides that she doesn't want to have to come up with a large amount of money for taxes next April. She would rather send enough now so that the sum of her April and June payments equals two quarters' worth of the total taxes that will be due for this year. She divides the $10,055 total tax liability by 4, multiplies it by 2 (for the two quarters that have gone by), which results in a total amount due for the two quarters of $5,028. Since Erin sent in $853 last quarter, she sends in the remaining $4,175 this quarter. This is a large amount to pay on her $12,000 income, but Erin is making up for the small amount sent in the first quarter.

When Erin files her tax return in April, the IRS will notice that Erin paid different amounts for the first and second quarters. The IRS will assume that Erin's income was the same both quarters and will think that Erin underpaid the amount owed for the first quarter. They will be ready to penalize Erin unless she sends Form 2210 with her tax return (see page 151–152) to show the IRS her first-quarter income and why she paid only $853 for that quarter. This information will enable them to see that she sent in the correct amount based on her true income.

CALCULATIONS ERIN DID THIS QUARTER:		YOUR CALCULATIONS:
$ 4,000	profit earned first quarter	
+ $ 12,000	profit earned second quarter	
$ 16,000	total profit for the first 5 months	
÷ 5	number of months that have gone by	÷ 5
$ 3,200	average net profit per month	
× 12	number of months in the year	× 12
$ 38,400	projected profit for the year	
× 92.35%	self-employed people pay self-employment tax on 92.35% of their net self-employment earnings	× 92.35%
$ 35,462		
× 15.3%	self-employment tax rate	× 15.3%
$ 5,426	projected self-employment tax for the year	
$ 38,400	projected net profit for the year	
− $2,800	personal exemption, available for each taxpayer, spouse, and dependent	
− $4,400	standard deduction for single taxpayers ($7,350 for married taxpayers)	
− $ 2,713	half of the projected self-employment tax	
$ 28,487	projected taxable income for the year	
− $ 25,750	15% bracket goes up to this amount for single people	
$ 2,737		
× 28%	federal income tax rate for a single person with taxable income over $25,750 and less than $62,450	× (see tax rate schedule)
$ 766	28% tax on this portion of the income	
+ 3,863	15% tax on the first $25,750 taxable income	
$ 4,629	projected federal income tax for the year	
$ 4,629	projected federal income tax for the year	
+ 5,426	projected self-employment tax for the year	
$ 10,055	total tax liability for the year	
÷ 4	the four quarters of the year	÷ 4
$ 2,514		
× 2	with this payment, Erin wants to have paid in 2 quarters' worth of the tax she'll owe	× 2
$ 5,028		
− $ 853	amount Erin sent first quarter	
$ 4,175	amount Erin needs to send this quarter	

CALCULATIONS ERIN DID THIS QUARTER:

YOUR CALCULATIONS:

$ 4,000	profit earned first quarter	....
+ $ 12,000	profit earned second quarter	....
+ $ 8,000	profit earned third quarter	_____
$ 24,000	total profit for first 8 months	....
÷ 8	number of months that have gone by	÷ 8
$ 3,000	average net profit per month	_____
× 12	number of months in the year	....
$ 36,000	projected profit for the year	× 12
× 92.35%	self-employed people pay self-employment tax on 92.35% of their net self-employment earnings	....
		× 92.35%
$ 33,246		_____
× 15.3%	self-employment tax rate	....
$ 5,087	projected self-employment tax for the year	× 15.3%
		....
$ 36,000	projected net profit for the year	....
− $2,800	personal exemption, available for each taxpayer, spouse, and dependent	....
− $4,400	standard deduction for single taxpayers ($7,350 for married taxpayers)	....
− $2,544	half of the projected self-employment tax	_____
$ 26,256	projected taxable income for the year	....
− $ 25,750	15% bracket goes up to this amount for single people	_____
$ 506	amount to be taxed at 28%	....
× 28%	federal income tax rate for a single person with taxable income over $25,750 and less than $62,450	× (see tax rate schedule)
$ 142	28% tax on this portion of the income	_____
+ $3,863	15% tax on the first $25,750 of taxable income	....
$ 4,005	projected federal income tax for the year	_____
		....
$ 4,005	projected federal income tax for the year	....
+ $5,087	projected self-employment tax for the year	_____
$ 9,092	total federal tax liability for the year	....
÷ 4	the four quarters of the year	÷ 4
$ 2,273		_____
× 3	with this payment, Erin wants to have paid in three quarters' worth of the tax she'll owe	× 3
		_____
$ 6,819		....
− $853	amount Erin sent first quarter	....
− $4,175	amount Erin sent second quarter	_____
$1,791	amount Erin needs to send this quarter	....

Just prior to the third-quarter payment due date, Erin again calculates the amount she needs to send. Payment is due on September 15 for money received between June 1 and August 31. Erin estimates her income for the year by adding together the $4,000 she earned in the first quarter, the $12,000 from the second quarter, and the $8,000 she earned in the third quarter. Adding those quarterly figures together, Erin sees that her year-to-date income is $24,000. She divides that figure by the 8 months that have gone by and gets an average income of $3,000 a month. She multiplies that figure by 12 months, which results in a yearly projected income of $36,000, very similar to what she projected last quarter, which was $38,400.

As in the previous quarters, Erin calculates the self-employment tax on $36,000. It is $5,087. She then subtracts out her personal exemption, her standard deduction, and half of her projected self-employment tax from $36,000. The end result is projected taxable income for the year of $26,256. Again, most of this amount is taxed in the 15% tax bracket, but some of it will be taxed at the 28% rate because it's more than $25,750. The income tax on Erin's projected taxable income is $4,005. Her estimated self-employment tax is $5,087, for a total projected tax for the year of $9,092. Erin divides that figure by the four quarters of the year. By the time she makes this payment, Erin wants to have sent in three quarters' worth of tax, or $6,819. So far she's sent in $5,028, leaving her $1,791 to send in this quarter.

On January 15, Erin's final payment of the previous year's tax is due. Since the tax year ended December 31, theoretically by this time Erin knows what she earned during the previous year. It turns out that Erin's net profit for the year was $30,000. This is quite a bit more than the $16,000 she originally projected, but it is less than the $38,400 and $36,000 she estimated in the second and third quarters.

Again Erin does the estimated tax calculation. The self-employment tax on her $30,000 net profit is $4,239. Erin subtracts her personal exemption, her standard deduction, and half of her self-employment tax from the $30,000 profit. The result is taxable income for the year of $20,680. This means that Erin is being taxed totally in the 15% income tax bracket because $20,680 is less than $25,750. The income tax on $20,680 is $3,102. Erin's total tax (income tax plus self-employment tax) for the year is $7,341. So far she's sent in $6,819 during the year, leaving her only $522 to pay for this quarter. Erin pays this very small amount because she overpaid in the second and third quarters, when she thought her taxable income for the year would be more. Erin pays the remainder of her estimated taxes on January 15 and files her tax return on April 15. No additional tax is due with her return.

CALCULATIONS ERIN DID THIS QUARTER:		YOUR CALCULATIONS:
$ 30,000	net profit for the year	....
× 92.35%	self-employed people pay self-employment tax on 92.35% of their net self-employment earnings	× 92.35%
$ 27,705		_____
× 15.3%	self-employment tax rate	....
$ 4,239	self-employment tax for the year	× 15.3%
		....
$ 30,000	net profit for the year	
– $2,800	personal exemption, available for each taxpayer, spouse, and dependent	....
– $4,400	standard deduction for single taxpayers ($7,350 for married taxpayers)	....
– $2,120	half of the self-employment tax	....
$ 20,680	taxable income for the year	_____
× 15%	federal income tax rate for this amount of income	....
$ 3,102	federal income tax for the year	× (see tax rate schedule)
		....
$ 3,102	federal income tax for the year	
+ 4,239	self-employment tax for the year	....
$ 7,341	total federal tax liability for the year	_____
– $853	amount Erin sent first quarter	....
– $4,175	amount Erin sent second quarter	....
– $1,791	amount Erin sent third quarter	....
$ 522	remaining tax liability to send this quarter	_____
		....

And that's how you do the estimated tax calculation!

SMALL BUSINESS
OWNERS

This section provides lists of resources helpful to small business owners. They include groups, publications, and Web sites of particular interest to women entrepreneurs.

TAXING AGENCIES

As you know, the Internal Revenue Service (IRS) is the federal agency that deals with your taxes—individual, business, and payroll. The IRS telephone number is 1-800-829-1040 (1-800-829-4059 for TTY/TDD help). One particularly helpful IRS department is the Problem Resolution Office. If you've had ongoing correspondence with the IRS over an issue that hasn't been resolved, you can call the main number and ask that your case be assigned to a worker in Problem Resolution. The personnel in that department will help to resolve the issue.

Unless you live in one of the states that doesn't have an income tax, your state has an agency that performs functions parallel to those of the IRS. A list of those state agencies can be found on page 184. In some states, this is the agency that handles your personal and business tax return, while a different agency deals with payroll taxes if you have employees.

If your state has an excise or sales tax and your product or service is taxable, look in the white (or blue) pages of your phone book, in the state section, to find the agency responsible for collecting this tax.

Look in the same area of the phone book, in the city section, to see if there's a business license division. If so, contact that office about requirements for operating your business within the city.

Some areas have "one-stop shops," which are a collaboration between city and county agencies to provide all the needed information about licenses, permits, sales taxes, and so on, in one location.

CLASSES, WORKSHOPS, AND INDIVIDUAL COUNSELING

The IRS offers free small business tax seminars covering general information for entrepreneurs, as well as tax information for employers. Check with your local IRS office for upcoming programs.

The Small Business Administration (SBA), a federal government agency, offers free and low-cost workshops for new and potential business owners. SBA centers may also offer small business management and computer classes and/or include a BIC (Business Information Center) that provides books, magazines, software, and other valuable resources for small business owners.

PHONE NUMBERS OF STATE TAX OFFICES

State Web site addresses are not included since they change frequently; http://www.irs.ustreas.gov/prod/forms_pubs/ftaframes.html provides a link from the IRS Web site to each state's site.

Alabama Department of Revenue
(334)242-1000

Alaska Department of Revenue
(907)465-2320

Arizona Department of Revenue
(800)352-4090

Arkansas Department of Finance
(800)882-9275

California Franchise Tax Board
(800)852-5711

Colorado Department of Revenue
(303)232-2446

Connecticut Department of Revenue
(800)382-9463

Delaware Department of Revenue
(302)577-3300

Florida Department of Revenue
(850)488-6800

Georgia Department of Revenue
(404)656-6286

Hawaii Department of Taxation
(800)222-3229

Idaho Department of Revenue and Taxation
(208)334-7770

Illinois Department of Revenue
(800)732-8866

Indiana Department of Revenue
(317)232-2240

Iowa Department of Revenue
(800)367-3388

Kansas Department of Revenue
(785)296-2461

Kentucky Revenue Cabinet
(502)564-4581

Louisiana Department of Revenue
(225)925-4611

Maine Revenue Service
(207)626-8475

Maryland Revenue Administration
(800)MD-TAXES

Massachusetts Department of Revenue
(800)392-6089

Michigan Department of the Treasury
(800)487-7000

Minnesota Department of Revenue
(800)652-9094

Mississippi State Tax Commission
(601)923-7300

Missouri Department of Revenue
(573)751-7191

Montana Department of Revenue
(406)444-3674

Nebraska Department of Revenue
(800)742-7474

Nevada Department of Taxation
(775)687-4892

New Hampshire Department of Revenue
(603)271-2191

New Jersey Division of Taxation
(609)292-6400

New Mexico Taxation & Revenue
Department
(505)827-0700

New York State Department of Taxation and
Finance
(800)225-5829

North Carolina Department of Revenue
(919)733-4684

North Dakota Tax Commissioner
(701)328-2770

Ohio Department of Taxation
(800)282-1780

Oklahoma Tax Commission
(405)521-3160

Oregon Department of Revenue
(800)356-4222

Pennsylvania Department of Revenue
(717)787-8201

Rhode Island Division of Taxation
(401)222-3911

South Carolina Department of Revenue
(800)763-1295

South Dakota Department of Revenue
(605)773-3311

Tennessee Department of Revenue
(800)342-1003

Texas Comptroller of Public Accounts
(800)252-5555

Utah State Tax Commission
(800) 662-4335

Vermont Department of Taxes
(802) 828-2557

Virginia Department of Taxation
(804)367-8031

Washington Department of Revenue
(800)647-7706

Washington, D.C., Department of Finance
and Revenue
(202)727-6103

West Virginia State Tax Department
(800)982-8297

Wisconsin Department of Revenue
(608)266-1911

Wyoming Department of Revenue
(307)777-7961

The SBA Web site *www.sba.gov* offers free online classes in subjects of interest to entrepreneurs. Classes are offered in Spanish, as well as English.

The SBA also funds the Service Corps of Retired Executives (SCORE), a group that offers free business counseling. Participants in this program are matched with a retired person who has operated a similar business and can provide guidance and support. In addition to in-person counseling, SCORE offers online help via e-mail. To find the location of the nearest SCORE program, look in the "United States Government" section of the phone book or go online to *www.score.org*

Other very helpful resources are the Small Business Development Centers (SBDCs) and Small Business Institutes located throughout the country. These organizations are funded jointly by the SBA and large corporations and are usually affiliated with local colleges. They offer free and low-cost workshops and individual counseling, specifically geared to small businesses. To locate your nearest SBDC, check with local colleges or look in the "Business Development" section of the SBA Web site at *www.sbaonline.sba.gov/SBDC*

Nationwide there are more than sixty-five SBA Women's Business Centers that provide training and individual counseling specifically for women entrepreneurs. The list of centers, as well as information about SBA loans and services designed for women can be found at *www.onlinewbc.org/docs/wbcs/index.html* An online SBA Women's Business Center is at *www.onlinewbc.org*

Small business classes are also often offered through adult education and community college programs.

On pages 186–187 is a listing of a number of national organizations that are helpful to women-owned businesses. Many have local chapters as well. While these organizations don't usually offer individual counseling, most have speaker and seminar programs, where you can make invaluable contacts with other small business owners. Some of the larger organizations may also offer such benefits as health insurance and travel discounts to their members.

TELEPHONE AND AUDIOTAPE HELP

The IRS offers telephone help with your tax questions. However, you may find that calling the IRS more than once with the same question will result in two or more dissimilar answers. If you prepare your tax return based on an answer you receive from the IRS, you are not protected from penalties if it turns out that you were given an incorrect answer. The IRS telephone number is 1-800-829-1040 (1-800-829-4059 for TTY/TDD help).

TeleTax is a program of taped information offered through the IRS. Two to three-minute tapes on various tax topics can be accessed twenty-four hours a day. Sample topics are "Who Must File a Tax Return" (tape 351) and "Business Use of Your Home" (tape 509). To listen to the TeleTax tapes, call (800) 829-4477. These topics are also available online at *www.irs.ustreas.gov/prod/tax_edu/teletax/index.html*

WOMEN ENTREPRENEUR AND SMALL BUSINESS ORGANIZATIONS

American Business Women's Association (ABWA)
9100 Ward Parkway
P.O. Box 8728
Kansas City, MS 64114-0728
(816) 361-6621
www.abwahq.org/
There are 2100 local chapters throughout the country. Seminars, magazine, and corporate discounts available to members.

Home Based Working Moms
P.O. Box 500164
Austin, TX 78750
(512) 266-0900
www.hbwm.com
Online and in-print magazines. Online bulletin board.

Independent Means
126 Powers Avenue
Santa Barbara, CA 93103
(800) 350-1816
www.anincomeofherown.com
Conferences and Camp Start Up offered for girls and young women, encouraging them to consider self-employment as they think about career choices.

National Association for Female Executives (NAFE)
135 W. 50th Street, 16th Floor
New York, NY 10022
(800) 634-NAFE
www.nafe.com
Nearly 200,000 members in affiliated chapters throughout the country. Programs are geared to corporate employees as well as to self-employed women. Offers health insurance, as well as other benefits to members.

National Association of Women Business Owners (NAWBO)
1100 Wayne Avenue, Suite 830
Silver Spring, MD 20910
(301) 608-2590
www.nawbo.org
Chapters throughout the U.S. Emphasis on building networks with other members. Speakers, conferences, and corporate discounts for members.

National Federation of Business and Professional Women's Clubs, Inc. (BPW)
2012 Massachusetts Avenue NW
Washington, DC 20036
(202) 293-1100
www.bpwusa.org
More than 200,000 members in sixty countries. Local chapters in cities throughout the U.S.

Women Incorporated
333 S. Grand Avenue, Ste. 2450
Los Angeles, CA 90071
(800) 930-3993
www.womeninc.com
Seminars for women business owners, loan programs, and corporate discounts.

Work At Home Moms (WAHM)
Box 366, Folsom CA 95763
(916) 985-2078
www.wahm.com
Print newsletter, online bulletin board, support, and information.

ONLINE SUPPORT AND RESOURCES

There are many online areas of interest to small business owners. Following are some sites that are specifically for women entrepreneurs or are especially helpful to all small business owners.

Helpful Web sites are also included in the information about agencies, classes, and groups listed earlier in this chapter.

Tax Sites

The IRS web page is at *www.irs.ustreas.gov/prod/cover.html* Federal tax forms and publications can be downloaded, and the answers to frequently asked questions are posted on this site. Links are available from this site to the 50 state sites.

www.fairmark.com Easy-to-understand tax site covering various topics. The focus is not self-employment but there are articles on retirement plans, investing, and making estimated tax payments.

www.naea.org Web site of the National Association of Enrolled Agents. Tax information, links to other tax sites, and nationwide directory for finding a tax advisor.

www.quicken.com Articles and message boards on various tax topics, including self-employment.

www.smbiz.com Easily understandable tax articles applicable to small businesses.

www.taxmamma.com Easy-to-understand tax articles and free e-mail tax newsletter.

www.taxsites.com Links to tax, accounting, and related resources on the Internet.

www.taxweb.com Tax information and links to other tax sites.

www.toolkit.cch.com Web site for Commerce Clearing House, a business that provides research materials for tax professionals. They've created a small business site with easy-to-understand explanations of tax laws and other business financial requirements.

Small Business Sites

az@azriela.com The e-mail address for Azriella Jaffe, author of *Honey, I Want to Start my Own Business: A Planning Guide for Couples; Let's Go Into Business Together: Eight Secrets to Successful Business Partnering*; and other business books. Azriella writes several free online newsletters including the *Entrepreneurial Couples Success Letter* that is designed to help business owners build a thriving business while enjoying an intimate relationship with spouse and family.

www.crafter.com/brabec Web site hosted by Barbara Brabec, author of *The Crafts Business Answer Book; Handmade for Profit*, and others. Focus is on the business side of making and selling crafts.

www.edgeonline.com Sponsored by the nonprofit Edward Lowe Foundation (he was the inventor of Kitty Litter), this site contains articles and tools to help entrepreneurs grow their businesses.

www.entreworld.org Sponsored by the Kauffman Foundation Center for Entrepreneurial Leadership, this site includes all kinds of information for new and not-so-new businesses.

www.gohome.com Helpful online magazine for entrepreneurs.

www.isquare.com The Small Business Advisor site. Resources and articles for small business owners. Free e-mail newsletter.

www.lowe.org/smallbiznet This Lowe Foundation site contains thousands of searchable documents, providing all kinds of information about running your own business. E-mail newsletter.

www.nolo.com Web site of Nolo Press, publishers of excellent law books for the layperson. Includes excerpts from their books and articles on related subjects.

www.paulandsarah.com Small business Web site hosted by Paul and Sarah Edwards, entrepreneur gurus and authors of many books about self-employment.

www.smalloffice.com The Web site for Home Office Computing and Small Business Computing magazines. Lots of small business information.

www.smartbiz.com Small business resources

www.startupbiz.com Small business resources

www.workingsolo.com Hosted by Terri Lonier, author of *Working Solo* and other small business books. In addition to articles and information helpful to small business owners, this site contains searchable portions of *Terri's Working Solo Sourcebook* which is packed with useful resources. Free e-mail newsletter.

Women in Business Sites

Major women's content sites such as *www.women.com*, *womenCONNECT.com*, and *www.ivillage.com* provide articles and message boards for women entrepreneurs.

www.advancingwomen.com Business center and tools for entrepreneurs and employees.

www.att.com/wib/ AT&T's Women in Business Web site. Message boards and business tools.

www.bizymoms.com Hosted by Liz Folger, author of *The Stay-at-Home Mom's Guide to Making Money*, this is a site for moms with (or wanting to have) home businesses.

www.digital-women.com Lots of freebies, e-mail newsletter, marketing tips, etc., for women in business.

www.en-parent.com Co-hosted by Lisa Roberts, author of *How to Raise a Family and a Career Under One Roof: A Parent's Guide to Home Business*, this site offers support and an e-mail newsletter for work-at-home moms.

www.fodreams.com Web site for the *Field Of Dreams*, a support site for women business owners. Free e-mail newsletter and My Online Mentor.

www.homeworkingmom.com Web site for Mothers' Home Business Network.

www.mlmwoman.com Bulletin boards, newsletter, and other tools for women involved in multilevel marketing.

www.pleiades-net.com Message boards for women entrepreneurs.

www.sbaonline.sba.gov/hotlist/women.html A link from the Small Business Administrations' Web site, this page contains an extensive list of non-SBA women-oriented sites.

www.witi.com Web site for Women in Technology International. Job listings and message boards.

www.womanowned.com The Web site for Woman Owned Workplaces Network. Lots of information, a message board, and links to other small business resources.

www.wwork.com The Women's Work site. Articles on work, using your computer, making your personal life less stressful, and lots more.

SELECTED IRS PUBLICATIONS OF INTEREST TO BUSINESS TAXPAYERS

1	Your Rights as a Taxpayer
15	Employer's Tax Guide
15A	Employer's Supplemental Tax Guide
17	Your Federal Income Tax (for individuals)
51	Agricultural Employer's Tax Guide
225	Farmer's Tax Guide
334	Tax Guide for Small Business
463	Travel, Entertainment, Gift, and Car Expenses
505	Tax Withholding and Estimated Tax
509	Tax Calendar for the Year
533	Self-Employment Tax
535	Business Expenses
536	Net Operating Losses
538	Accounting Periods and Methods
541	Tax Information on Partnerships
542	Tax Information on Corporations
544	Sales and Other Dispositions of Assets
551	Basis of Assets
553	Highlights of Tax Changes
556	Examination of Returns, Appeal Rights, and Claims For Refund
560	Retirement Plans for Small Business
583	Starting a Business and Keeping Records
587	Business Use of Your Home
589	Tax Information on S-Corporations
595	Tax Guide for Commercial Fisherman
910	Guide to Free Tax Services
911	Direct Sellers
946	How to Depreciate Property
954	Tax Incentives for Empowerment Zones
969	Medical Savings Accounts
1518	Tax Calendar for Small Businesses
1542	Per Diem Rates
1544	Reporting Cash Payments of Over $10,000

BOOKS AND OTHER PUBLICATIONS

PUBLICATIONS

The Small Business Administration (SBA) has a number of low-cost publications helpful to small business owners. The SBA's phone number is in the blue or white section of the phone book, in the "United States Government" section or find them online at *http://www.sbaonline.sba.gov*

Some cities publish booklets, with names such as *Starting a Business in [Name of city]* which will tell you all the requirements for operating a business in your locale. Your city or state Chamber of Commerce may publish a business guide specific to your area.

Check also with any professional associations to which you belong for publications that might be helpful.

A list of relevant IRS publications can be found on page 189 The IRS publication that covers the issues of most concern to sole proprietors is Publication 334, *Tax Guide for Small Businesses*. Booklets covering corporation and partnership tax law are also available. To get these publications, you can call the IRS (delivery may take several weeks), go to an IRS office, or download them from the IRS Web site at *www.irs.ustreas.gov/prod/cover.html*

One IRS publication directed especially to new small businesses is the annual *Tax Tips Calendar for Small Businesses.* This oversized calendar contains helpful hints, general tax information, a listing of the most common tax filing dates, and more. For a free copy, call 1-800-829-3676 and ask for Publication 1518, catalog number 12350Z.

Small Business Success is an annual magazine with excellent articles and extensive resources. Published by Pacific Bell. Call for a free copy (800) 848-8000.

There are a number of small business magazines which you can find at bookstores and libraries. Among them are *Home Office Computing, Entrepreneur, Home Business Magazine, Black Enterprise,* and *Success. Working Woman Magazine* also frequently has articles relevant to entrepreneurs.

BOOKS

The following books are available in bookstores, libraries, and at online bookstores.

About My Sister's Business: The Black Woman's Road Map to Successful Entrepreneurship, by Fran Harris. This includes ideas and advice for African American women starting a business.

Business Capital for Women: An Essential Handbook for Entrepreneurs, by Emily Card and Adam Miller. This is a comprehensive guide to resources available for women who are looking for money to start or expand a business.

Business Mastery: A Business Planning Guide for Creating a Fulfilling, Thriving Business and Keeping it Successful, by Cherie Sohnen-Moe. This book combines the practical and psychological aspects of owning a business. Originally written for healing arts professionals, this book is appropriate for business professionals in all fields.

The Crafts Business Answer Book; Handmade for Profit; and *Homemade Money* by Barbara Brabec. These three books give guidance to small business owners selling crafts.

422 Tax Deductions For Businesses and Self-Employed Individuals by Bernard B. Kamoroff. Here is an alphabetical encyclopedia of tax deductions. Not sure if you can deduct clothes or bribes? Look it up!

The Frugal Entrepreneur: Creative Ways to Save Time, Energy, and Money In Your Business by Terri Lonier. This provides hints (from Terri and other entrepreneurs) on ways to save time, money, and energy in running your business.

Girl Boss: Entrepreneurial Skills, Stories, and Encouragement for Modern Girls by Stacy Kravetz. Know a young woman who wants to get a business started? This is the book for her. Subtitled *Running the Show Like the Big Chicks*, this is a fun guide to being an entrepreneur.

Hers: The Wise Women's Guide to Starting a Business on $2,000 or Less, by Carol Milano. Here is a good beginner's guide for someone thinking of becoming self-employed. In bookstores or from Allworth Press at (800) 289-0963.

The Home Office and Small Business Answer Book, by Janet Attard. This is a reference book rather than a quick read. In question and answer format, you'll learn about publicity, insurance, saving time, and most other facets of operating a small business.

The Home Team: How Couples Can Make a Life and a Living by Working at Home, by Scott Gregory and Shirley Siluk Gregory. This provides ideas and inspiration for couples who want to build a better life by working at home.

Honey, I Want to Start My Own Business: A Planning Guide For Couples, by Azriella Jaffe. This book provides information and support for couples in which one partner is self-employed.

How to Raise a Family and a Career Under One Roof: A Parent's Guide to Home Business, by Lisa M. Roberts. Here is a discussion of the real-life issues facing parents who want to operate a business from home. Hints for household scheduling as well as information about the details needed to get a business started.

Inc. Your Dreams, by Rebecca Maddox. This is not a book about how to legally incorporate your business but rather a book about how to incorporate what you love to do into a business of your own.

Keeping the Books: Basic Recordkeeping and Accounting for the Small Business, by Linda Pinson and Jerry Jinnett. This book provides very complete information on using financial statements to measure the health of your business. Jerry and Linda have also written an excellent book on marketing and another on preparing a business plan.

Mompreneurs: A Mother's Practical Step-By-Step Guide to Work-At-Home Success, by Ellen H. Parlapiano and Patricia Cobe. It provides hints for setting up your home office, getting help with the kids, time management, and preventing the business from taking over your family life.

Moneymaking Moms: How Work at Home Can Work for You, by Caroline Hull and Tanya Wallace. This includes time management tricks, marketing ideas, and tips to solve other issues faced by moms working at home.

Money Smart Secrets for the Self-Employed, by Linda Stern. This discusses saving money in your business, collecting what's due to you faster, and just about everything else that has to do with small businesses and money.

The NAFE Guide to Starting Your Own Business: A Handbook For Entrepreneurial Women, by Marilyn Manning and Patricia Haddock. This book was co-published with the National Association of Female Executives. It provides advice for those making the transition from employee to entrepreneur.

101 Best Home-Based Businesses For Women, More 101 Best Home-Based Businesses for Women, and *101 Best Small Businesses For Women* are three of the books Priscilla Y. Huff has written. If you need some ideas for the type of business to start, here they are.

101 Best Home-Business Success Secrets for Women, by Priscilla Y. Huff. Here is a guide to everything a new entrepreneur needs to know to start, manage, and profit from operating a business.

Our Money, Ourselves: Redesigning Your Relationship with Money, by Dr. C. Diane Ealy and Dr. Kay Lesh. This isn't specifically for entrepreneurs but addresses the money issues that many women are dealing with.

Our Wildest Dreams: Women Entrepreneurs Making Money, Having Fun, Doing Good, by Joline Godfrey. Here is a look at how women can change the face of business. By talking about her own experiences in the corporate world and providing interviews with women entrepreneurs, Joline helps us consider a new definition of business success.

Prince Charming Isn't Coming: How Women Get Smart About Money, by Barbara Stanny. This book is not specifically directed to women entrepreneurs but addresses money issues faced by many women. Stanny is the daughter of one of the founders of H&R Block.

Running a One-Person Business, by Claude Whitmyer and Salli Raspberry. This book covers the psychological issues of being in business for yourself: How do you keep from feeling isolated? How do you go on vacation when you're self-employed? How do you keep your business life separate from your personal life?

Sister CEO, by Cheryl Broussard. Here is a look at the businesses operated by 50 women who were interviewed by the author. Their hardships, triumphs, and lessons are shared with the reader.

Small Business Tax Savvy and *Stand Up to the IRS*, by tax attorney Frederick Daily. Here are two comprehensive tax publications. The first is a guide to tax regulations affecting small businesses; the second provides information on how to deal with the IRS.

Small Time Operator: How to Start Your Own Small Business, Keep Your Books, Pay Your Taxes, and Stay Out of Trouble, by Bernard Kamaroff, CPA. This is an easy-to-understand book that's been around in revised editions for more than 20 years.

The Small Business Money Guide: How to Get It, Use It, Keep It, by Terri Lonier. This book provides information on using money to start, manage, and grow a business.

The Smart Woman's Guide to Starting a Business by Vickie L. Montgomery. This book provides guidance and resources for new business owners.

The Stay-at-Home Mom's Guide to Making Money: How to Choose the Business That's Right for You Using the Skills and Interests You Already Have, by Liz Folger. This book provides ideas and tips for getting a business going at home.

The Women's Guide to Starting a Business, by Claudia Jessup and Genie Chipps. Here is a step-by-step guide to everything that must be considered when starting a business. Includes information on marketing, insurance, goal setting, and so on.

The Women's Business Resource Guide, by Barbara Littman. This is full of information about programs, organizations, and information for women who are starting or are already in businesses of their own.

201 Great Ideas for Small Businesses, by Jane Applegate. This book isn't specifically geared to women entrepreneurs but the ideas will help you grow your business.

Working Solo Sourcebook: Essential Resources for Independent Entrepreneurs, by Terri Lonier. This book is packed with listings of helpful organizations, publications, tapes, and more. It is helpful on its own or as a companion title to Lonier's book *Working Solo: The Real Guide to Freedom and Financial Success with Your Own Business*. Portions of this book are searchable online at www.workingsolo.com.

All the small business and home-based business books by Paul and Sarah Edwards are highly recommended. Paul and Sarah write small business columns for a number of publications, host a small business Web site, and also have a radio show for entrepreneurs. Their titles include *Working from Home; Finding Your Perfect Work; Home Businesses You Can Buy; Getting Business to Come to You; Making Money with Your Computer at Home;* and *Secrets of Self-Employment*. These books are widely available in bookstores, libraries, and online bookstores.

Nolo Press publishes all types of self-help legal and small business guides. They have books on forming your own corporation, partnership law, and so on. You can read select chapters of books at their Web site www.nolo.com. Nolo books are widely available in bookstores, libraries, and online bookstores.

Redleaf Press publishes books for child care centers. Although the focus of many of their books is in helping the child care worker be more effective in working with children, Redleaf also publishes the *Family Child Care Tax Workbook* and related recordkeeping books. Phone (800) 423-8309.

Craftsman Book Company publishes books and software for business owners in the construction industry. Their titles include *Builders Guide to Accounting* and *Contractor's Year-Round Tax Guide*. Phone (800) 829-8123.

There are numerous other small business books in print. Look in the business section of your library or bookstore. If you're looking for tax information, check the copyright year in the front of the book. Anything more than a year or two old will be somewhat out of date and should be relied on only for general advice.

INDEX